Teacher Preparation in the United States

Emerald Studies in Teacher Preparation in National and Global Contexts

Series Editors: Teresa O'Doherty, Marino Institute of Education, Dublin, Ireland; Judith Harford, University College Dublin, Ireland; and Thomas O'Donoghue, University of Western Australia, Australia

Teacher preparation is currently one of the most pressing and topical issues in the field of education research. It deals with questions such as how teachers are prepared, what the content of their programs of preparation is, how their effectiveness is assessed, and what the role of the "good" teacher is in society. These questions are at the forefront of policy agendas around the world.

This series presents robust, critical research studies in the broad field of teacher preparation historically, with attention also being given to current policy and future directions. Most books in the series will focus on an individual country, providing a comprehensive overview of the history of teacher preparation in that country while also making connections between the past and present and informing discussions on possible future directions.

Previously Published

Historical Perspectives on Teacher Preparation in Aotearoa New Zealand
By Tanya Fitzgerald and Sally Knipe

Teacher Preparation in Northern Ireland
By Séan Farren, Linda Clarke and Teresa O'Doherty

Catholic Teacher Preparation
By Richard Rymarz and Leonardo Franchi

Teacher Preparation in South Africa
By Linda Chisholm

Teacher Preparation in Australia: History, Policy and Future Directions
By Thomas O'Donoghue and Keith Moore

The Emergence of Teacher Education in Zambia
By Brendan Carmody

Teacher Preparation in Scotland
By Rachel Shanks

The Peripatetic Journey of Teacher Preparation in Canada
By Rosa Bruno-Jofré and Joseph Stafford

Historical Development of Teacher Education in Chile
By Beatrice Ávalos and Leonora Reyes

Teacher Preparation in Singapore: A Concise Critical History
By Yeow-Tong Chia, Alistair Chew and Jason Tan

Forthcoming in This Series

Teacher Preparation in France: History and Policy
By Imelda Elliott and EmelineLucuit

Teacher Preparation in the United States: History, Current Conditions, and Policy

BY

KELLY KOLODNY

Framingham State University, USA

And

MARY-LOU BREITBORDE

Salem State University, USA

emerald
PUBLISHING

United Kingdom – North America – Japan – India – Malaysia – China

Emerald Publishing Limited
Howard House, Wagon Lane, Bingley BD16 1WA, UK

First edition 2022

Reprints and permissions service
Contact: permissions@emeraldinsight.com

British Library Cataloguing in Publication Data
A catalogue record for this book is available from the British Library

ISBN: 978-1-80071-688-9 (Print)
ISBN: 978-1-80071-687-2 (Online)
ISBN: 978-1-80071-689-6 (Epub)

Printed and bound by CPI Group (UK) Ltd, Croydon, CR0 4YY

ISOQAR certified Management System, awarded to Emerald for adherence to Environmental standard ISO 14001:2004.

ISOQAR REGISTERED
Certificate Number 1985
ISO 14001

INVESTOR IN PEOPLE

To the memory of Louise Boyle Swiniarski, PhD, Professor of Education, global educator, teacher educator extraordinaire. Our friend and colleague, whose support for children's universal rights – to play and grow and learn in peace – lives on in the thousands of teachers and teacher educators she influenced around the world.

Table of Contents

About the Authors

Kelly Kolodny is Professor of Education at Framingham State University. Her research and writing address the fields of educational biography, the history of state normal schools in the United States, contemporary schooling, and the learning and development of children. She is the past president of the New England Philosophy of Education Society (NEPES).

Mary-Lou Breitborde is Professor Emerita of Education at Salem State University, where she teaches courses in the social foundations of education and served as Associate Dean and Chair in the School of Education. Her research, publications, and international presentations focus on the social and cultural history of education; the lives and work of social-reconstructionist educators; and global/multicultural education.

Acknowledgments

We appreciated the invitation to include this book in the Emerald Studies in Teacher Preparation in National and Global Contexts series, and for this opportunity we especially thank Tom O'Donoghue from the University of Western Australia. We are grateful to staff at Emerald Publishing for their superb assistance with this book, especially Kimberley Chadwick and Hemavathi Rajendran. Many archivists and teacher educators provided patient and invaluable assistance with this project. We extend a special thank you to Daniel Mulcahy, Professor Emeritus from Central Connecticut State University, for his support. Deep thanks to our colleagues at Framingham State University and Salem State University for their consistent support of our work and to our students for what they have taught us and for their own dedication to the students and families with whom they work. Our students are a source of inspiration and insight.

Kelly Kolodny would like to thank her family – particularly her husband Doug and her children Jonathan, Anna Grace, Joshua, and his significant other Megan.

Mary-Lou Breitborde would like to thank her partner Bob for his support and good editorial eye and her sons, daughters-in-law, and grandkids for being exemplars of teaching and learning at their best.

Introduction

At the start of the second decade of the twenty-first century, 50.7 million children are enrolled in public elementary and secondary schools in the United States. Another 3.1 million children are enrolled in public charter schools and 5.7 million are enrolled in private schools (NCES, 2020). These children represent an increasingly diverse student population with 47.6% identifying as White, 15.2% Black, 26.7% Hispanic, 5.5% Asian/Pacific Islander, 1% American Indian/Alaska Native, and 3.8% two or more races (NCES, 2020). Approximately one in four of all public school students in the United States are immigrants, for a significant number of whom English is not their first language.

Today's American school-aged children find themselves in varied economic circumstances. In 2018, 18% of children under age 18, approximately 12.6 million children, were living in poverty (NCES, 2020). This number would have been significantly higher if the data were expanded to include children whose families' yearly income fell slightly above the official poverty line. Poverty rates, and economic hardships, clearly influence the academic achievement of students, their success in schooling, and overall general health.

Twenty-first century children display different learning abilities and challenges with regard to their formal studies. In 2018–2019, for example, 14% of public school students, or 7.1 million children, received special education services (NCES, 2020). The Council for Exceptional Children (CEC) reminds us that learning disabilities "may impact a student's ability to read, write, spell, think, speak, listen, or do mathematics" (CEC, 2021).

Wider events in communities and throughout the country also have shaped the learning of twenty-first century children, as well as their larger lives and sense of well-being. School shootings have resulted in political movements, and connected policies, focused on stricter gun control laws. The past few years have seen a significant rise in the use of opioids and in rates of addiction which have compromised the stability of families. Children in the United States also have witnessed mass protests unfold in response to continued systemic racist practices in the country. The murders of African Americans, at times in police custody, have made headlines and filled courts across the nation.

In 2019, 2020, and 2021, children in the United States and throughout the world saw the COVID-19 pandemic shutter their schools as teaching and learning moved to remote formats. For some children, the shutdown of schools and workplaces meant that they saw more of their parents and their siblings. Many were able to access appropriate tools successfully to engage in remote learning;

Teacher Preparation in the United States, 1–7

Published under exclusive licence by Emerald Publishing Limited
doi:10.1108/978-1-80071-687-220221001

they learned how to use new software and how to type faster. But other children were left alone at home without supervision or help and struggled to secure technology or find safe, quiet places to learn. Misinformation propagandized about the source of the COVID-19 pandemic led to a rise in hate crimes against Asian Americans, including Asian American students.

Young people of the twenty-first century are growing up in increasingly challenging and complex circumstances. Through challenging times, they draw support from teachers and other professional educators. These are the individuals who guide them with formal academic learning experiences as well as with other social and emotional aspects of their lives. Drawing support from education professionals is something that children in the United States have been doing for hundreds of years. The contexts of life, work, and school have certainly changed, but common elements in the work of teachers have persevered. These common elements include a sense of the larger purposes connected to the teaching profession and a moral persistence that many teachers bring to their work with young people. The twenty-first century educator Rita Pierson, who conducted professional development workshops for thousands of teachers during her career, was well known for her view that, "We're educators. We're born to make a difference."

The purpose of this book is to explore how teachers have been prepared in American history to work with young people, to understand and be responsive to their diverse circumstances, in order to help them live and learn. In this book, we highlight both the opportunities and challenges connected to teacher preparation initiatives during different periods in the United States. Formal teacher preparation is an undertaking that millions of individuals have pursued. In 2017–2018 alone, for example, 3.5 million full- and part-time practicing public school teachers were employed in the United States who had completed formal teacher preparation programs (NCES, 2020). Our aim in this book is to present an authentic, comprehensive account and analysis of the programs and routes to teaching which so many individuals have chosen to pursue.

It is difficult to identify a starting point for examining teacher preparation initiatives in the United States. For tens of thousands of years, meaningful educations took place in Native American and First Nation groups. Native teachers educated young people in the art and science of surviving, using and appreciating the Earth; and in the beliefs, practices and traditions of the group, using storytelling and other oral traditions, rites of passage, modeling, and observation. Some of these educational traditions were shared with the European colonists who arrived in the United States in the 1500s and 1600s. Disease, warfare, and racism, however, saw the educational traditions of the colonists dominate. These European colonial traditions shaped the teacher preparation and initiatives and programs that unfolded from the 1600s to the current day. For these reasons, the authors commence our history of teacher preparation programs with the early academies and seminaries of the seventeenth and eighteenth centuries, and continue into the nineteenth, twentieth and twenty-first century with the development of private, municipal, and state normal schools; teacher institutes; public and private colleges with education programs; and newer "alternative" models.

We open this book by offering a working definition of the term *teacher preparation program*, as well as provide a sense of the evolution of these programs from the 1600s, when very little, if any, formal preparation of teachers was required, to the contemporary context when a baccalaureate degree and licensure are minimum requirements to teach in public school. Connected to this timeline, and throughout this book, we explore the impulses (thematic threads) that have shaped teacher preparation programs. These threads center on (1) the wider historical, social and economic contexts, processes, and policies guiding teacher preparation programs, (2) the structure, content, and pedagogy of these programs, and (3) participant experiences, including issues of equity and accessibility. Also woven into this book are short biographies of diverse individuals who have influenced or have been affected by teacher programs at different historical periods and in various contexts. Philosopher of education Jane Roland Martin (2011), who reconceptualized our understanding of the transmission of education broadly defined, reflected on the encounters that occur between individuals and wider contexts and cultures. In these encounters, the capacities of an individual or individuals and the stock of a wider culture become yoked together. These encounters are both an instant of individual learning, as well as one of cultural transmission. Applying Martin's theory to our study of teacher preparation programs, we believe that while teacher preparation programs certainly are shaped by larger societal contexts and structures, we cannot divorce the stories of individuals who also are intricately connected to them. We include these stories to provide a more holistic understanding of the historical and contemporary contexts of teacher preparation programs and the threads that bind them.

Teacher Preparation Programs

The definition, or defining characteristics, of *teacher preparation programs* have changed and evolved over time in response to changing milieus and policies. In the contemporary context, teacher preparation programs prepare undergraduate and graduate students for licensure in a variety of fields, including early childhood, elementary and secondary education, as well as specialist roles. It is assumed that students in these programs have completed the minimum equivalent of a high school diploma prior to entering them. Contemporary teacher preparation programs are approved at the state level, demonstrating that candidates enrolled in them meet specific state standards. They encompass both content and pedagogical studies, as well as require mastery of teacher licensure tests. Pre-practicum and practicum experiences also are embedded into these programs. In addition, these programs may be accredited at the national level by the Council for the Accreditation of Educator Preparation (CAEP). Attributes connected to contemporary teacher preparation programs reflect societal contexts which are joined powerfully to accountability movements. The term teacher preparation programs also are referred to as teacher education programs.

Historically, however, teacher preparation was less bound to state and national standards. When the roots of these programs were budding in the United States, they reflected more of a moral and religious focus, in addition to an academic and pedagogical one. The requirements of these programs were less defined and intense. Indeed, educational historian James Fraser (2007) wrote that in the seventeenth and eighteenth centuries, the majority of teachers actually had no formal preparation. "Teachers were simply hired by school boards seeking the best person willing to work for the low pay offered" (Fraser, 2007, p. 3). Therefore, the definition of teacher preparation initiatives in early contexts differs tremendously from the twenty-first century.

When the United States was developing as a young nation in the late 1700s, following the American Revolution, teacher preparation programs reflected a particular political context bound to the period. An example of this is seen in the state normal school movement, introduced in the 1830s to help prepare teachers to work with a growing school-age population in a young nation. The early state normal school programs were often only two years or less in length. A smaller number of these programs were three or four years in length. Though these programs, too, encompassed academic and pedagogical studies, a concern centered on the low-academic preparation of students who entered these programs, particularly in the nineteenth century (Herbst, 1989). Requirements were less structured than the contemporary context, though these students were assessed by a board of examiners. Many of the state normal schools eventually would develop into four-year state teacher colleges and then universities. A smaller number of these schools became high schools and community colleges.

Teacher institutes also flourished in mid 1800s and usually met once or twice a year for a period of two to four weeks (Ogren, 2005). These were considered teacher preparation programs, but often lacked substantial content. These were not guided by local or state requirements. Various private colleges and universities began to offer teacher preparation programs, starting in the nineteenth century and increasing in the twentieth century. A sequential review of teacher preparation programs reveals how these initiatives expanded and evolved over the past 400+ years, as well as how defining characteristics changed to meet new contexts.

Research Methodology

Our approach to writing this book included historical research through which we examined primary and secondary sources connected to teacher preparation programs. Primary sources included school catalogs, educational speeches, committee reports, and student journals. Secondary sources included academic journal articles and books related to the field of teacher education. Our research also included document analysis connected to teacher preparation programs in the contemporary context. Some of the documents that we reviewed included reports from the American Association of Colleges of Teacher Education (AACTE) and National Center for Educational Statistics (NCES). While undertaking this research we looked for themes that emerged related to teacher preparation programs, as well as outliers. We searched for the stories of individuals who significantly shaped teacher preparation programs in the United States and/or were impacted by them.

Format of the Book

This book is divided into two sections. Part One focuses on the historical contexts and policies of teacher preparation programs in the United States. Part Two focuses on the contemporary circumstances and policies shaping teacher preparation programs. Within these two parts, there are six chapters.

Part One

Chapter 1 provides an overview of the colonial era and early national period when formal teacher preparation programs had not yet been implemented in the United States. There was an assumption that if one was educated enough to know as much as an eighth grader, and if one could keep a classroom of multi-age children, including farm boys who are 14+ years old, under control, then one could teach. This changed in the early nineteenth century with the growth of the population and the need to educate children for a new country and national language and culture. At this time upper class women increasingly sought a formal education. There were new female seminaries whose purpose was to prepare women to use their "true womanhood" – their presumably higher character and disciplined ways – to educate children either in the home as mothers or in formal schools as teachers. Chapter 1 highlights the influence of Samuel Read Hall, Joseph Emerson, Catharine Beecher, Emma Willard, Mary Lyon, Myrtilla Miner, and others, who established schools for this purpose and for the expanding country.

Chapter 2 analyzes formal teacher education in the United States starting in the 1830s with the commencement of state normal schools. It examines how the state normal schools reflected the political and social contexts of a new nation. It examines the schedule and length of teacher preparation programs in the nineteenth century, connected curriculum, model schools where practice teaching occurred, and the informal networks that formed among students. It highlights the movement through which teacher education expanded throughout the South and West during the nineteenth century. It explores the unique contexts of these areas and the factors that shaped them; for example, the quest for an American identity; the role of women in society; the growth of state responsibility; early immigration; slavery, the Civil War and Reconstruction; and the White settlement of the West. This chapter also examines how the growth of the state normal schools in the US drew attention from representatives from other countries, including Argentina and Japan, who wanted to replicate the movement. This chapter features a biographical sketch of Horace Mann and information about Henry Barnard. Biographies of nineteenth century normal school graduates Mary Swift, Olivia Davidson, and Charlotte Forten also are highlighted.

Chapter 3 examines the dual contexts of the post-Reconstruction Jim Crow era and the Progressive Education movement of the late nineteenth and early twentieth century. It describes as well the evolution and destiny of normal schools as higher education grew and transformed in the United States. The chapter analyzes changes in educational methods and materials in response to research and developments in the new disciplines of psychology and sociology. Biographies of Progressive teacher educators John Dewey and Fanny Jackson Coppin are included in this chapter.

Chapter 4 spotlights the mid-to-late twentieth century and how teacher education evolved during this time. It showcases the influence of the Civil Rights movement, War on Poverty, arms race, and space race on teacher preparation programs. It explores the growth of STEM education, multicultural education, special education, and peace education. Biographies of influential teacher educators during this period including James Banks, Geoffrey Canada, Eleanor Duckworth, Jaime Escalante, Maxine Greene, Ian Harris, Sonia Nieto, Nel Noddings, and Christa McAuliffe are highlighted in this chapter.

Part Two

Chapter 5 explores the contexts of twenty-first century teacher preparation programs in the United States. It examines federal legislation that shaped teacher preparation programs, transitioning from the twentieth century into the twenty-first century. This includes Goals 2000, Improving America's Schools Act (IASA), No Child Left Behind Act (NCLB), and Every Student Succeeds Act (ESSA). It examines the length of teacher preparation programs, curriculum, and connected licensure requirements. It explores the roles of state departments of education in approving teacher preparation programs, as well as the national accrediting role of the Council for the Accreditation of Educator Preparation (CAEP). It looks at national organizations such as the American Association of Colleges of Teacher Education (AACTE). The impact that diverse geographical contexts have on contemporary teacher preparation programs are explored, as well as controversies over the relative place of standards and assessment in teacher education and in the public schools. Featured teacher educators in this chapter include James Comer and Linda Darling-Hammond.

Chapter 6, the final chapter of the book, reviews the challenges facing teacher education at present and proposes policy recommendations to address them. Issues discussed include the disparity between who are the students in today's US and who are their teachers, the looming shortage of teachers in particular places and fields, and the recognition that attention to conditions in families, communities, and the larger society must be included in the business of schools. Recommendations target antiracist curricula and culturally sustaining pedagogies; holistic knowledge of students; and the need to prepare teachers to teach in a fast-changing society and a globally connected world.

Formal teacher preparation in the United States has a robust and varied history intimately connected to the robust history of this relatively young country and to its ideals and realities. The book describes the forward movement to formalize and professionalize the work of teachers whose work extended to increasing populations of increasingly diverse children and families. As the lens of teacher education and education policy widens, we present a history that extends the story into the twenty-first century, a time of crises that, we hope, will spawn a clearer view of our problems, our accomplishments, and our possibilities.

References

Council for Exceptional Children. (2021, November). Students with learning disabilities (LD) have difficulty acquiring basic skills or academic content due to difficulty using or understanding spoken or written language. Retrieved from https://exceptionalchildren.org/topics/learning-disabilities

Fraser, J. (2007). *Preparing America's teachers: A history*. New York, NY: Teachers College Press.

Herbst, J. (1989). *And sadly teach: Teacher education and professionalization in American culture*. Madison, WI: The University of Wisconsin Press.

Martin, J. R. (2011). *Education reconfigured: Culture, encounter, and change*. New York, NY: Routledge.

National Center for Education Statistics. (2020). *The condition of education 2020*. Washington, DC: U. S. Department of Education.

Ogren, C. (2005). *The American state normal school: An instrument of great good*. New York, NY: Palgrave Macmillan.

Chapter 1

The Young Republic Needs Teachers

Education in the Early America and the New Republic

In early America, the education and schooling of the children of colonists were two different phenomena, occurring separately, together, or not at all. Depending on where children lived and their race, social class, and gender, they might be taught at home by their parents or elders, tutored by people who might be students themselves, attend lessons given by a neighbor woman in her own home, sent abroad to a school in England, or, as in the case of most poor White farm children and enslaved Black children, have no formal education at all. Where they existed, schools were likely sectarian and concerned as much or more with piety and virtue than with intellectual or academic learning. There were great regional differences in the content, form, and oversight of education.

In colonial New England, education was a public responsibility for towns of a certain size. In 1647 Massachusetts Bay (which included Maine and parts of New Hampshire at the time) enacted the first education law in the country, which mandated that parents ensure their children's "ability to read & understand the principles of religion & the capitall lawes of this country, and…impose fines upon such as shall refuse to render such accounts to them when they shall be required." This "Old Deluder Satan Act," copied later in Connecticut, was meant to ensure that the young could read the Bible, which would protect them from evil urges and influences (Old Deluder Satan Act, 1647). As long as they could themselves read and write, teachers were hired and approved by town selectmen or school committees on the basis of their fealty to the Puritan religion that dominated and, second, for their ability to keep order in multi-age classrooms. Little attention was paid to their subject matter knowledge or pedagogical skill. In the Middle Atlantic region, where religion was less tied to political dominance, schools were typically sponsored by the various sects, including Quakers, German Lutherans, and Moravians. In the American South, the very existence of education varied with race and class: The children of wealthy planters had private tutors, sometimes shared with other plantation families. Their sons continued their education in the private academies of the North or in England. The children of poor White farmers were lucky to have any education at all, which would have been only as much as their parents or neighbors or ministers had the time or ability to teach them. Education for enslaved children was incidental, accidental, and hidden, gleaned from the overheard lessons of planters' children or from the rare literate

Teacher Preparation in the United States, 9–34

doi:10.1108/978-1-80071-687-220221002

older enslaved adult who managed to teach them. Following the dissemination of insurrectionist tracts like David Walker's *Appeal* (1995 (1829)) and the slave revolts of the 1830s, Southern states outlawed the teaching of reading to the enslaved, fearing, with good reason, that Black literacy would lead to Black rebellion and liberation.

The call for a widespread system of free public "common" schools began with America's fight for independence from England and the need to ensure a civically educated public with a distinctly American identity. Thomas Jefferson's 1779 "Bill for the More General Diffusion of Knowledge" (1950 (1779)) filed with the Virginia General Assembly called for three years of tax-supported schools for White boys and girls, with more schooling for boys with academic talent. Virginia planter lawmakers were not ready to fund general education, wary of upsetting the caste system of race and class, which kept poor White and Black laborers from reading or dreaming about a different, better life. Jefferson's effort, however, resulted in the founding of the University of Virginia, which allowed White boys with academic talent and professional interests to stay "at home" in the South for their higher education. In the North, advocates of public education had better luck: for example, Vermont's post-Revolutionary War 1777 Constitution called for the establishment of a system of publicly funded schooling that included primary to university education (Zoracki, 2006).

The founding of the new republic attracted waves of immigrants from Germany, Ireland, and Northern Europe, who helped grow cities in the eastern part of the United States and expand White settlements in the "western" (now midwestern) territories in the first part of the new century. In a society increasingly comprising diverse religions, languages, and ways of life, many thought a standard system of public education necessary to create a national identity and preserve social order. Systematized schooling would help newcomers assimilate to a distinctly American (meaning "Anglo") culture, a new American (rather than British) English, and the White Anglo-Saxon Protestant norms, values, and virtues deemed necessary to the functioning and growth of the nation. Those who did not or could not fit in (e.g., Natives, Blacks and, often, Catholics and Jews) were not part of the process. While Vermont's 1777 constitution had separate laws aimed at establishing schools "for the instruction of youth" and encouraging "virtue," by 1793, its official, state constitution had combined the two purposes: "Laws for the encouragement of virtue and prevention of vice and immorality ought to be constantly kept in force, and duly executed; and a competent number of schools ought to be maintained in each town…" (Zoracki, 2006).

Nineteenth century America also saw an extension of suffrage, industrialization, and rising nationalism. The new nation was taken up with the business of creating a robust economy and a sense of civic responsibility in a now self-governing people. It was argued that broad civic participation required a literate public and general literacy required schools and teachers, an argument that reached state legislatures. In 1827, the Great and General Court of Massachusetts enacted a law that provided free elementary schooling for all children. By mid-century, New York had a robust educational system and in new Midwestern states like Ohio there were one-room schools "within walking distance of virtually every child. It was a truly phenomenal expansion." Out of this rapid expansion of public schools emerged demands for teacher education (Cremin, 1953, p. 163).

A Patchwork of Programs for Teacher Preparation

The earliest criteria for hiring teachers for the new public schools were far more about character and respectability than they were about knowledge or teaching skills. If one could convince the local school directors, (or, in Massachusetts, the local ministers and the town selectmen) that he or she knew as much as the graduate of a typical eight-grade school and could keep order in a roomful of children of mixed ages, including 14-year-old farm boys unused to sitting indoors for long hours on hard benches, then one was qualified to teach – provided, that is, that one was a regular church-goer (Cole, 1957). Early school terms were brief – typically, boys attended three months in the winter and girls three months in the summer, with fall and spring reserved for their help with planting and harvesting. Because the work was part-time and the pay minimal, early schoolteachers tended to be young men who were farmers looking for extra income in the slow winter season, students looking for a temporary position to support their studies, or men without a trade or land or the ability to sustain steadier work. Richard Hofstadter, arguing that America's interest in schooling has always been limited and "antiintellectual" describes the prevailing view of early American teachers as men who were fit for nothing else:

> There was a train of stereotypes of this order: the one-eyed or one-legged teacher, the teacher who had been driven out of the ministry by his weakness for drink, the lame teacher, the misplaced fiddler.
>
> (Hofstadter, 1963, p. 314)

Growing industrialization brought with it both the need and the opportunity to extend the school term beyond the agriculture-focused three-month winter session for boys and three-month summer session for girls. As both the population and the economy grew, so did the need to add more years of schooling, organize larger schools into age-graded classrooms, and hire teachers with specialized content knowledge and skills in presenting it. There were now examinations for prospective teachers, developed at either the local, county, or state level. The great majority of test questions assessed general content knowledge, the assumption being that if one had enough knowledge, one could teach it.

At first, whatever attention was given to the knowledge and skills required of those who taught the young was given to men. Most people believed that male children needed more education than females – after all, the vote belonged only to them, as did property rights within married couples. Men were more available to teach, as they were free of the domestic responsibilities that were considered women's primary responsibility. And men had access to a network of preparatory academies that had sprung up to educate them. While the first teacher preparation programs were informal and brief, offered in the form of private classes and summer- or short-term institutes, the college preparatory academies soon took on some responsibility for educating prospective teachers.

The first formal teacher preparation programs appeared in these academies as ancillary curricula or specialized training. Some academies in New York state added "teacher departments" which, with state funding, supported young men with financial need with a curriculum comprising the "common branches," along with a few lectures on methods of teaching, health, "general school-keeping," and moral responsibilities. In Massachusetts, Amherst Academy, founded in 1820 for "indigent" young men with a Classical – Greek and Latin – department for the college-bound and a more practical English department for those not pursuing college, added a third department in 1827 to prepare schoolteachers. Phillips Andover Academy followed with a Teaching Seminary in 1830, an alternative to its classic college preparatory program.

Andover Teaching Seminary's first principal was Samuel Read Hall, a teacher and teacher of teachers who had opened what is considered the first "normal school" for teachers in 1823 in Concord, Vermont. Hall saw teaching as a distinct profession with its own set of knowledge, values, and tools. He is reported to have been the first to use a blackboard as a teaching tool. His book, *Lectures on School-Keeping*, was widely read and well-respected. Its chapter on the "requisite qualifications of an instructor" seems remarkably prescient. Critical in a school-teacher, he wrote, were "literary attainments" and… "a highly cultivated mind": a good teacher needed to know the rules of language, the properties of numbers, geography, history, and the civil and political history of the United States, writing/rhetoric, natural philosophy, chemistry, and moral philosophy. But Hall thought subject matter knowledge was insufficient. Good teaching also required common sense – "that faculty by which things are seen as they are…the exercise of reason, uninfluenced by passion or prejudice…very different from genius or talent… and better than either" (Hall, 1829, pp. 30–31). Furthermore, good teachers needed an even temper: "It is impossible for [a teacher of uneven temperament] to gain and preserve respect among his pupils. No one who comes under the rule of a person of uneven temper, can know what to expect or how to act" (1829, p. 31). Fore-shadowing what we now know about learning and personality differences, he added to his list of teacher qualifications "a capacity to understand and discriminate" the varied dispositions of children. "The instructer [*sic*] who considers all alike does injury to many. A word of encouragement [is] sufficient to excite attention in some, while another will require…every motive that can be placed before him" (p. 31). Hall's good teacher was decisive, purposeful and consistent, but also caring. "A kind interest manifested in their welfare…exhibited in action as well as words" earned the love and good will of one's "scholars" (p. 32). Finally, he advised prospective teachers to study moral philosophy, to give them a knowledge of themselves, of human nature in general, and of their God, and to lead them to prioritize the welfare of their students and the community. Hall felt that a teacher's role as moral agent was even more important than the cultivation of student intellect, as teachers were "forming characters for this world and the next" (p. 40).

Many young male graduates of the classic academy programs or of their teacher departments did become teachers. But the wider opportunities for men in the growing nation and the low pay–given teachers made it unlikely that their numbers would meet the need for teachers nationwide. The teacher shortage in the early-to-mid-nineteenth century was, in fact, solved by women in search of meaningful work and some independence and adventure. But the solution would carry with it some variation in the kind and quality of preparation offered to prospective and practicing teachers and disagreement over the public's responsibility for funding it.

Biographical Sketch

Samuel Read Hall.
"Caring teachers will generally excite the same in their scholars."
Source: Courtesy of the Old Stone House Museum, Brownington, VT.

Samuel Read Hall was born in 1795 in Croydon, N. H. Suffering from bouts of ill health in an area with few schools, he attended school only minimally, educating himself by reading through his father's library of classic works. At age 19, he was hired as a teacher in Rumford, Maine, where he earned great respect for his ability to teach compositional writing to young children and in 1816, pioneered the use of a blackboard for instruction. "One of the first convictions fastened on my mind after I became a teacher," he wrote later in life, "was, that…the whole system of education in the country was defective, that the time of Scholars in the common schools was, in a great measure, lost. I determined, therefore, to do what I could by my feeble influence, to reform abuses and correct evils" (Rev. Samuel Read Hall Obituary, 1877).

Teaching was still considered a part-time occupation, and Hall turned to the ministry, studying theology with several noted ministers in the region. In 1823, he was invited to be pastor of a Congregational church in Concord, Vermont. Touring the town's schools, he concluded that the greatest service he could do for its children was to teach their teachers. Hall, therefore, accepted the post with the condition that he be allowed to establish a seminary "as a means of elevating the character of teachers, and advancing the usefulness of schools" (Barnard, 1858, p. 383). His seminary opened in March, 1823 and is considered the first normal school in America.

Henry Barnard, nineteenth century educational leader from Connecticut and the first US Commissioner of Education, wrote,

> Here in an obscure corner of New England, under the hand of one who was, to a remarkable degree, self-taught, self- prompted and alone in planning it, was an institution with all the essential characteristics of a normal school, eighteen years before the Massachusetts movement had reached that point of development which secured the establishment of the [first state] normal school at Lexington.
>
> (Barnard, 1858, p. 377)

The above quotation comes from Barnard's, 1858 lengthy article on Hall's importance in the *American Journal of Education*, in which he extolled not only the excellence of his teaching ("it must by no means be supposed that Mr. Hall's success was due solely to his intellectual activity...and the stimulating effect...upon young minds. His influence through the conscience and the affections was still more decided and important") (Barnard, 1858, p. 376), but also Hall's place in the history of teacher education. Hall's lectures on school-keeping came "some years earlier than any other of the kind was ever made...written without any aid from books or periodicals. When first delivered, there was not a single tract...furnishing even 'hints' on the subjects discussed" (Barnard, 1858, p. 377).

Hall's Teacher Seminary could be completed in three years, with the understanding that students would be engaged in teaching by their second year. The curriculum included English Grammar, rhetoric, "intellectual" and written arithmetic, algebra, geometry, trigonometry, chemistry, natural history, logic, civil engineering, theology, moral philosophy, surveying, US and English history, ancient and modern geography, "construction of maps," "use of globes," astronomy, political economy, "evidences of Christianity," philosophy, linear drawing, bookkeeping, and the "art of teaching" (Barnard, 1858, p. 378). He invited several young children to participate in the normal school activities for the purpose of demonstration and practice, thus introducing the idea of practice teaching."

To supplement his earnings to meet his expenses, Hall published several books on teaching, which were widely praised and sold well, and used in many schools across the country. His first book, *A Child's Assistant to a Knowledge of the Geography and History of Vermont*, published in 1827, dismissed the typical way that teachers taught geography by presenting the child with a map of the world, advocating instead that they begin with the immediate community and move outward to the state, region, nation, and world. "Why should he learn the names of continents, islands, oceans, seas and lakes, rivers and mountains many thousands of miles distant before he is taught the geography of his own town, county, state and country?" (Hall, 1829, p. 89). Teachers should learn all they can about the history and details of the town or village where they teach, and "carry the young learners to as many as possible of these places... The health of the pupils is benefitted by the fresh open air ... [and] everything wears the aspect of reality, and of nature, and of life" (Hall, 1829, p. 96). Anticipating the eminent educational philosopher John Dewey by some 70 years, Hall urged teachers to begin with the child's interests and leave the four walls of the classroom to use real environments to teach real things. Hall fleshed out this child-centered philosophy in his *Lectures on School-Keeping* (1829), a book that was widely read by both prospective and working teachers and that brought him national renown. With great prescience and exercising the common sense and critical thinking he required of teachers, he described effective teaching as the ability to recognize and respond to the great differences among children in their motivations and "dispositions," and to use themselves as models for the persistence and kindness they wanted to see in their students. "The human heart...cannot resist the influence of kindness; caring teachers will generally excite the same in their scholars (Hall, 1829)."

Hall was invited to lead schools all over America. In 1830 he accepted the role of principal of the English Normal School of Phillips Academy in Andover, Massachusetts, where he served until 1840. He had helped organize the American Institute of Instruction in 1829, the oldest educational association in the US, in which he gave lectures on "The Necessity of Educating Teachers" and "School Government." A meeting of the Institute in Boston in 1836 featured a debate on the professional education of teachers. The debate produced a resolution: "that the business of teachers should be performed by those who have studied the subject of teaching as a profession..." therefore, that "there ought to be one seminary, at least, in each state devoted exclusively to the education of teachers, and that the board of directors memorialize the legislature on the subject of establishing a seminary for the education of teachers." Signed by Hall and others, the resolution was presented at the next session of the state legislature. It resulted the following year in the creation of a Board of Education in Massachusetts, the appointment of Horace Mann, who had been influenced by Hall's work, as its first Secretary, and two years afterward, the establishment of the first normal school endowed by any state (cited in Barnard, 1858; Levy, 1991).

Hall was offered the first presidency of Oberlin College in the early 1830s but turned it down. In 1840 he moved back to his home state of New Hampshire to take a position as head of Holmes Plymouth Academy, on condition that he be able to establish a coeducational teaching department. His support for preparing and hiring women teachers had been reflected in his 1832 book, *Lectures to Female Teachers*. Plymouth Academy evolved into

Plymouth State Normal School, now Plymouth State University. Though he had spent three years at Kimball Academy studying for the ministry, due to illness, Hall himself had never attended college. He was awarded honorary degrees for his ground-breaking, progressive work in pedagogy and teacher education by both Dartmouth College and the University of Vermont. From his founding of the normal school in Vermont to the opening of the first public normal school in Massachusetts, which he had helped happen, Hall was the only professional educator of teachers in America (Barnard, 1858; Levy, 1991).

Teaching as "Women's Work"

Several factors merged to make teaching attractive and available to women as the nineteenth century progressed: the industrialization of the northeast and reduction in farm work that occupied women's days; the migration of New Englanders and Europeans to the new "West" (current Midwestern US) in search of land and opportunity; the lengthening of school terms; more formalized schools with age-graded classrooms led by women teachers under the supervision of male principals; and growing expectations for women's education, including by women themselves. When school terms expanded from three months to eight, teaching could no longer fit into a man's winter farming lull or a college break; it became a full-time job without a full-time salary. Rising standards for teacher qualifications privileged girls who had more time and opportunity to attend high schools than their brothers whose work on the farm or in the shop began early. And when the Civil War (1860–1865) enlisted almost three million men, leaving women behind to do the work they had done, local (male) school committees quickly realized that women could teach as well as, if not better than, men, and for much lower pay. They could refer to some nineteenth century views on women's "natural sphere," assumptions about women's "inherent" kindness and nurturing personalities, and the responsibility of "Republican womanhood" to inculcate the norms and values that their sons would need to make political decisions in the future (Kerber, 1976; Nash, 1997). By the middle of the nineteenth century, the nation's teaching workforce was moving toward three-quarters female. In Massachusetts, women teachers outnumbered men by a factor of two to one in 1842. Surveying 70 county records, Strober and Langford found that the percentage of teachers who were female rose from 38% in 1850 to 62% in 1870 (Sklar, 1973, p. 181; Strober & Lanford, 1986). As the economy and geography of the nation changed, the need for public schools heightened and the science of pedagogy deepened, educational opportunities for prospective women teachers grew.

In 1859, the abolitionist social reformer and champion of women's suffrage Thomas Wentworth Higginson wrote an article for *The Atlantic Monthly* facetiously entitled, "Ought Women to Learn the Alphabet?". In it, he argued with those, presuming that women were inherently distinctly different from, and inferior to, men and worried about threats to male privilege and domestic upheaval, would hold women back from the educational (and professional) opportunities that were available to men. Higginson expressed sympathy for women teachers whose annual salary of 200 dollars was "embittered by the knowledge that the young college stripling in the next school-room is paid a 1000 dollars for work no harder or more responsible than her own, – and that, too, after the whole pathway of education has been obstructed for her and smoothed for him…" Higginson demanded that women receive a "fair share of training, of encouragement, [and] remuneration."

> Nothing can be more absurd than to impose entirely distinct standards…on the two sexes, or to expect that woman, any more than man, will accomplish anything great without due preparation and adequate stimulus…Give an equal chance, and let genius and industry do the rest…First give woman, if you dare, the alphabet, then summon her to her career.
>
> (Higginson, 1859, p. 11)

Even without the access to the formal schooling that subsequent years would provide, many young women in the early years of the republic took it upon themselves to learn as much as their brothers, with or without their family's support. To satisfy the desire for learning that her high intelligence and curiosity demanded, Emma Willard taught herself geometry at age 13 and read her nephew's college texts in mathematics and philosophy. She would later establish Troy Female Seminary in New York, whose curriculum included the sciences and mathematics, winning some public funds by arguing that the future of the nation depended on the character of its citizens, character largely formed by their mothers (Lutz, 1964). Margaret Fuller's father set before his talented daughter a rigorous reading list that included classic literature, history, and Latin to supplement the more limited "ornamental" curriculum offered to girls in the local Cambridge, Massachusetts, schools. Margaret was then enlisted as teacher for her younger brothers. Despite her parents' concern as she entered her twenties that she pay more attention to her marriageability than her education, she continued a program of self-study into her adulthood and became a feminist journalist and member of the Transcendentalist philosophers and educators (Marshall, 2013).

A few forward-thinking men had established secondary schools for women that often included some preparation for teaching. The earliest incorporated high school for girls was the Young Ladies' Academy in Philadelphia, cofounded by Benjamin Rush in 1792. Rush argued that women needed knowledge and skills "useful" in influencing the behavior and values of the men and children in their lives but also useful in their own daily lives: rational, scientific thinking, business skills, and the tools of writing and mathematics would prepare them to contribute both economically and morally to the young nation. Pupils studied literature, mathematics, geography, history, rhetoric, chemistry, and natural philosophy.

Graduates were examined in public ceremonies featuring student speeches and awards for academic merit, attended by leading Philadelphians (Nash, 1997; Rush, 1787). Thirty years later and further north, Boston's High School for Girls opened using a monitorial system of instruction, whereby older girls acted as teaching assistant for younger students. The (male) School Committee anticipated that many teachers for the city's primary schools would be drawn from these experienced class monitors (Boston in the 1830s, 2018; Nash, 2005). The school closed after two years, a victim of its own popularity: three times as many girls qualified and persisted in their studies than were expected, and the school committee deemed it too expensive to keep. It reopened 25 years later with a curriculum that offered for prospective teachers: "suitable lectures on the art of imparting instruction to children…[to] qualify said pupils to become teachers of youth" (Boston School Committee, 1848, p. 8).

Notions of women's responsibilities in nurturing the young republic, combined with growing industrialization and urbanization and the freeing of middle- and upper-class women from farm life, gave women more time and purpose for an education similar to their brothers. Moreover, in a nation undergoing rapid growth and change, many women found themselves without the security of traditional family work and support and needed a way to support themselves. Teaching provided work that was acceptable to all social classes and much needed in the new economic order. Even the wealthy urged their daughters to prepare to teach: A North Carolina plantation mistress wrote in 1840 to her daughter away at one of the new seminaries for women, "In this changing world you may hereafter find that your education may be worth more to you than any fortune you might receive in any other" (Sweet, 1985, p. 50).

Female Seminaries Prepare Missionary Teachers

Some early efforts to prepare women to teach had religious roots. The Christian religious revivals of the first part of the nineteenth century – the "Second Great Awakening" – set before many young women the goal of living with high spiritual purpose – the virtues of usefulness and responsibility for one's own soul and that of others. What better way to carry out the Lord's work – to answer the call, to be useful – than to teach Christian values, to prepare themselves and others for the millennium, along with literacy and numeracy? To carry out their vocation, they would need an education themselves. The first decades of the nineteenth century saw a plethora of private academies and "seminaries" for women spring up, often helped with some public funding. "Teachers prepared in these seminaries, many believed, could do as much or more to enlighten the world and introduce the millennium than persons of any other profession except ministers of the gospel" (Sweet, 1985, p. 48). While a student at Litchfield Academy Susan Nye underwent a religious conversion, which affirmed her intention to carry out her Christian responsibility to help build the nation through teaching and benevolent work, she took her conviction to North Carolina in 1815 to teach at Raleigh Academy, a well-respected school for White wealthy and middle-class young women. On her own time, however, Nye extended her teaching to the slaves she saw around her, using her Sundays to read to them from the Bible and surreptitiously teaching them to read, an act that was outlawed in that state. Nye was an example of the many teachers – Black and White – who responded to Blacks' thirst for literacy in secret (Tolley, 2015).

Joseph Emerson, principal of the Byfield Academy for women, offered a rational argument for teaching as women's work, in 1822: "If preaching [is] committed to men, if the lucrative & honorable prof of law & med exercised by them…does it not seem reasonable that the business of teaching should be in a greater measure consigned to the other sex?" (Emerson, 1822). At the opening of Rutgers Female Institute in 1839, Isaac Ferris observed that just as the men had made New York City a center for business and finance, now women bore the responsibility for making it into America's foremost intellectual and moral center (Sweet, 1985, p. 48). Among the best known of these seminaries were Emma Willard's Troy Female Seminary (1821), Catharine Beecher's Hartford (CT) Female Seminary (1823), Zilpah Grant's Ipswich Female Seminary (1824), and Mary Lyon's Mount Holyoke Female Seminary (1837). The combined efforts of their founders probably account for the birth of the idea that teaching is a "natural profession" for women.

Living in Middlebury, Vermont, teacher Emma Willard was struck by the vast difference between her own formal education and Middlebury College's curriculum. Denied admission to the male-only college she nevertheless "completed" courses by reading her nephew's college texts and notes. When New York Governor Dewitt Clinton suggested she open a school for women across the border in New York, she secured public funds from the town of Troy to buy land and build Troy Female Seminary. The school was among the first to prepare women with rigorous academic content for what she saw as their primary roles as informed, confident teacher-mothers whose responsibility was to serve the nation in ways differentiated by their gendered tasks. She authored textbooks and treatises on women's education and her school earned wide respect as a serious academic institution; it exists today as the Emma Willard School, a college preparatory academy (Lutz, 1964). Always private and independent, most of its students were wealthy, although in its first years, Willard secured scholarships for the 10 percent of her students who intended to become schoolteachers (Baym, 1991, pp. 9–10). But Willard defined all women as "teachers," whether they were employed in schools or not. Her aim was to create effective, patriotic, moral, righteous "governors of themselves and others," for, "if the female character be raised, it must inevitably raise that of the other sex…[and]…the whole character of the community" (Willard, 1819).

Believing that women should have an education of serious purpose and content that would fit them for their highest purpose – teaching children – within families and/or in schools, Catharine Beecher probably deserves the credit for the idea that professional teaching requires professional preparation. In 1823, she and her sister founded the Hartford (Connecticut) Female Seminary, whose curriculum eschewed the "ornamental" and focused on a range of academic subject matter as well as classes in physical education and health. The daughter and sister of a minister, she went west to Ohio with her minister father, opened a school for women, contributed to the McGuffey early reading books and saw the great need for new schools led by well-qualified Christian teachers. The US Land Ordinance of 1785 had mandated the use of western public lands for public schools, stipulating that each new township should set aside 1/16 of its land area whose lease or sale should be used to support a school. The Ordinance of 1787 defined the new schools' educational purpose: "Religion, morality and knowledge, being necessary to good government and the happiness of mankind, schools and the means of education shall forever be encouraged" ("An Ordinance," 1787). Returning to Connecticut, Beecher responded to the need for new teachers for the frontier settlements by establishing the Board of National Popular Education, which recruited evangelical Protestant teachers and trained them in a six-week program. Beecher's pedagogy stressed reading aloud as a technique of modeling language and thinking, and the importance of teaching to all aspects of children's development: moral, physical, cognitive, and artistic. While Beecher's National Board sent some 600 women west to teach, some to open new schools, the Board was not without critics, who found the Easterners too narrow in their views and unappreciative of the diverse settlers and their hardships and talents (Cordier, 1997, p. 29).

McGuffey's Readers: Lessons for Children and Their Teachers

William Holmes McGuffey (1800–1873), US educator and Presbyterian clergyman, developed a series of early reading books (readers) for primary school students that blended instruction in reading with lessons in the moral code that was part of his religion and the social, political, and religious values and norms of behavior that he considered particularly American. First published in 1836, they sold over 125 million copies and were used in schools throughout the nation well into the twentieth century. McGuffey's Readers offered lessons in grammar, spelling, and punctuation contexted in proverbs, didactic poetry, and selections from literature – what might be deemed the "Great Books" of the Western canon, written by writers such as William Shakespeare, Charles Lamb, Charles Dickens, and Louisa May Alcott. The books contained author biographies, pedagogical suggestions for teachers, and beautiful illustrations by noted painters and engravers of the era.

Having taught school in country schools from the age of 14 (after completing grammar school), McGuffey entered Washington and Jefferson College in western Pennsylvania. While there, he was contacted by a Cincinnati publisher, who had first asked Catherine Beecher to write a series of schoolbooks. She had turned them down, saying she was too busy, but recommended her friend McGuffey for the job. Frustrated with the materials available for his own teaching, he had already written two such books. With his degree in hand and his book project underway, McGuffey began a career in higher education, first as professor of languages at Ohio's Miami University, then to the presidencies of Cincinnati College and of Ohio University and finally a professorship in moral philosophy at the University of Virginia. While in Ohio, he helped organize the state's public school system. His "Eclectic Readers" for first through sixth grades were published from 1836 to 1857 and were continually revised and reprinted, with the help of his brother Alexander Hamilton McGuffey ("McGuffey and His Readers," 2007). By today's standards, McGuffey's readers were unabashedly narrow in cultural and historical perspective, racist, sexist, and imbued with a religion not shared by all American children. But their use of real literature ranging over a variety of subject areas and their inclusion of questions that teachers might ask pupils revolutionized reading and language teaching methods which, before McGuffey, comprised lists of syllables and words to be memorized and recited. The popular readers addressed children's comprehensive development and offered pedagogical guidance that invited children to consider meaning in what they were reading and how it might apply to their lives.

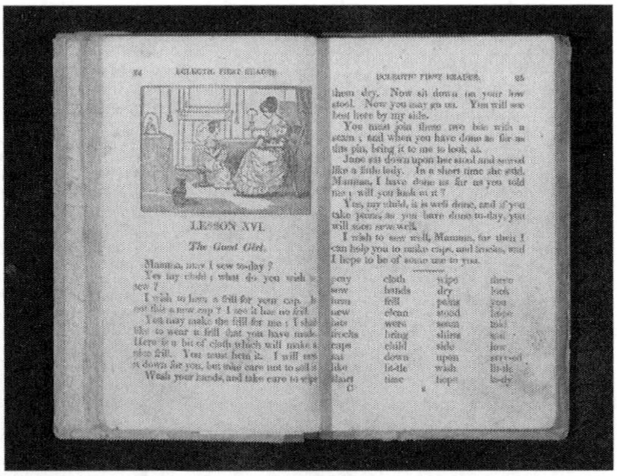

Source: Courtesy of the McGuffey House and Museum, Miami University (images in the public domain).

National Board recruits were joined by many students at the other female seminaries founded in the early nineteenth century. At Byfield Academy, student Zilpah Grant's intelligence and interest in teaching quickly earned the respect of Joseph Emerson, who hired her as a teacher there, which began her rapid ascension to leadership. The first principal of New Hampshire's Adams Female Academy (est. 1824), she returned to Massachusetts in 1828 to lead the Ipswich

Female Academy for many years, assisted by her Byfield friend Mary Lyon. Renamed the Seminary for Teachers in Ipswich, it was one of the first schools to advertise a purpose of explicit teacher preparation; the school offered instruction on how to teach children "of different capacities" and in "different stages of improvement," in methods of gentle "correction," on how to "awaken attention," "excite inquiry," "arouse the indolent" and "encourage the diffident," and improve a student's whole character (Ipswich Female Academy catalog quoted in Capen & Labaree, 1947, pp. 347–348). Ipswich graduates often returned to the school for additional training from its leader, whose understanding of children and pedagogy seems remarkably prescient. Below are notes taken by one student attentive to her lecture:

> On what subject should we first instruct a child. On such subjects as he can understand...When children begin to read short sentences or even words let them learn some idea in connection with it. Talk about it, make it interesting & never let them learn anything which they cannot understand. Let every subject or study be made interesting. It requires some preparation on the part of a teacher to simplify a subject so that minds of small capacity may be interested...How can we gain the affections of scholars? Treat them as if you desired their best good; with affection, & kindness. Strive to love them.
>
> (quoted in Capen & Labaree, 1947)

Grant's assistant principal, Mary Lyon, left Ipswich in 1834 to found two other Massachusetts academies that later became Mount Holyoke and Wheaton Colleges for women.

A Botany Class at Wheaton Female Seminary, 1885.
Source: Courtesy of Gebbie Archives at Wheaton College (Massachusetts).

It is worth noting that, although all these academies were private, requiring tuition, several of their leaders were concerned that promising young women of limited financial means be able to attend. Willard successfully secured some public funding from the state of New York to defray some of its expenses. Troy and Ipswich seminaries allowed needy students to attend "on credit," with the understanding that they would repay their tuition from their teaching salaries. Mary Lyon's Mount Holyoke operated on a "domestic system," whereby both students and teachers shared in cooking, cleaning, and growing their own food. Lyon also tirelessly collected funds from middle-class neighbors to support her school and its students. Catharine Beecher, strongly advocating for recruiting prospective teachers from the middle and upper classes, gave tuition reductions for the daughters of clergymen (Nash, 2005, pp. 66–70; Navaree, 1977, p. 145).

Biographical Sketch

Catharine Beecher.
"[I]t is in the power of American women to save their nation."
Source: Schlesinger Library, Harvard Radcliffe Institute.

Catharine Beecher was born into an evangelical Christian family of religious and social reformers that included her sister Harriet Beecher Stowe, author of the antislavery novel *Uncle Tom's Cabin* and father and son ministers Lyman and Henry Ward Beecher. At her mother's death, it fell to Catharine, the eldest, to run the household and raise her siblings. Fittingly, she became a teacher and teacher of teachers, imbued with religious mission and social/educational reform, sensitive to the shadowed place of women in early American society. While she subscribed to the prevailing theory that women's natural sphere was the private home (and a man's, a more public arena), she thought the separate spheres are equally important to society. As a single woman, she understood the need for women to have "honorable independence and extensive usefulness," whether within their homes or in the working world, but in roles that remained within "the proscribed boundaries of feminine modesty." Women, by nature nurturant and empathic, were "the best... guardian[s] and teacher[s] of childhood." Professional teaching, therefore, furnished women with respectable, socially and morally necessary, and remunerative work. It would allow women to be both professional and womanly (quoted in Speicher, 2017, n.p.).

Beecher was a prolific speaker and writer on all matters relating to women's responsibilities, from housekeeping and health tips to religion, abolitionism, and education. She sought to recruit female teachers from among America's middle class, many of whom looked for ways to apply their knowledge and skills to work that had spiritual and patriotic meaning. "This is the way, and the only way, in which our nation can be saved from impending perils… the work to be done enormous, yet it is in the power of American women to save their nation" (Beecher, 1845, n.p.). The "perils" that she foresaw were threats to the White Anglo-Saxon Protestant "civilization": increasing immigration, rising number of Catholics, and the unruly, godless, culturally diverse wasteland that were the new midwestern and western settlements.

> Soon in all parts of our country in each neglected village, or new settlement, the Christian female teacher will quietly take her station, collecting the ignorant children around her, teaching the habits of neatness, order and thrift; opening the book of knowledge, inspiring the principles of morality, and awakening the hope of immorality.
>
> (Beecher, 1846, p. 12)

The army of woman teachers she sought needed a substantive education. She founded the Hartford Female Seminary in 1823 in Connecticut, Western Female Institute in Ohio in 1833 and the Milwaukee Female College in 1850, urging their graduates to go west to teach where millions of children had no access to schools and lived with parents many of whom spoke no English and/or were illiterate. In 1846 she established the National Board of Popular Education, whose purpose was the recruitment of women of good character, background, and education and prepare them in a six-week program for their Western mission. Beecher then embarked on a tour of eastern cities (e.g., Philadelphia, New York, Baltimore, Washington, D.C.) to publicize the program and secure donations, winning the endorsement of major educational leaders like Henry Barnard of Connecticut and Horace Mann of Massachusetts. The Board sent some 600 new teachers into the Midwest and Western communities and many new schools were opened where there had been none before. The program was not without criticism, however, especially from the westerners themselves. For one thing, the Board accepted only Presbyterians, Methodists, Congregationalists, Baptists and Episcopalians – no Unitarians, no Catholics, no Jews, no Quakers. For another, there was resentment against many teachers' attitudes of superiority. Most of these women were independent and self-supporting, with some years of teaching experience. All had evangelical motives; Beecher's application included an essay on their "conversion" experiences as well as testimonials from ministers or educators regarding their moral character and piety, "cheerful, hopeful spirit," "devotion to Christ" as a "means of doing good in the destitute, valley of the West," as well as their teaching skills. Accepted students underwent intensive training in pedagogy and discipline, as well as writing, music, mathematics, and physiology; then sent West. The training was free, but the teachers were on their own once they arrived. They had to teach at least two years and, if possible, refund her training expenses. They taught in seminaries, one-room schools, in homes or churches. Some were welcomed, and others were met with hostility toward Easterners, women teachers and/or evangelicals. The hostility may have been justified, judging from letters from teachers reporting that their students were ignorant, uninterested in education, and that their schoolhouses and boarding houses were inadequate. Most teachers were underpaid; some, not paid at all. Beecher went West on occasion to provide teachers money and support. In 1852 she established the American Woman's Educational Association, to endow professional schools in Iowa, Illinois, and Wisconsin to train young women from Western communities, women who would "encounter less prejudice and suspicion" than teachers from the East. The Milwaukee Female College became part of the University of Wisconsin-Milwaukee.

Catharine Beecher was not a champion of women's political equality; for example, she was against women's right to vote. She was, however, a champion of the "moral economy of women's educational labor, a social formation that placed women directly into the national life of the United States" (Sklar, 1973, p. 174), whose contributions she elevated by labeling teaching a "profession" offering influence, respectability, and independence. In her lectures, lobbying, writing, and organizing, she joined Horace Mann and Henry Barnard in influencing the development of the common school movement and specialized teacher preparation (see Chapter 2).

By the 1850s, school oversight, teacher qualifications, and preparation in the midwestern states were more organized. Indiana's Rebecca Russel, whose own schooling had been completed in the "common" schools of her town supplemented by some higher courses, including one for prospective teachers, had to pass a test of grammar, spelling, geography, and arithmetic to qualify for a two-year teaching license. Her diary records the fact that she kept up her professional development by subscribing to the *Indiana School Journal*, reading *The Teacher's Friend*, and attending monthly meetings of the local teachers' association (Kaestle, 1988).

Oberlin College in Ohio, founded in 1833 for men only, began admitting women four years later, becoming the first coeducational higher education institution in the US. It had, in 1835, been the first to regularly admit African Americans. Its founders, Presbyterian missionaries, sought "to train teachers and other Christian leaders for the boundless most desolate fields in the West." The school's "grand object" was "the diffusion of useful science, sound morality, and pure religion, among the growing multitudes through education of ministers and pious schoolteachers; secondarily, the elevation of female character; and thirdly, the education of the common people with the higher classes, in such a manner as suits the nature of republican institutions." The education was free; students were expected to labor as well as learn, helping to build and sustain the community, the men growing food for the community, the women cooking, laundering, and sewing. Women were not admitted to the bachelor's program until 1837, but teacher preparation did not generally require a college degree in the US at that time. The early "Ladies Course," was four years of study but required only a "good common school education" (8th grade) for admission. It included mathematics and the sciences, philosophy, literature, and languages, "requiring about a year more time than is devoted to study in the best female academies." Committed to the abolition of slavery, Oberlin was a stop along the Underground Railroad, the system of safehouses that aided enslaved African Americans in their escape to freedom. Of importance in the history of education, and of teacher preparation, in the US, is Oberlin's role in educating the freed people during and after the Civil War. Black and White male and female graduates of Oberlin carried out their mission not only in the new "West" but in the South, teaching and leading schools for the formerly enslaved (Fairchild, 1860).

The opportunity to help the formerly enslaved brought some 3000 teachers South who had prepared at Oberlin, in female seminaries, in the public normal schools arising in the Northeast and Midwest, or in a few Eastern universities, to answer the African American demand for an education. While the great majority of the earliest groups of teachers were female and White, there were men and there were African Americans. After the war, some were Southern Blacks who had attended normal programs in the schools established during Reconstruction. Part of the "Port Royal Experiment" on the South Carolina sea islands, the Penn School was one of the earliest in 1862 of these schools, joined later by the Schofield Normal and Industrial School in the same state. Two graduates of Oberlin – Carolyn Putnam and Sally Holley – founded the Holley School in Virginia. Established by White northerners during and just after the Civil War, these schools and others responded to the demands of Black southerners for an education they had been deprived of for 250 years and which they knew to be linked to liberation and citizenship. Eventually they would help prepare teachers, principals, and school founders from the very communities they served (Butchart, 2013).

The Education of Black Americans and Their Teachers

In the eighteenth and early nineteenth century South, there were few opportunities for education for Black children; any education available to slaves was rare, accidental, hidden, and generally illegal. There were few publicly supported schools in the South for poor Whites, and none for free Blacks. Northern cities and towns typically provided schools for local children, though, in most cases they were segregated. Philadelphia Quakers, for example, had long provided schools for Black children, but they were separate and often inferior to what was available to Whites. Such was the case in Boston until the state legislature banned segregated schools in 1855, the first state to do so. Here and there were bright spots of Black education, often the work of progressive or reformed White citizens. Philadelphia, for example, hosted the first institution of higher education for free Blacks. Richard Humphreys, the son of British Virgin Island slave-holding planters who had immigrated to Philadelphia as a young man, converted to Quakerism and in doing so began to see the struggles of free Blacks to earn a good living in the city. On his deathbed in 1831, he granted one-tenth of his substantial wealth to establish "a benevolent society or institution [for] the instructing the descendants of the African race in school learning, in the various branches of the mechanic arts and trade, and in agriculture, in order to prepare and fit and qualify them to act as teachers in…those branches of useful branches." By 1851, in his legacy "Institute for Colored Youth," a staff of Black male and female teachers of advanced mathematics, physical and social sciences, English, philosophy, classical languages, and moral and religious studies were preparing young African Americans for teaching and other professions. Those planning to teach could do so by completing the Institute's boys' or girls' high school program or continue to the collegiate level. The Institute offered the wider Black community a library and lectures by leading Black intellectuals and activists and produced many Black community leaders, physicians, lawyers, business owners, and teachers. Eventually, the curriculum narrowed to normal and industrial education, and by 1914, had been renamed the Cheyney Training School for Teachers, today Cheney University of Pennsylvania (History of the Institute for Colored Youth, n.d.; Hornick, 1975).

The same year that the Philadelphia Institute for Colored Youth opened, some 140 miles south in Washington, D.C., Myrtilla Miner established the Normal School for Colored Girls who wanted to teach. Miner, a White woman from New York state, had been teaching at a female academy in Mississippi. Abhorring slavery, she asked to teach African American girls, and was refused. Moving north to Washington, she opened a school in a room of the house of a Black man and then secured funding from Harriet Beecher Stowe and others for a permanent building. Despite hostility and harassment from Whites, attempts to burn down the school, and denouncements from the mayor, she prevailed; the Institute was the only postelementary school for African Americans in the city until the Civil War. To one of her students, she was "one of the bravest women I have ever known." To Frederick Douglass, who had tried to dissuade her from her plan, she was a hero. From the 1870s through World War II, Miner Teacher's College educated the majority of African American elementary schoolteachers employed by the D.C. schools. In 1879, the school was renamed the Myrtilla Miner Normal School in her honor, and later merged with other institutions to create the University of the District of Columbia (Foner & Pacheco, 1984; Velez, 2013).

Countering a too-long-prevailing view that the education of Black Americans and teachers was accomplished primarily by the generosity of White allies and advocates is evidence that the movement began and persisted with bravery and seriousness of their own efforts. In the same year that Laura Towne opened the Penn School on St. Helena Island, S.C., Clement Robinson, a Virginia slave who had bought his own freedom and gone north to Philadelphia for an education returned to Virginia to establish a "colored school" in Alexandria for children and adults. Its upper school – called Beulah Normal and Theological Institute – was the first secondary school preparing Black teachers and ministers in the South and the first with African American teachers. Five years later in 1867, seven Black citizens of Fayetteville, N.C., established the Howard School, which later became the first public normal school in that state and the first state-sponsored teacher training institute in the South. It is now Fayetteville State University, one of many Historically Black Colleges and Universities in the US (Huddle, 1997).

Post-war Reconstruction had brought federal aid to the South via Congress's establishment of a federal Bureau of Refugees, Freedmen, and Abandoned Lands. This "Freedmen's Bureau" provided help both to emancipated African Americans and to poor White Southerners who had lost land, homes, and sources of income in the war. The Bureau led the effort to relieve their poverty and displacement but also to help reconstruct a society that included full citizenship for Blacks. It provided food, clothing, jobs, legal and medical services; pensions for soldiers, both Black and White; and negotiated labor contracts and land settlements. It received complaints and petitions about violent voter repression and the repressive new Black Codes. It was, however, unable to secure long-term policies ensuring equality and civil rights; while the "Radical Republicans" in Congress – including newly elected Black representatives – supported the Bureau, President Andrew Johnson's general policy of appeasement of Southern Whites led eventually to its being dismantled in 1872. The election of Rutherford B. Hayes in 1876 resulted in the withdrawal of federal troops from the South and, in effect, of support for the formerly enslaved.

Where the Freedmen's Bureau did make a lasting impact, however, was in education. Led by Bureau Commissioner O.O. Howard, the Bureau helped "a whole race trying to go to school" (Washington, 1901, p. 30) by establishing and overseeing tax-supported schools for both Blacks and Whites where there had been none. Howard collaborated with religious and secular benevolent societies, sympathetic southern and formerly enslaved African Americans to distribute funds, resources, and staff. The result of this public-private partnership was that by the end of Reconstruction, every Southern state had established a system of public schools, though now racially segregated and markedly inferior to their White counterparts (Butler, 2013). At the federal level, President Andrew Johnson established a Department of Education in 1867 to collect information on the nation's schools, but to appease Southern politicians concerned with the possibility of federal control over local schools, the department was reduced a year later to an Office of Education within the Department of the Interior (U.S. Department of Education, 2010).

The need for more teachers to staff and lead the growing number of southern Black schools was critical. The wartime US Congress had passed the Morrill Act of 1862, an act similar to the Homestead Act which had mandated public schools in the new settlements of the Midwest. The Morrill Act aimed to do the same for higher education; it provided states with public land that could be sold for the support of "at least one college where the leading object shall be... branches of learning related to the agricultural and mechanic arts...to promote the liberal and practical education of the industrial classes in several pursuits and professions in life" ("Transcript of Morrill Act," 1862). After emancipation, Black educators and their White allies asked that the funds be used for "public people's colleges" (high schools) and normal schools for African Americans. But southern state legislators, largely White, refused to use Morrill funds for Black normal schools; and only three southern states used the money to support Black agricultural and technical secondary schools (Reid, 2015, pp. 143–144).

Southern Blacks looked elsewhere for other ways to prepare teachers. In the absence of public secondary schools, the new elementary schools sometimes offered a normal program in the upper grades, a practice also common in the North and Midwest. Older students who had the ability, interest, and talent required for teaching were given special instruction in how to manage children, how to teach reading, etc., and then given teaching positions in the primary classes. Secondary normal programs were established with private donations. By 1866, Beulah Normal School was just one of many separate normal schools supported by churches or relief societies. The New York and Pennsylvania Freedmen's Relief Associations and the American Missionary Society funded networks of Black normal schools. The Presbyterian Church sponsored normal schools, including one in Baltimore and all-female Scotia Seminary in Concord, NC, founded in 1867 by Rev. Luke Dorland. Later renamed Scotia College, it counted among its alumnae, noted Black educator Mary McLeod Bethune, a member of President Franklin Roosevelt's "Black Cabinet" (Butchart & Rolleri, 2004).

Historically Black Colleges and Universities (HBCUs)

With support from the American Missionary Society and the Methodist and other Protestant churches, the Freedmen's Bureau established higher education institutions and normal schools to prepare Black teachers. By 1870, seven higher education institutions, all with normal programs, had received charters. These first "Historically Black Colleges and Universities" were Berea College in Kentucky, Fisk University in Tennessee, Atlanta University, Hampton Normal School (later Hampton Institute) in Virginia, Talladega College in Alabama, Tougaloo College in Mississippi, and Straight College and Union Normal Schools, which merged to form today's Dillard University in Louisiana. By 1876, 14 normal high schools were opened and by 1888, these schools had educated 7,000 African American teachers. Howard University in Washington, D.C., began with a partnership that included the Freedmen's Bureau, the Washington, D.C. Congregationalist Church, and the Reconstructionist US Congress who, in 1867, created Howard College to prepare Black teachers, ministers, and lawyers. Today's Howard University was named for the Freedmen's Bureau Commissioner, who served as its first president. Baptists, Presbyterians, African Methodist Episcopalian, and other churches were responsible for establishing additional colleges and universities for Black students, most with teacher preparation programs. They include what are now Morehouse, Spelman, and Stillman Colleges and Lincoln and Johnson C. Smith Universities, among the 107 HBCUs existing today (Johnson & Harter, n.d.; Pierce, 1904, pp. 78–79; Talladega College: Our History, n.d.).

The founders of many of these early universities, normal schools, and high schools were abolitionists and/or religious leaders dedicated to helping the formerly enslaved to rise as a race from the degraded conditions in which they had been forced to live. Some were committed to racial equality and integration. The forward-thinking among them were committed to preparing Black educational leaders. Oberlin graduates Caroline Putnam and Sally Holley, for example, described by a fellow Oberlin student as "the only two ultra-radicals there" and who established the Holley School in Virginia, willed their school to the 11 African American trustees after their deaths. Of note, however, is the fact that many of these institutions were established or inspired by African Americans themselves; Talladega College began at the initiative of a group of former slaves from Mississippi committed to the education of their people: "We regard the education of our children and youths as vital to the preservation of our liberties, and true religion as the foundation of all real virtue, and shall use our utmost endeavors to promote these blessings in our common country" (Talladega College: Our History, n.d.). The school they created educated those who needed elementary-level instruction as well as those in need of a "normal program" to prepare as teachers. In Atlanta, Georgia, former slaves James Tate and Grandison Daniels opened the first school for Black children in 1862 in a Black

Baptist church. At the war's end, Tate and Daniels accepted the help of the American Missionary Association to expand the program and charter Atlanta University. For African American educators like Clement Robinson at Beulah Normal, Robert Harris in Fayetteville, N.C., and Tate and Daniels in Atlanta, creating their own institutions of higher education and preparing their own teachers were important exercises of Black autonomy and control of their own lives.

Conclusion: The Call to Widen Access, Assume Public Responsibility for Teacher Preparation

In the first part of the nineteenth century, normal classes and programs that prepared teachers received their funding from private organizations, philanthropists, and/or the Freedman's Bureau to support young men and women whose families could not provide for their further education or the expenses of their living away from home. Given the nation's growing population, including new immigrants and Black Americans freed by the war; the Western migration and rapid growth of new towns and cities; and the growing, industrializing economy, there was rising awareness that the public bore some responsibility for the preparation of teachers for the young nation's new public schools. Parallel to the establishment of private academies to educate young women and men as teachers, of new high schools and colleges with "normal programs," and of normal schools funded by religious and philanthropic organizations, there were calls for tax-funded teacher education institutions – normal schools – of the kind that European nations like Prussia were pioneering. In New England and the Northeast, there was a great disparity in the level and quality of credentials and preparation between teachers in the larger cities – typically graduates of high schools, academies, or colleges – and teachers in rural "common" schools, who had only just been graduated from them. Leading educators pushed for state funding to allow students who were financially unable to attend private academies and colleges to receive a high-quality preparation at state expense for the important work of educating the children in the common schools. Four years after Samuel Read Hall began his normal institute at Concord, James Carter opened a teacher's seminary at Lancaster, Massachusetts, with a group of interested local citizens. For the next 10 years, he and others would petition the state legislature to support the seminary effort and attach a model school. It would take the new Massachusetts Secretary of Education and a wealthy donor to convince the legislators to approve a new experiment in state-funded normal schools that would spread throughout the nation (Wright, 1930). The next chapter tells the story.

References

An Ordinance for the government of the Territory of the United States northwest of the River Ohio. (1787). *Adopted by the confederation congress*. Washington, D.C.: The National Archives and Records Administration. Retrieved from https://www.ourdocuments.gov/document_data/document_transcripts/document_008_transcript.html

Barnard, H. (1858). Samuel Read Hall. *American Journal of Education*, *5*(14), 372–385. Retrieved from https://ia803103.us.archive.org/21/items/americanjournalo05barn/americanjournalo05barn.pdf

Baym, N. (1991, March). Women and the republic: Emma Willard's rhetoric of history. *American Quarterly*, *43*(1), 1–23. Retrieved from https://www.jstor.org/stable/2712964

Beecher, C. E. (1845). *The duty of American women to their country*. New York, NY: Harper & Brothers. Retrieved from https://www.gutenberg.org/files/53739/53739-0.txt

Beecher, C. E. (1846). *The evils suffered by the American women and American children*. Address to the Protestant clergy of the United State. New York, NH: Harper & Brothers. Retrieved from https://babel.hathitrust.org/cgi/pt?id=hvd.32044009733171&view=1up&seq=10

Boston School Committee. (1848, May 8). *Additional report of committee on high school for girls. City document no. 25 city of Boston archives*. Retrieved from https://cityofboston.access.preservica.com/uncategorized/IO_19d2ab60-c2cd-45da-b1e6-4badc7a701ad/

Boston in the (18)30s: The Girls High School Experiment. (2018, January 17). City of Boston archives and records management. Retrieved from https://www.boston.gov/news/boston-30s-girls-high-school-experiment

Butchart, R. E. (2013). *Schooling the freed people: Teaching, earning, and the struggle for Black freedom, 1861–1876*. Chapel Hill, NC: University of North Carolina.

Butchart, R. E., & Rolleri, A. F. (2004). Secondary education and emancipation: Secondary schools for freed slaves in the American South, 1862–1875. *Paedagogica Historica*, *40*(1–2), 157–181. doi:10.1080/00309230310001649243

Butler, A. J. (2013). *A union of church and state: The Freedmen's Bureau and the education of African Americans in Virginia from 1865 to 1871*. Ed.D. Dissertation, College of William and Mary in Virginia, 1539618383. doi:10.25774/w4-0k2t-pw52

Capen, E. P., & Labaree, L. W. (1947). Zilpah grant and the art of teaching: 1829. *The New England Quarterly*, *20*(3), 351–353. Retrieved from https://www.jstor.org/stable/361444

Cole, N. M. (1957, Winter). The Licensing of schoolmasters in colonial Massachusetts. *History of Education Journal*, *8*(2), 68–74.

Cordier, M. H. (1997). *Schoolwomen of the prairies and plains: Personal narratives from Iowa, Kansas, and Nebraska, 1860s–1920s*. Albuquerque NM: University of New Mexico.

Cremin, L. A. (1953). The heritage of American teacher education. *Journal of Teacher Education*, *4*, 163–170.

Emerson, J. (1822, January 15). Female education, a discourse, delivered at the dedication of the seminary hall in Saugus, to which is added the little reckoner, consisting principally of arithmetical questions for infant minds. *Maine Bicentennial, 88*. Retrieved from https://digitalcommons.library.umaine.edu/mainebicentennial/88

Fairchild, J. H. (1860). Joint education of the sexes: An address before a meeting of college presidents at Springfield, Ill. Retrieved from https://www2.oberlin.edu/external/EOG/LucyStonewalk-a-thonTour/FairchildCoEducation.html

Foner, P. S., & Pacheco, J. F. (1984). *Three who dared: Prudence Crandall, Margaret Douglass, Myrtilla Miner–Champions of antebellum Black education*. New York, NY: Praeger.

Hall, S. R. (1829). The Old Stone House Museum. Retrieved from https://web.archive.org/web/20100405231650/http://www.oldstonehousemuseum.org/srhallbio.html

Hall, S. R. (1830). *Lectures on school-keeping*. Boston, MA: Richardson, Lord and Holbrook. Retrieved from https://play.google.com/books/reader?id=SAETAAAAIAAJ&hl=en&pg=GBS.PP5

Higginson, T. W. (1859, February). Ought women to earn the alphabet. *Atlantic Monthly*, 3–23. Retrieved from https://www.theatlantic.com/magazine/archive/1859/02/ought-women-to-learn-the-alphabet/306366/

History of the Institute for Colored Youth (n.d.). Villanova, PA: Falvey Library, Villanova University. Retrieved from https://exhibits.library.villanova.edu/institute-colored-youth/institute-history

Hofstadter, R. (1963). *Anti-intellectualism in American life*. New York, NY: Knopf.

Hornick, N. S. (1975, October). Anthony Benezet and the Africans' school: Toward a theory of full equality. *The Pennsylvania Magazine of History and Biography*, *99*(4), 399–421. Retrieved from https://www.jstor.org/stable/20091000

Huddle, M. A. (1997, April). To educate a race: The making of the first state colored normal school, Fayetteville, North Carolina, 1865–1877. *North Carolina Historical Review*, *74*, 147–150.

Jefferson, T. (1950/1779). A Bill for the more general diffusion of knowledge. In J. P. Boyd (Ed.). *The papers of Thomas Jefferson* (Vol. 2, pp. 526–535). Princeton, NJ: Princeton University Press.

Johnson, C. J., & Harter, C. (n.d.). Biographical Note. *American missionary association archives, 1828–1969*. New Orleans, LA: Amistad Research Center at Tulane University. Retrieved from http://amistadresearchcenter.tulane.edu/archon/?p=collections/findingaid&id=19&rootcontentid=12505

Kaestle, C. F. (1988, March). Public education in the old Northwest: "Necessary to good government and the happiness of mankind". *Indiana Magazine of History*, *84*(1), 60–74. Retrieved from https://www.jstor.org/stable/27791140

Kerber, L. (1976, Summer). The republican mother: Women and the Enlightenment–An American perspective. *American Quarterly*, *28*(2), 187–205.

Levy, T. (1991, Fall). First in his class: The many contributions of Samuel Read Hall. *Organization of American Historians Magazine of History*, *6*(2), 38–41. Retrieved from https://www.jstor.org/stable/25162822

Lutz, A. (1964). *Emma Willard: Pioneer educator of American women*. Boston, MA: Beacon Press.

Marshall, M. (2013). *Margaret Fuller: A new American life*. Boston, MA: Houghton Mifflin Harcourt.

Nash, M. A. (1997, Summer). Rethinking republican motherhood: Benjamin Rush and the young Ladies' academy of Philadelphia. *Journal of the Early Republic*, *17*(2), 171–191. Retrieved from https://www.jstor.org/stable/3124445

Nash, M. A. (2005). *Women's education in the United States, 1780–1840*. New York, NY: Palgrave-Macmillan.

Navarre, J. P. (1977). *The female teacher: The beginnings of teaching as a "woman's profession"*. Ph.D. Dissertation, Bowling Green State University, Ohio. Retrieved from https://etd.ohiolink.edu/apexprod/rws_etd/send_file/send?accession=bgsu1566463048515457&disposition=inline

Old Deluder Satan Act. (1647). *The laws and liberties of Massachusetts*. Reprinted from the copy of the 1648 Edition in the Henry E. Huntington Library, with an introduction by Max Farrand. Cambridge, MA: Harvard University Press. Retrieved from https://www.mass.gov/files/documents/2016/08/ob/deludersatan.pdf

Pierce, P. S. (1904). *The Freedmen's Bureau: A chapter in the history of reconstruction*. Iowa City, IA: University of Iowa Press.

Reid, D. A. (2015). People's colleges for other citizens: Black land-grant institutions and the politics of educational expansion in the post-Civil War Era. In A. I. Marcus (Ed.), *Science as service: Establishing and reformulating American land-grant universities, 1865–1930* (pp. 141–174). Tuscaloosa, AL: University of Alabama.

Rev. Samuel Read Hall, L.L.D. Obituary. (1877, July 7). Bellows Fall, VT: Vermont Chronicle. Newspapers by Ancestry. Retrieved from https://www.newspapers.com/clip/27665122/vermont-chronicle/

Rush, B. (1787). Thoughts upon female education. The Albert M. Greenfield Digital Center for the History of Women's Education. Retrieved from http://greenfield.brynmawr.edu/items/show/2828

Sklar, K. K. (1973). *Catharine Beecher: A study in American domesticity*. New Haven, CT: Yale University Press.

Speicher, A. (2016–2017, Winter). Catharine Beecher educates the West. In *Connecticut explored: The Magazine of Connecticut history*. Retrieved from https://www.ctexplored.org/catharine-beecher-educates-the-west/

Strober, M. H., & Lanford, A. G. (1986, Winter). The feminization of public school teaching: Cross-sectional analysis, 1850–1880. *Signs*, *11*(2), 212–235. Retrieved from https://www.jstor.org/stable/3174046

Sweet, L. I. (1985, March). The female seminary movement and woman's mission in antebellum America. *Church History*, *54*(1), 41–55. Retrieved from https://www.jstor.org/stable/3165749/

Talladega College. (n.d.). Talladega college: Our history. Retrieved from http://www.talladega.edu/our-history/

Tolley, K. (2015). *Heading south to teach: The world of Susan Nye Hutchison, 1815–1845*. Chapel Hill, NC: University of North Carolina Press.

Transcript of Morrill Act. (1862). Washington, DC: The National Archives and Records Administration. Retrieved from https://www.ourdocuments.gov/doc.php?flash=false&doc=33&page=transcript

U.S. Department of Education. (2010, September). An overview of the US department of education. Retrieved from https://www2.ed.gov/about/overview/focus/what.html

Velez, D. O. (2013, December 8). Myrtilla Miner: Teaching 'Colored Girls' to teach. *Daily Kos*. Retrieved from https://www.dailykos.com/stories/2013/12/8/1260525/-Myrtilla-Miner-Teaching-colored-girls-to-teach

Walker, D. (1995/1829). *David Walker's appeal, in four articles: Together with a preamble to the coloured citizens of the world, but in particular, and very expressly, to those of the United States of America*. Revised edition with an Introduction by Sean Wilentz. New York, NY: Hill and Wang.

Washington, B. T. (1901). *Up from slavery: An autobiography*. New York, NY: Doubleday & Company.

Willard, E. (1819). *An address to the public particularly to the members of the legislature of New York proposing a plan for improving female education*. Middlebury, VT: J.W. Copeland. Retrieved from https://ia802702.us.archive.org/13/items/aplanforimprovi01willgoog/aplanforimprovi01willgoog.pdf

Wright, F. W. (1930, January). The evolution of the normal schools. *The Elementary School Journal*, *30*(5), 363–371. Retrieved from https://www.jstor.org/stable/994569

Zoracki, S. M. (2006). Vermont's tradition of education and the Vermont constitution. *Albany Law Review*, *69*, 581. Retrieved from http://www.albanylawreview.org/Articles/Vol69_2/69.2.0581-Vermonts_Tradition_of_Education_and_the_Vermont_Constitution.pdf

Chapter 2

The States Take Responsibility for Teacher Preparation

In the early nineteenth century, the formal educational experiences of young people in the United States were neither consistent nor cohesive, but could be characterized as a mismatch of encounters. Imbalances and inequities in the schooling that children received stemmed from differences in how much instruction was allowed or reliably offered, the quality of school buildings and materials, and the availability of teachers and resources. As a result of these differences, there were increased calls for uniform and centralized educational experiences for children. Appeals for schools that would be common for all students multiplied.

At the same time there was increased pressure to develop an educated citizenship in the United States to support a growing nation following the war with England in the late 1700s. The evolving common school structure, precursor to the contemporary public school system in the United States, was viewed as the channel to develop this learned citizenship. The significant concern about the mixed academic experiences that young people were receiving in their schooling, coupled with recognition of the important role of education in developing a strong nation, drew attention to the need to prepare high quality teachers who would educate students in the new common schools. This chapter explores the seminal roles of the state normal schools in preparing effective and dedicated teachers for a young, developing, and expanding nation.

State Normal Schools

Massachusetts' first Secretary of Education in 1837, Horace Mann, was a key advocate of the state normal schools – institutions aimed at preparing teachers for their work in common schools. Mann believed that teacher preparation programs should be overseen at the state level to help with consistency and quality. He saw teaching as an arduous profession that deserved to be viewed as such, rather than as a stepping stone to other careers. He persuasively proposed that formal teacher preparation programs, specifically state normal schools, would help to foster advantageous perspectives about teaching and its connected possibilities. Not one to labor alone, Mann drew from the work of other early advocates of formal teacher preparation. These supporters included Governor Edward Everett of

Teacher Preparation in the United States, 35–57

Published under exclusive licence by Emerald Publishing Limited
doi:10.1108/978-1-80071-687-220221003

Massachusetts who served in this role from 1835–1838 and philanthropist and state board member Edmund Dwight who donated $10,000 to support the Commonwealth of Massachusetts' first state normal schools. Reformer James G. Carter from Massachusetts also published essays on the topic, including *Influence of an Early Education* in 1826, which provided strength to the teacher preparation movement that Mann championed (Fraser, 2007).

Biographical Sketch

Horace Mann. First Secretary of Education in Massachusetts in 1837.
Source: Collections of Massachusetts Historical Society.

Horace Mann was a strong advocate for the establishment of formal teacher preparation in the nineteenth century. Born in Franklin, Massachusetts in 1796, Mann was one of five siblings. As a child, he lived on his family's farm. Mann, however, did not find that his childhood was a happy one as he experienced great loss when he was 13 years old when his father died of tuberculosis. He also lost one of his siblings at a young age. Mann continued to live with his mother in Franklin until he was 20. He attended the town church regularly, but strongly disagreed with the Calvinist teachings of the minister. This would influence his later work in the field of education (Mann, 1865).

As a young person, Mann encountered meager opportunities with formal schooling. He sporadically attended the poor district school not far from his home, but did not find that his teacher was inspiring of the students. He, however, developed a love for knowledge and learning and often visited the town library, which was said to be the first public library in the United States (Mann, 1865).

Mann went on to study at Brown University in 1816 and then at Litchfield Law School in 1821. He won a seat in the state legislature in 1833 and became president of the senate in 1836. He also maintained a law practice in Dedham, Massachusetts. However, the field of education was of close interest to Mann.

Horace Mann became the first Secretary of the Massachusetts Board of Education in 1837. In this role, he worked to ensure that every child received a free education supported by taxation. Mann's wife, Mary Mann, wrote "Mr. Mann's wish was to restore the ... custom of having the rich and the poor educated together ... he desired to make the public schools as good as schools could be made" (1865, p. 63). He believed that stability and social harmony depended upon a basic education, a set literacy level, and common ideals. He supported progressive ideas and wanted teachers to move away from Calvinist beliefs surrounding corporal punishment in school.

Horace Mann was influential in the development of teacher preparation programs. He played a crucial role in the establishment of the first state normal school in Massachusetts in 1839 in Lexington. He recognized that the quality of schooling experiences of children needed to be raised and believed that this would occur through a state normal school program for teachers. Mann argued for the recruitment of women into teacher training programs and into the ranks of teaching. Toward the end of Mann's career, he moved to Yellow Springs, Ohio and became the first president of Antioch College, the first college that was founded as a coeducational institution in the United States (Mann, 1865).

The state normal schools were modeled after Prussian institutions which had met significant success in preparing quality teachers in Germany. These normal schools also drew their name from the French ecole normal. State normal schools received funding from the state level, as well as from local and private sources. The initial momentum and optimism in starting these schools, however, was not met without its foes. Indeed, it was said that "a bitter controversy raged about these institutions during the early years, and especially during the years 1839–1842" (Norton, 1926, p. xiv). Among the factors that opponents cited against the normal schools were concerns about paying for them and whether there truly was a need for them. Opponents believed that the practice of teaching could be learned without formal training.

The first state normal school opened on July 3rd in 1839 in Lexington, Massachusetts. This was a town with strong historic roots to the American Revolution – the location of the first battleground. There were only three students who showed up on the first day, partly due to rainy weather conditions, though this number would increase in the weeks that followed. This school was open to female students only and initially overseen by the principal, Cyrus Peirce. Not only was he the principal of the school, but he also was the sole teacher of the students, manager of the financial affairs of the school, and primary connection to the state representatives. He arrived at the Lexington Normal School from the island of Nantucket, at that time considered the whaling capital of the world, where he had gained recognition for his work as an educator, specifically with advocating for the integration of schools. His wife, Harriet Peirce, also accompanied him and spent time with the normal school students, at times teaching them botany (Norton, 1926). These students called themselves – normalites (Kolodny, 2014). This school would relocate to West Newton, Massachusetts in 1844 and then to Framingham, Massachusetts in 1853 (Norton, 1926).

Lexington Normal School.
Source: Drawing by Electa N. Lincoln Graduate of 1843 Class. Photo Courtesy of Framingham State University Archives and Special Collections, Framingham, MA.

After this first state normal school opened, additional institutions were established in locations throughout Massachusetts. The second state normal school, a coeducational institution, opened in Barre, Massachusetts in 1839. On the first day that the Barre Normal School opened, 20 students came to start their studies in teacher education (Dodge, 2014). The first principal was Dr Samuel P. Newman who hailed from Bowdoin College. This school, however, closed in 1841 due to geographical isolation (Dodge, 2014). It later relocated to the town of Westfield, Massachusetts in 1844 which, at the time, was a thriving industrial community located between Springfield, Massachusetts and Albany, New York (Dodge, 2014). By 1844, 49 students sought admission to the school.

The early state normal schools were situated in particular towns in Massachusetts as a result of an application process. Town members, for example, were asked to describe the buildings and materials they could provide to support these endeavors. The accessibility of these towns was another important factor of consideration. The first two state normal schools were followed by others opening in Massachusetts in Bridgewater (1840), Salem (1854), Worcester (1874), Fitchburg (1894), and North Adams (1894) (Breitborde & Kolodny, 2014). An art normal school in Boston also opened in 1873 which provided drawing instruction and curricular for the common schools (public schools) (Dobbs & Hetland, 2014).

Historian of education Christine Ogren (2005) wrote that within a decade of the establishment of the first state normal school, there were others that opened in Connecticut and New York. In 1850, for example, the State Normal School in New Britain, Connecticut launched. It was the result of an act of the legislature during the May session of 1849 (Gillette, 1850, p. 3). Similar to the normal schools in Massachusetts, the establishment of this school was the result of a bidding process. In Connecticut, the community which offered the highest bid was granted the normal school. The community of New Britain offered $16,250, while the state of Connecticut contributed $10,000 over a four-year period toward this school. This normal school building contained three large study halls, nine classrooms, a lecture hall, and an office. There also were three houses in the village which were utilized as primary schools for practice teaching (Gillette, 1850, p. 3).

State Normal School at New Britain.
Source: Photo courtesy of the Special Collections Department, Elihu Burritt Library, Central Connecticut State University.

Henry Barnard was named the first principal of the State Normal School in New Britain (Muirhead, 1999). Barnard previously had served as a member of the Connecticut House of Representatives from 1837–1839. In this role, he sought increased supervision of the common schools in Connecticut demonstrating clear interest in the field. While Barnard served as principal of the State Normal School at New Britain, he also was the superintendent of the common schools in the state. In addition, he became the editor of the *American Journal of Education* from 1855 to 1881. He became a vocal advocate of formal teacher preparation.

Henry Barnard's American Journal of Education

Henry Barnard edited the *American Journal of Education* from 1855 to 1881. Issues highlighted in this journal included proceedings from the American Association for the Advancement of Education, the conditions and supervision of schools, issues related to colleges and universities, biographies of well-known educators, teaching methods, educational discipline, as well as teacher qualifications, advancement, and compensation. The majority of the articles initially were written by males, though women contributed. In 1856, for example, Catharine McKeen from the Mount Holyoke Seminary contributed an article titled "Mental Education of Woman." The *American Journal of Education* contributed to the discourse and movement surrounding teaching preparation in the nineteenth century (Barnard, 1856).

Early state normal schools also opened in Rhode Island, including the Rhode Island State Normal School in Bristol, Rhode Island in 1854. In New Jersey, the Paterson City Normal School opened in 1855. "By 1870, 18 (of 37) states had at least 1, and a total of 39 state normal schools were located in New England, the mid-Atlantic States, the Midwest and California" (Ogren, 2005, p. 1). The state normal school movement, however, was still taking shape. It continued to expand into the early twentieth century and provided formal teacher preparation to thousands of students throughout the growing country. The Branch State Normal School of California in Los Angeles, for example, was established in March of 1881 as a two-year teacher preparation program. At this time, railroads had arrived to California and the population of Los Angeles was growing. A group of 200 citizens raised $8,000 to purchase a five-acre hilltop in the area for the school. This purchase thereafter was transferred to the State of California. When this school officially opened in 1882, there were 61 students. Forty-eight students were women and 13 were men. By the end of the first term, there were 84 students, demonstrating steady growth in enrollment. Similar to other state normal schools, there was a training school (a model school) for students on the first floor of the building that engaged the pupils in practice teaching under the supervision of experienced educators. The name of this school was changed to Los Angeles State Normal School in 1887 (Andersen, 2015).

The Branch State Normal School of California in Los Angeles, 1886. *Source:* Photographer E. A. Foxley, Thelner and Louise Hoover Photographic Collection, University Archives, Charles E. Young Research Library, UCLA.

Following the Civil War, state normal schools also were established in the South, specifically for African American students. In 1867, for example, the Lincoln Normal at Marion in Alabama opened. Initially, the school was established by the American Missionary Association, while also receiving funding from the Freedmen's Bureau of the federal government. In 1870, the state of Alabama appropriated $486 for this school. This increased to $1,250 the following year. In 1873, the Alabama Legislature established the State Normal School and University for the Education of Colored Teachers and Students. Peyton Finley, the first Black man to be elected as a member of the Alabama State Board of Education, was influential in the establishment of this school (Westhauser, Smith, & Fremlin, 2005). The assets of the Lincoln Normal School at Marion thereafter became part of this state normal school. The State Normal School and University for the Education of Colored Teachers and Students in Alabama was one of the first state-supported educational institutions for African American students in the United States (Westhauser et al., 2005). In 1874–1875, lawmakers from Alabama appropriated $2,000 to the institution. Though this was an increase from previous years, it was less than 10% of the funds that were appropriated to the University of Alabama in Tuscaloosa that same year (English, 2020).

Students at this school initially attended for free, as long as they agreed to teach in Alabama's Black public schools for two years. Schools were segregated in Alabama at this time. In 1874, it was estimated that 30 to 40 students attended this institution under the direction of one teacher. Approximately 30 of these students worked in the state's Black public schools after they completed their studies. It was observed that the demand for teachers in Black segregated schools in Alabama was greater than this school could supply. During the session of 1878–1879, enrollment further grew, and there were 127 students enrolled in this school. As this normal school evolved, however, the Black students who attended experienced steady racial violence and discrimination. One incident resulted in White petitions for the abolition of this school. The school subsequently was relocated to Montgomery, Alabama in 1887 (Clark, 1889). In 1873, a state normal school also opened in Florence, Alabama that was open to White students only. Segregation was a prevailing context of schooling in Alabama from the 19th to mid and late twentieth centuries.

A small number of state normal schools also were opened to prepare American Indian teachers. In 1887, for example, the Croatan Normal School was established as a result of legislation from Representative Hamilton McMillan and enacted by the General Assembly of the state of North Carolina. The Croatan Normal School initially was to train teachers for those of the Croatan background. There were 15 students enrolled during its first year (Catalogue of Cherokee Indian Normal School, 1938). This school moved to Pembroke, North Carolina in 1909. In 1911 its name was changed to the Indian Normal School of Robeson County. In 1913, the name was changed again to the Cherokee Indian Normal School of Robeson County. It remained a state institution (McIntosh, 1920).

A Spanish-American Normal School also opened in El Rito, New Mexico in 1909 for Spanish-speaking teachers. "The object of the school was to educate Spanish-American young men and women of the territory as teachers" (Department of the Interior, 1910, p. 650). This area was very rural at that time; roads were not yet fully established. School participants arrived at the normal school by horse, wagon, and by foot. Memoirist Sigfredo Maestas (2011) wrote that the students "came from villages and small towns of northern New Mexico. Four students came from farther south in the territory, and two students were from the forty-six that then comprised the United States of America" (p. 11). Not many of the communities in the area had common schools (public schools) during that time. Those that did have public schools were ones in which the teachers had not reached a high level of educational attainment which subsequently shaped the schooling experiences of the students. The Spanish-American Normal School was located on a plateau surrounded by gray sagebrush. In the early years of the school, there was no running water nor electricity. Outhouses were built for the students. The buildings and real estate of the Spanish-American Normal School, at that time, were valued at $26,177 (Maestas, 2011). A board of regents helped to oversee the school (Lucero, 1915). New Mexico, though still a territory at this time, would be admitted to statehood with restrictions in 1911 and full statehood in 1912. The Spanish-American Normal School was supervised at the state level by 1912 and received state funding. In 1912, there were 99 students in attendance (White, 1913).

Though the fate of the state normal school movement was uncertain at its inception and the contexts differed greatly between these institutions, they became a significant source for formal teacher preparation in the United States in the mid-to late-nineteenth century (Ogren, 2005, p. 55). There were other institutions which offered studies in teacher preparation. For example, there were private and municipal normal schools that opened and were not overseen at the state level. Academies and institutes also provided studies in teacher education, as well as some high schools. In addition, colleges and universities began to offer this area of instruction. Some even established normal departments. Randolph-Macon College in Virginia, for example, added a normal department in 1839 (Ogren, 2005, p. 17). However, by 1870, the state normal schools had entered their heyday, as described by historian Christine Ogren (2005).

As the state normal schools expanded and gained increased recognition, educational advocates and reformers from outside of the country also sought to replicate the movement. Argentina's Minister of Education Domingo Sarmiento, for example, sought to bring this movement to his country. In 1883, 22 American teachers went to Argentina for this purpose. One of these teachers was Jennie Howard who had graduated from the Framingham Normal School in 1864. Howard became the regent and vice-directress of the Girls' Normal School of Cordoba. After two years she transferred to the Mixed Normal School of San Nicholas as regent and professor of Pedagogic Criticism and Arithmetic. A book about her experiences, "*In Distant Climes and Other Years*" was published in 1931. She believed the work of the normal schools was deep and lasting in Argentina.

Shuji Isawa, from the Ministry of Education in Japan, came to Massachusetts in 1878 to study teacher preparation at the Bridgewater Normal School program. Upon his return to Japan, he directed the Tokyo Normal School in 1879 and became an esteemed pioneer in the field of education in Japan (Battaglino, 2014). In addition to bringing information about teacher preparation to Japan, he also brought knowledge of music education, which was an area of keen interest to him.

Shuji Isawa, Ministry of Education in Japan. *Source:* Courtesy of Bridgewater State University Archives and Special Collections, Bridgewater, MA.

Structure and Curriculum of State Normal Schools

Some common elements related to the structure and curriculum of the state normal schools were instituted as the movement in teacher preparation grew. For example, nineteenth century state normal schools largely were intended to be one to two-year programs. Smaller numbers of state normal schools that opened during the latter part of nineteenth century were three- or even four-year programs (Fraser, 2007). Most students, however, did not stay this full amount of time.

The state normal schools were set up in terms. For example, when the State Normal School at New Britain in Connecticut commenced in 1850, it had two terms – a summer and a winter term (Gillette, 1850, p. 4). The winter term was 14 weeks, and the summer term was 12 weeks. Other state normal schools in Massachusetts, in comparison, held three or four terms a year (Kolodny, 2018, p. 72). At the coeducational normal schools in the Northeast, female students often attended during the summer terms, when they were not engaged in teaching in district schools. Male students participated during winter terms when they were free from responsibilities on farms. Albert Boyden (1876) who wrote a history of Bridgewater Normal School recorded:

> The young men were out in the winter, the young women in the summer. Some terms the school would be composed almost entirely of different pupils from those of the term before. A new class was received at the commencement of each term.
>
> (p. 26)

There were enrollment goals that were set for the state normal schools, though capacity levels differed among the institutions. At the State Normal School in New Britain, for example, attendance was capped at 220 students per term (Gillette, 1850, p. 4). One factor that significantly shaped the capacity level of these institutions was the size of the building in which the programs were held.

Students at the state normal schools routinely were required to participate in an examination prior to admission. In the earliest state normal schools, many students entered with the equivalent of a common school or elementary school education (Fraser, 2007). As the state normal schools expanded, however, the educational requirements of the students rose. In the twentieth century, many state normal schools required a high school education for admission. The educational requirements for admission generally increased in connection to the growth of public education in the area in which the state normal school was located (Fraser, 2007).

Different admission procedures were followed when students entered the state normal schools. When the opening terms commenced at the Barre Normal School in Massachusetts, for example, the "applicants for admission" were divided into divisions. The males were taken to one area of the school building and the females to another area. The students then were arranged in alphabetical order and required to supply their present address, name, and occupation of guardian, health data, and information about previous teaching experience, as well as future intent to teach in the Commonwealth of Massachusetts upon completing their studies at the normal school (Mann, 1845).

The early state normal schools provided a formal curriculum that offered a review of the common branches of knowledge including spelling, reading, writing, grammar, geography, arithmetic, and advanced studies of languages. In addition, the curriculum centered on the professional preparation of teachers, provided information about the governance of schools, as well as hands-on teaching experience in a model or experimental school (Norton, 1926, p. xviii). In a letter to Henry Barnard in 1841, the first principal at Lexington, Cyrus Peirce, reflected on teaching and curriculum. He wrote:

> Two things I have aimed at, especially at this school. 1) To teach thoroughly the principles of the several branches studied, so that the pupils may have a clear and full understanding of them. 2) To teach the pupils by my own example, as well as by precepts, the best way of teaching the same thing effectually to others.
>
> (Norton, 1926, p. 1)

At the State Normal School at New Britain in 1850, a list of 58 discussion topics related to the theory and practice of education was developed. Some of these topics included the circumstances which make a teacher happy in school, requisites of success in teaching, causes of failure in teaching, monitoring student attendance and progress, and length and frequency of recess (Barnard, 1850). The progressive curriculum of the state normal schools reflected a move away from the Calvinist influences on schooling, specifically surrounding issues of corporal punishment (Kolodny, 2018). In Massachusetts, Secretary of Education Horace Mann, a frequent visitor to the state normal schools, "argued publicly against corporal punishment in schools in a lecture titled 'On School Punishments'" (Kolodny, 2018, p. 75).

Though there were a number of timely topics addressed at the state normal schools related to teaching, others were missing and not yet considered to be of importance. At this time, for example, there was not a lot of attention devoted to, or even knowledge of, the field of special education, or working with students of diverse abilities. Rather, the discussion topic closest to this area was how to work with "backward" children. It would not be until the time of the Civil Rights movement in the United States, when laws would be enacted to create more equitable schooling experiences for children of diverse abilities, that these topics would be more adequately addressed in teacher preparation. In addition, there was a dearth of attention focused on multicultural education or culturally sustaining pedagogy at this time.

Model schools were set up in connection to the state normal schools. These were places where students engaged in practice teaching. Children who were from the neighborhoods surrounding the state normal schools participated in the model schools. At the Lexington Normal School, for example, the model school was located on the first floor of the building (Kolodny, 2018, p. 74). At other normal schools, the model schools were located in the surrounding villages. Educational historian James Fraser (2007) wrote "the experience of student teaching was essentially invented in the first normal schools, and most of the time these institutions offered supervised practice teaching in their own lab school or a nearby school with time for reflection and successes and failures for their students" (p. 116).

Religion also was integral to the state normal school experiences in the nineteenth century. Scripture was read at the start of each school day. Mary Swift (Lamson), a member of the first class in 1839 at the Lexington Normal School, recorded the following note in her journal.

> Wednesday, Sept. 18th The first exercise was reading a portion of the Scriptures commencing the 50th verse, 27th Chap. Matt. Mr. P. made some remarks upon the 52nd verse.
>
> (Norton, 1926, p. 114)

There often were notable visitors to the state normal schools. In Lexington, for example, students met with Bronson Alcott, a transcendentalist. They likewise met with well-known phrenologists. Historian Arthur Norton (1926) provided a description of the visitors who came to the Lexington Normal School during its first years.

> Certain of the visitors from out of town brought news of the intellectual movements and social reforms which were then rising to prominence. Phrenology, the Peace Movement, Non-Resistance, Temperance Reform, and Transcendentalism were represented by talks from various men.
>
> (Norton, 1926, p. xxiii)

In addition to the formal curriculum, there also was an informal curriculum that unfolded with the students. At the Lexington Normal School, for example, students formed a reading society that met during the evening hours. At times, these students read books focused on women's issues. In the 1840s at the Bridgewater Normal School, in contrast, a men's lyceum met on Friday evenings and was open only to men. This, however, changed by the late 1800s when women joined the lyceum which was renamed "The Normal Congress" (Kolodny, 2018). Through formal and informal learning experiences, the normal school students became acquainted. Once they completed their studies, some students remained in contact with each other. They became professional supports to each other, and at times, they became friends.

In the early years of state normal schools, students often attended six days a week – Monday through Saturday. Students who boarded at the schools also attended church together on Sundays. In Massachusetts, as well as in some other states, tuition initially was free of charge at the state normal schools, as long as students committed to teaching in the common schools in their state for a period of time (Breitborde & Kolodny, 2014).

The state normal schools were carefully monitored. A board of visitors typically called on the normal school principal and students a few times a year to assess the overall progress that was being made. The board of visitors attended classes and asked questions of students. These visits were stressful affairs at times. Information about the schools also was shared publicly in various state reports and journals. In Massachusetts, for example, information about the state normal schools was shared in *The Common School Journal.*

The Common School Journal

Massachusetts Secretary of Education, Horace Mann, founded and edited *The Common School Journal* in 1838. At its inception, the journal was to be published twice a month for a total of 24 issues a year. It was to serve as a "depository of the laws of the Commonwealth in relation to schools, and of the reports, proceedings, etc., of the Massachusetts Board of Education" (Mann, 1839, p. 1). In the first volume of the journal, various topics were discussed. For example, the importance of developing a learned citizenship was addressed, as well as the benefits of physical education, and moral and religious, education. There also was a sample lesson about the atmosphere. In the second volume of *The Common School Journal*, libraries were addressed (Mann, 1839). In volume six of the journal, the Lexington Normal School was discussed, and in volume eight, information was provided about the Barre Normal School (Mann, 1839). In volume nine, laws related to the district schools were presented, as well as information about school committees (Mann, 1839). *The Common School Journal* was an avenue to provide information about teacher preparation in Massachusetts, along with other topics related to the field of education.

There were no formal graduation requirements during the earliest years of the state normal schools. Students typically received a note from the principal of the school at the end of their studies, stating that their program had been completed. They also received recommendations from their principals for particular teaching positions (Kolodny, 2014). This practice would change and evolve as the state normal school movement gained momentum in the late nineteenth century and early twentieth century. At times, the principals of the normal schools would visit their former students at the one-room schools at which they assumed these positions. Sometimes, these principals also would bring a normal school student along for the visit.

Students

When the state normal school movement commenced, women increasingly moved into the field of teaching. They took part in the normal school programs from their inception. The students who attended Massachusetts state normal schools were supposed to be 16 or older, though records indicate that a few young women joined when they were 15. Male students were supposed to be 17 or older when they commenced their studies. Age requirements, however, differed between the state normal schools. In North Carolina, for example, at the Cherokee Indian Normal School of Robeson County, no young person (either sex) under the age of 13 was to be admitted. However, if a young person who was 11 could pass an approved examination, they potentially could be admitted (McIntosh, 1920). The background experiences of the students, likewise, varied at the different normal schools. At the Barre Normal School, records "suggest that many of these students came from families who farmed, though on occasion the registers also showed a father listed as a mechanic, tailor, merchant, or physician" (Kolodny, 2018, p. 72). Many of these students were considered to be in need of bolstering their academic skills, though some came with a solid foundation in their previous schooling. In the Spanish American Normal School in New Mexico, students were the children of farmers and ranchers with minimal formal schooling experiences (Maestas, 2011).

Though not all state normal schools were integrated, from their implementation, state normal schools in the Commonwealth of Massachusetts were open to students of all races. Mary Miles Bibb, a daughter of free Black Quaker parents, for example, was a student at the Lexington Normal School, graduating in 1843. After completing her studies, Bibb taught in schools in Boston, Albany, and Cincinnati. She thereafter married escaped slave and abolitionist, Henry Bibb, in 1848. She and her husband moved to Canada where they published an abolitionist newspaper – *Voice of the Fugitive*. Bibb also continued to teach school to young people, as well as adults, in Canada.

Voice of the Fugitive

The *Voice of the Fugitive* was Canada's first Black newspaper. It was founded by Henry Bibb and Mary Miles Bibb in 1851. The newspaper was published from 1851 until 1853 when the newspaper office was burned down. After a brief respite, it was published again until 1854 when Henry Bibb died. The *Voice of the Fugitive* was a four-page paper that was published bi-weekly. The paper included news from around the world, poetry, and stories of slaves and fugitive slaves. Questions relating to Canadian colonization also were addressed. In addition, the paper was used as an important means of communicating with Underground Railroad supporters (Jones, 2020).

Charlotte Forten, a free Black woman from Philadelphia, attended the integrated Salem Normal School in Massachusetts where she completed her studies in 1856. The location of the Salem Normal School, the fourth school established in Massachusetts, was known for its "maritime history, beautiful architecture, and prominence in American history" (Brietborde, 2014, p. 59). Similar to the Lexington Normal School in Massachusetts, the school at Salem was for women only. After Forten completed her studies at the Salem Normal School, she became a notable teacher, writer, and abolitionist (Breitborde, 2014).

Biographical Sketch

Charlotte Forten. Student in Salem Normal School in Salem, Massachusetts in 1856.
Source: Courtesy of Salem State University Archives and Special Collections.

Charlotte Forten, a free Black woman, was born on August 17, 1837. Her grandfather, James Forten, was a successful sailmaker who employed both Black and White workers, hosted both abolitionist meetings and escaped former slaves in his home, and helped fund Black schools and William Lloyd Garrison's abolitionist *Liberator*. Charlotte's parents and aunts and uncles were prominent speakers and writers promoting the rights of Blacks and women. She grew up surrounded by people who valued justice, political activism, education, the arts, and high-minded work. She also grew up in a loving, supportive family village: When at three, she lost her mother to consumption (tuberculosis) and was cared for by loving grandmothers and aunts.

During Forten's early years she was educated at home by tutors and her parents, as the city's Quaker schools were segregated. At 16, her father sent her to Salem, Massachusetts to attend the city's top-notch, integrated schools. In Salem, she lived with the Remonds, a prominent Black family, several of whom lectured on abolition in America and abroad. Forten attended the Higginson Grammar School and thereafter Salem Normal School, where she was named class poet. With the help of her two school principals, she was appointed to a teaching position at the Epes Grammar School in the city, the first African American teacher of White children in Salem, and possibly the state.

Although a committed and fine teacher, Forten's heart was in writing. She was a poet and an essayist. In 1858, her essay "Glimpses of New England" appeared in the *National Antislavery Standard* and her poetry in *The Liberator*. In 1862, at the beginning of the Civil War, at the urging of her friend and mentor John Greenleaf Whittier and with the sponsorship of the Port Royal Relief Society of Philadelphia, she sailed to St. Helena Island in South Carolina to teach hundreds of formerly enslaved individuals whose planter-masters had fled the sea islands during the Battle of Port Royal. The federally sponsored "Port Royal Experiment" was a test of Blacks' abilities to work on their own ("free labor") and to learn; the speed with which Forten's students, youngsters to adults, learned to read, clearly proved the case for their independence and self-sufficiency (Breitborde, 2014). With the help of her friend and mentor John Greenleaf Whittier, she published the two-part series "Life on the Sea Islands" in *The Atlantic Monthly* to bring the history, conditions, talents and intelligence, and aspirations of the formerly enslaved to the attention of Northerners. In South Carolina, Forten befriended and aided Colonels T.W. Higginson and Robert Gould Shaw, commanders of the earliest troops of Black soldiers and Harriet Tubman. After the war's end, she worked for the Freedmen's Bureau placing teachers in Reconstruction schools and taught in one of them (the new school named for Shaw in Charleston, SC) herself. In 1872, Forten moved to Washington, DC, to serve as assistant principal at the Preparatory High School for Negro Youth. There, she met and married Francis Grimke, born into slavery and now a Presbyterian minister, later co-founder of the National Association for the Advancement of Colored People (NAACP). The Grimkes became part of the growing Black aristocracy in Washington DC, joining Frederick Douglass, Anna Cooper, Mary Church Terrell, and others. In later life she was active in the "colored" and integrated women's clubs, co-founding the National Association of Colored Women, and the settlement house movement, whose aim was to improve the lives and futures of women and children. Forten died in 1914, leaving a strong legacy in her work as an exceptional teacher, dedicated activist for civil and social justice, and gifted writer (Breitborde, 2014).

When students completed their normal school studies, many taught in one-room schools in their respective states. Some of these students taught for relatively short periods of time. When many nineteenth century White women teachers married, for example, they left the teaching field. However, others made a career of teaching. Some of these teachers, such as Louisa Harris from the Lexington Normal School in 1839, took short breaks from teaching in the common schools to serve as private tutors for families (Kolodny, 2014).

Some students also worked as teachers in schools with unique missions. Several of the students from the Lexington Normal School, for example, went on to work at the Perkins Institution for the Blind with Dr Samuel Gridley Howe, though they had no formal preparation in working with the blind. One of these students was Mary Swift (Lamson), a member of the first class at Lexington Normal School. She worked closely with Laura Bridgeman, a student who was deaf and blind and could not speak (Kolodny, 2014).

Biographical Sketch

Mary Swift Lamson. Student in First State Normal School in Lexington, Massachusetts in 1839.

Source: Photo Courtesy of Framingham State University Archives and Special Collections, Framingham, MA.

Mary Swift (Lamson) was born on June 22, 1822 in Nantucket, Massachusetts. She attended school on Nantucket, where she met Cyrus Peirce (her school teacher) who later became the principal of the first state normal school in Lexington, Massachusetts. With encouragement from Cyrus Peirce, Swift entered the normal school in Lexington on July 10, 1839. At the normal school, she studied natural philosophy, moral philosophy, and arithmetic.

She kept a copious journal. She also helped teach in a model school for young students. While at the normal school she also met other scholars who remained her friends throughout her life. They met consistently for reunions, to share their news, sorrows, and joys. She completed her studies on April 4, 1840 (Kolodny, 2014).

Following her normal school studies, Swift was recruited by Dr Samuel Gridley Howe to work at the Perkins Institution, now known as the Perkins School for the Blind in Watertown, Massachusetts. Initially she worked with two blind male students, Joseph Smith and Merchant Sturtevant, and taught Latin and Greek, so they could attend college. Smith attended Harvard College, and Sturtevant attended Dartmouth College. Swift also worked with Oliver Caswell, a blind and deaf child. Within half hour of meeting Oliver, she was able to communicate with him. He previously had not been able to communicate, beyond using rudimentary gestures with others (Kolodny, 2014). Swift also was a teacher of Laura Bridgeman, a "blind, deaf, mute" child. She later wrote a book about Laura Bridgeman that is still reproduced in the twenty-first century (Lamson, 1879). In addition, it was Swift's work and successes that inspired Helen Keller to face the challenge of learning to communicate orally. In 1890 Helen Keller wrote, "Mrs. Lamson…who had just returned from a visit to Norway and Sweden, came to see me, and told me of Ragnheld Kaata, a deaf and blind girl in Norway who had actually been taught to speak. Mrs. Lamson had scarcely finished telling me about this girls' success before I was on fire with eagerness. I resolved that I, too, would learn to speak" (Keller, 1902, p. 59).

During Swift's life she served for nine years on the Board of Trustees of the Lancaster State Industrial School and served on the School Board of the town of Winchester. She was a pioneer in the Young Women's Christian Association work. She was aware of the conditions of working girls in Boston during the mid-nineteenth century and sought to assist with those circumstances. The Young Women's Christian Association in Boston led to the organization of the International Board of Young Women's Christian Associations (Kolodny, 2014).

Other graduates went to teach in schools that had been established for African American students following the Civil War during the period of Reconstruction. One of these students was Olivia Davidson who was a graduate from the Framingham Normal School in 1881. Davidson went to teach at the Tuskegee Normal and Industrial Institute, where she worked closely with Booker T. Washington. The classes for Tuskegee Institute initially were held in a church. Thereafter, Booker T. Washington purchased a former plantation as grounds for the school.

Biographical Sketch

Olivia Davidson. Student at Framingham Normal School in 1879.
Source: Photo Courtesy of Framingham State University Archives and Special Collections, Framingham, MA.

Born in Mercer Country, Virginia, on June 11, 1854, Olivia Davidson was the daughter of a former slave and a freeborn mother. She had several siblings. Her family moved to Ohio in 1857 when she was three years old as it was a free state (Dorsey, 1985). In Ohio, Davidson studied in the common schools. At a young age, she experienced her first great loss with the death of her father.

Davidson began teaching at the age of 16 in Ohio and then in Mississippi. While in Mississippi one of her students became ill with small pox. When members of the community became frightened, Davidson closed her school and remained with the child until he recovered, demonstrating both her commitment and compassion for her students. In 1878, Davidson studied at Hampton Normal Agricultural and Industrial School in Virginia. She delivered her class' commencement address. Booker T. Washington (class of 1875) was the postgraduate speaker at this ceremony (Washington, 1901).

Davidson entered Framingham Normal School in 1879 (Dorsey, 1985). Upon graduating in 1881, at age 27, she joined Booker T. Washington at his request to help him in the formation and development of the Tuskegee Normal and Industrial Institute in Alabama, a coeducational school established for African American students (Dorsey, 1985). At that time, the Tuskegee Institute was a farm of 100 acres. Booker T. Washington drew from the Hampton Normal School's model of industrial education including farming and domestic work. Industrial education was combined with practical knowledge, including hygiene, hard work, and financial prudence.

When Davidson first arrived at the school, she recognized that there was a tremendous need for resources. The students lacked wealth. Though in frail health, Davidson's commitment to the school was said to be as strong as Washington's. She worked as an equal partner with Washington and developed curriculum materials, taught and assisted with the administration of the school, and raised money. Davidson was said to have a gift for raising money and organized suppers, entertainment, and benefits. She also went from door to door, asking for contributions (Dorsey, 1985). During this time, Davidson maintained communication with the Framingham Normal School. In one letter, she wrote to a former class member, Mary Jewett, on September 12, 1881 and described her work at the Tuskegee Institute. She wrote, "Our school is fast growing. Already there are nearly seventy in attendance and although they are mostly young men and women in age." In describing the resources at the school, she wrote, "Not a reference book of any kind belonging to the school! Think of it – A Normal School without even a Dictionary or map of the U.S!!" (Davidson, 1881). In addition to her work at the Tuskegee Institute, Davidson also worked with women in the surrounding rural areas of Alabama, specifically Macon County, and organized reading societies. She also was an invited speaker at various meetings. In April of 1886 she spoke to the Alabama State Teacher's Association on the subject of "How shall we make the women of our race stronger?" (Dorsey, 1985).

When Booker T. Washington's first wife, Fanny Smith, died in 1884, he looked increasingly to Olivia Davidson for companionship; they married in 1886. She was 32 years old, and Washington was 30. Davidson thereafter became a stepmother to Washington's daughter, Portia Washington. She also gave birth to two children, Booker, Jr., and Ernest. Olivia Davidson died in 1889 of tuberculosis. Booker T. Washington (1901) recorded the following about Olivia Davidson in his book, *Up From Slavery*:

> At the end of the first six weeks a new and rare face entered the school as a co-teacher. This was Miss Olivia A. Davidson, who later became my wife…Soon after her graduation from the Framingham Institution, Miss Davidson came to Tuskegee, bringing into the school many valuable and fresh ideas as to the best methods of teaching, as well as a rare moral character and a life of unselfishness that I think has seldom been equaled. No single individual did more toward laying the foundations of the Tuskegee Institute as to insure the successful work that has been done than Olivia A. Davidson.
>
> (pp. 81–82)

By the early twentieth century, the Tuskegee Institute employed several faculty members. Ten buildings had been constructed, and the financial assets were said to be worth over three million. Olivia Davidson died of tuberculosis on May 9, 1889 at Massachusetts General Hospital (Dorsey, 1985).

In addition, some state normal school graduates also moved into positions in college teaching. One of these students was Rebecca Pennell who attended the Lexington Normal School in 1839. Pennell, the niece of Secretary of Education Horace Mann, went on to teach at the coeducational Antioch College (Kolodny, 2014). The paths that the state normal school students followed after graduation varied. Most, however, contributed to the field of education in various ways.

Conclusion

The state normal school movement, initially conceived of as the great uncertain experiment, grew strong roots during the 19th and early twentieth centuries. Originating in Massachusetts, the state normal schools expanded throughout the United States, providing formal teacher preparation to thousands of students from diverse backgrounds. Though there were some commonalities with the state normal schools, their contexts differed a great deal. Indeed, in their early years, it was argued that there was no typical state normal school (Fraser, 2007). Some of the state normal schools were awarded state funding from their inception, while others were awarded state funding after they were established. Whereas some of the state normal schools in areas such as Massachusetts were integrated during this time period, in other parts of the United States they were segregated. These schools also had varying levels of funding and resources. Though contrasting contexts surrounded the state normal schools, the establishment of common standards for these institutions began to be addressed in 1858 with the formation of the American Normal School Association. In 1866 this association evolved into the Department of Normal Schools. This organization examined the curriculum of state normal schools, as well as uniform requirements for admission and those for a diploma (Fraser, 2007).

Graduates of the state normal schools taught in common schools. Others became high school teachers or school principals. Some students taught in specialized schools, such as the Perkins Institution for the Blind. Others traveled to different countries to help open normal schools in those locations. Initially one to two-year programs (and occasionally three- and four-year programs), a number of the state normal schools grew into four-year state teacher colleges in the early part of twentieth century and then into state colleges by the mid-twentieth century. Other state normal schools, in contrast, evolved into high schools and community colleges. The history of the state normal schools in the field of teacher preparation, in the nineteenth and twentieth centuries, is one that was marked by opportunities and struggles, possibilities and complexities. It is one that addressed the increased needs for qualified teachers to work with children and young adults in the United States.

References

Anderson, K. (2015). *The Los Angeles state normal school: UCLA's forgotten past: 188–1919*. Keith W. Anderson.

Barnard, H. (1850). *Extract from the fifth annual report of the superintendent (Henry Barnard) of the common schools of Connecticut to the general assembly, May session, 1850*. Retrieved from https://www.jstor.org/stable/24884994?seq=1#metadata_info_tab_contents.

Barnard, H. (Ed.). (1856). *American Journal of Education* (Vol. 1). Hartford, CT: London, Trubner & Company.

Battaglino, L. (2014). Bridgewater normal school (1840). In M. Breitborde & K. Kolodny (Eds.), *Remembering Massachusetts state normal schools: Pioneers in teacher education* (pp. 48–57). Westfield, MA: Institute for Massachusetts Studies.

Boyden, A. (1876). *History and alumni record of the state normal school, Bridgewater, Mass, to July 1876*. Boston, MA: Noyes and Snow.

Breitborde, M. (2014). Salem normal school (1854). In M. Breitborde & K. Kolodny (Eds.), *Remembering Massachusetts state normal schools: Pioneers in teacher education* (pp. 58–77). Westfield, MA: Institute for Massachusetts Studies.

Breitborde, M., & Kolodny, K. (2014). *Remembering Massachusetts state normal schools: Pioneers in teacher education*. Westfield, MA: Institute for Massachusetts Studies.

Catalogue of Cherokee Indian Normal School. (1938). Retrieved from https://lib.digitalnc.org/record/109581#?c=0&m=0&s=0&cv=2&r=0&xywh=2305%2C2570%2C3358%2C2040

Clark, W. (1889). *History of education in Alabama: 1702–1889*. Washington, DC: Government Printing Office.

Davidson, O. (1881, September 12). [Letter to Mary Jewett]. Framingham State University archives and special collections.

Department of the Interior. (1910). *For the fiscal year ended June 30 1909: Volume II Indian affairs territories*. Washington, DC: Government Printing Office.

Dobbs, P., & Hetland, L. (2014). Massachusetts normal art school (1873). In M. Breitborde & K. Kolodny (Eds.), *Remembering Massachusetts state normal schools: Pioneers in teacher education* (pp. 78–97). Westfield, MA: Institute for Massachusetts Studies.

Dodge, M. (2014). Westfield normal school (1839). In M. Breitborde & K. Kolodny (Eds.), *Remembering Massachusetts state normal schools: Pioneers in teacher education* (pp. 34–47). Westfield, MA: Institute for Massachusetts Studies.

Dorsey, C. (1985). Despite poor health: Olivia Davidson Washington's story. *SAGE*, *2*(2), 69–72.

English, B. (2020). *Civil wars, civil beings, & civil rights in Alabama's black belt*. Tuscaloosa, AL: The University of Alabama Press.

Fraser, J. (2007). *Preparing America's teachers: A history*. New York, NY: Teachers College Press.

Gillette, F. (1850). *First annual circular of the trustees of the state normal school of Connecticut*. Retrieved from https://www.jstor.org/stable/44749450?seq=1#metadata_info_tab_contents

Howard, J. (1931). *In distant climes and other years*. Buenos Aires: The American Press.

Jones, J. (2020). Voice of the fugitive: Newspaper used to communicate with underground railroad supporters. Retrieved from https://blackthen.com/voice-fugitive-newspaper-used-communicate-underground-railroad-supporters/

Keller, H. (1902). *The story of my life*. New York, NY: Grosset & Dunlap Publishers.

Kolodny, K. (2014). *Normalites: The first professionally prepared teachers in the United States*. Charlotte, NC: Information Age Publishing.
Kolodny, K. (2018). The endorsed and spontaneous reading and writing exercises of students in early state normal schools in Massachusetts (1839–1850). In M. Nash (Ed.), *Women's higher education in the United States: New historical perspectives* (pp. 69–91). Palgrave Macmillan.
Lamson, M. S. (1879). *Life and education of Laura Dewey Bridgman, the deaf, dumb, and blind girl*. Boston, MA: New England Publishing Company.
Lucero, A. (1915). *The New Mexico blue book or state official registrar*. Santa Fe, NM.
Maestas, S. (2011). *Children of the normal school: 60 years in El Rito, 1909–1969*. Santa Fe, NM: Sunstone Press.
Mann, H. (Ed.). (1839). *The Common School Journal for the year 1839* (Vol. 1). Boston, MA: Marsh, Capen, Lyon, and Webb.
Mann, H. (1845). *Lecture on education*. Boston, MA: Marsh, Capen, Lyon and Webb.
Mann, M. (1865). *Life of Horace Mann*. Boston, MA: Walker, Fuller, and Company.
McIntosh, A. C. (1920). *Consolidated statues of North Carolina*. Raleigh, NC: Edwards & Broughton Printing Company, State Printers.
Muirhead, G. (1999). *Images of America: Central Connecticut State University*. Charleston, SC: Arcadia Publishing.
Norton, A. (1926). *The first state normal school in America: The journals of Cyrus Peirce and Mary Swift*. Cambridge, MA: Harvard University Press.
Ogren, C. (2005). *The American state normal school: An instrument of great good*. New York, NY: Palgrave Macmillan.
Washington, B. (1995/1901). *Up from slavery*. Mineola, NY: Dover Publications.
Westhauser, K., Smith, E., & Fremlin, J. (2005). *Life and learning at Montgomery's black university*. Tuscaloosa, AL: The University of Alabama Press.
White, A. (1913). *Biennial report of the superintendent of public instruction to the governor of New Mexico: For the years 1910–1911 and 1911–1912*. Santa Fe, NM: New Mexican Printing Co.

Chapter 3

The Nation Expands and the Teaching Profession Grows

The early history of teacher education in the US began with the assumption that if you were educated to a degree beyond that of your "scholars," and if you could control their behavior, you were qualified and prepared to teach. If you had finished the eight grades of "grammar school," you were seen as a prospective teacher of the very young; high school graduates were deemed ready to teach the older grammar school children. College students often taught school during summer breaks, or until a better job opportunity opened up (Labaree, 2008). When teachers themselves realized that the work required planning and technique, they formed associations and held summer institutes to exchange ideas, institutes that were later supported by district superintendents and state educational leaders like Henry Barnard of Connecticut. As Chapter 2 recounts, in light of the rapid growth of public common schools, the growing body of knowledge of pedagogy, and the influence of European teacher education programs, by mid-century many states had established "normal schools" to prepare teachers, first in the Northeast, then in the Midwest and West, and eventually, throughout the country. This chapter traces that expansion as it reflected the growth of the profession and new ideas about how best to offer teacher education: under whose aegis, with what structure and content, and for whom. These developments and changes in teacher preparation in the late nineteenth and early twentieth century occurred in the context of expanding public schools and higher education, the birth of the progressive education movement and, perversely, regressive racial policies that institutionalized inequity but that also spawned creative resistance from oppressed communities and their teachers. In academia, the fields of psychology and sociology grew to include new theories of child development, learning, and motivation; a deeper understanding of the impact of class, social institutions, and social change on individuals and communities; and new ideas and expectations about the role of public schools and the work of teachers. Teacher education varied across geographical settings, populations, and the boundaries of state law. One wide structural change brought the incorporation or transformation of state normal schools into comprehensive public colleges and regional state universities, a change with arguably both positive and negative long-term impact on the status of teacher education within higher education in general.

Teacher Preparation in the United States, 59–89

doi:10.1108/978-1-80071-687-220221004

Expanding Access to Teacher Education: Teacher Institutes and In-System Programs

During the Civil War, the Union Congress had passed the Morrill Land-Grant Act, giving the states acres of land – taken from Native tribes – which they could sell to fund higher education institutions for the "agricultural and industrial classes." While some educators, including Black educators, hoped that the funds would apply to new institutions preparing teachers, most state legislators interpreted the law to apply narrowly to agricultural and industrial education, arguing that their states had already established normal schools for the local population. After the war, Black veterans and those formerly enslaved, whose only access to education beyond grammar school had been privately supported normal programs (see Chapter 1), lobbied their state legislators to use Morrill money to fund teacher education as critical to the agricultural and industrial advancement of their people. Despite the support of the US Congress, their state legislators refused to use the funds for that purpose and Congress refused to intervene. In practice, therefore, the 1862 Morrill Act benefitted Whites in the North and South, including those who would become teachers. As will be described later in this chapter, 30 years later Congress would pass a second Morrill Act that explicitly funded both teacher preparation and agricultural and industrial education (Reid, 2015). But African Americans were not the only group deprived of a publicly supported higher education route to a teaching credential. Most would-be teachers didn't have the money or time for a college education or even a private academy. In a nation largely rural at the time, most would have had to travel far to attend one. Despite the proliferation of state normal schools in the mid-to-late nineteenth century, their numbers were insufficient to keep up with the supply of teachers needed.

The problem was most acute in one-room "country schools." In 1850, 75% of pupils in American schools were enrolled in one-teacher schools, a number that declined only to 50% in 1913. In midwestern and western states, the numbers were much higher (in 1936, 71% of Illinois schools, 79% of schools in Minnesota and Wisconsin, and 88% of schools in South Dakota were single-teacher). Teachers in these schools, whose only qualification might be the fact that they had completed the eight grades of their own rural school and passed an oral exam administered by a county superintendent, or simply that they could produce a signature in English, struggled to teach students aged four to 20 with diverse abilities, speaking diverse languages, and of diverse cultures and religions. The need for teachers was so great in the new western settlements that literacy was sometimes the only requirement. When one young girl, a 14-year-old graduate of a country school in Iowa, moved further west with her family to Kansas where "There was something for everyone to do," she immediately became a teacher (Cordier, 1997, p. 45).

Smith School Near Sunflower, Mississippi. Teacher distributes grapefruit from Florida, donated to the Red Cross, during drought of 1930–1931. *Source:* Lewis Hine, photographer. Library of Congress. https://www.loc.gov/pictures/item/90714883/.

The work of rural teaching began early in the morning, when a teacher lit the wood stove that would provide warmth for the room and for heating students' lunches, sharpened pens, filled the water bucket, swept the floor, checked the outdoor privies (lavatories), and laid out slates and other teaching materials. School maintenance enlisted the help of local farmers who supplied wood and older boys who stacked it. For this physically and professionally long, hard day, the country schoolteacher's salary was less than half that of her town and city peers. The conditions of teaching in country schools daunted even future US Presidents. James Garfield, who taught in five rural schools in the 1850s, wrote a friend, "You and I know that teaching is not the work in which a man can live and grow." Warren G. Harding called it "the hardest job I've ever done." As late as 1944, when more than 60% of country schoolteachers lacked a college degree and most had no formal higher education, President Franklin D. Roosevelt contrasted the condition and quality of schools in urban and rural settings as shameful: "[W]e are justifiably proud of the splendid, modern schools in our cities and towns [but] we cannot be proud…that many of our rural schools…have been sadly neglected" (Zimmerman, 2009, pp. 17, 19, 29, 116).

Lacking professional preparation, rural teachers taught the way they had been taught, or took their cues from local school boards. Jonathan Zimmerman records the account of one early 1900s teacher who had had the benefit of a normal school education and who faced a moral, and professional dilemma when his hiring school board advised him to, "Make them toe the line. Lick 'em, lick 'em like the dickens." The young man found that he was unprepared to teach eight subjects to 57 students: "How was I to teach Tommy to follow his historical bent in reading..., cultivate Mary in literature, and give Robert his start in political research" while other students were carving up their desks and running around the room? Despite the voice of the normal school instructor who abhorred corporal punishment ringing in his ears, he "whipped a few of the big boys," after which, he could "hear the tick of his watch" (Zimmerman, 2009, pp. 32–33).

As communities grew and the number of schools with them, district, county, and state governments took responsibility for raising teacher requirements. By the 1870s, there were written examinations for teacher certification, with questions ranging over "the common branches" of knowledge and skills in reading, spelling, arithmetic, and grammar. Candidates might be asked, for example, to cite the principal rules for the use of capital letters ("orthography"), to estimate the cubic feet of stone needed to build a wall around a well of a particular diameter and depth, or to list the causes and results of the Revolutionary War. Questions on "the art of teaching" on some exams might include how to determine a pupil's grade level or the purposes behind asking different types of questions, content that might have influenced the curriculum of normal programs and schools (Cordier, 1997, p. 51). But on other exams they were so general that Mary Bradford, age 16, could answer them well enough to earn a passing grade and a certificate despite her being "innocent of ever having read a book on pedagogy..." "The questions... were such as anybody with common sense and with the recollections of one or two good teachers, could have answered" (quoted in Kliebard, 1995, p. 550).

In the absence of sufficient numbers of normal schools, high schools or colleges, however, most teachers in nineteenth century America – especially the rural majority – received their training in part-time "institutes," very often after they had already been engaged in the work. As late as the turn of the twentieth century, only 5.5% of Nebraska teachers had attended a college or university. Forty percent held a high school diploma, and another 29% had some high school, but 15% percent had no high school education at all. For 84% of Nebraska teachers, the only professional training they had received had been in teacher institutes (Cordier, 1997, p. 69). At their best, these teacher institutes combined a chance to extend one's subject matter knowledge with information on the latest teaching and discipline techniques and opportunities to share with colleagues techniques that worked in country school settings. Held in central locations – for example, county seats – their form and content was set by county and state superintendents of instruction and included lectures and presentations by normal school educators and experienced teachers on the "common branches" taught in single-teacher schools – reading, spelling, penmanship, grammar, geography, history, civics, arithmetic, physiology and hygiene, drawing, music, some practical arts like sewing and carpentry, and school management. Lectures and demonstrations on methods of instruction were supplemented by opportunities for practice with volunteer pupils in late afternoon and evening sessions. The institutes were funded by the state or county; teachers paid a small registration fee and paid for their accommodation in private homes in the community, often a room with kitchen privileges.

Teacher institutes had a respected history. In the first decades of the nineteenth century, when the Connecticut state legislature refused to fund normal schools, the state Secretary of Education Henry Barnard – later, the first US Commissioner of Education – developed a four-to-six-week program of lectures and a "traveling model school" to prepare people for the "art of teaching." Barnard described his ideal institute as an organization of the teachers of a town, county, or state "for improvements in their profession...meeting for a thorough review of the studies of the public schools, under teachers of acknowledged reputation, as well as for lectures discussions, and essays on various methods of school discipline and instruction." Expert teachers would model new methods of instruction and classroom management, and attendees would have opportunities to try them out. Working teachers could exchange strategies and advice. Evening lectures and performances were open to the public, so that the community at large could engage with teachers and benefit from the experience (Fraser, 2007, pp. 62, 64–65).

Besides keeping teachers up to date and refreshing their knowledge and skills, the institutes were designed to strengthen teachers' motivation and collegiality. The *American Journal of Education* 1846 version described "conventions for mutual improvement and excitement...[where] raw and timid teachers are initiated into their new business, older teachers receive valuable suggestions and apply them...[and] an enthusiasm in their business is excited" (quoted in Fraser, 2007, p. 65). The expectations for standards of content, discourse, and practice were high; Barnard thought attendance at an institute twice a year for three years was equivalent to a normal school preparation, which, at the time, was little more than a year.

Educational administrators and legislators saw institutes as an efficient and relatively low-cost way to convey information and new techniques and to facilitate professional development and persistence. They rose to great popularity in the second half of the century. In the northeast, where the new normal schools proliferated and many academies offered normal programs, experienced teachers used institutes to refresh their knowledge and skills. Elsewhere in the nation, institutes were the primary means of professional learning for beginning as well as experienced teachers. They were also a way for teachers in remote settlements to gain professional friendships and support. Massachusetts-born Sarah Ballard, who had a school of 66 "scholars" from age 3 to 23 in Rosendale, Wisconsin, in 1851, wrote the director of the National Board of Popular Education that had sent her there that she had recently attended two common school conventions in that state ("it was estimated that there were 5,000 people present at the last one") and was also looking forward to an upcoming teacher's institute (Letter from Sarah Ballard to Nancy Swift, in Kaufman, 1984, p. 208). In 1877, 8,000 teachers attended institutes in Illinois. In 1880, Michigan held 65 institutes for almost 4,482 teachers. In the 1886–1887 academic year, the then-US Commissioner of Education reported 2003 institutes serving 138,946 teachers – about half of all teachers in the nation (Fraser, 2007, p. 67).

In the nineteenth century, the nation's largest cities faced the problem of great numbers of poor and immigrant children in need of public education to help them learn English, to teach them "American" norms and values, to prepare them for the workplace, and to keep them off the streets. The structure and methods of one-room, single-teacher schools where teachers heard small group recitations while other students worked quietly at their desks, would not work in overcrowded urban school settings. Philadelphia, Baltimore, New York, and other cities turned to a Europe-based alternative approach to teaching purporting to be far more efficient as well as cost-effective. New York City adopted the "monitorial" system early. Until the establishment of the city's Normal College in 1870, the preparation of its public schoolteachers was limited to in-district training in this method that would characterize the district for the first half of the century (Reigart, 1916, p. 90).

The model originated with Englishman Joseph Lancaster, who had invented a way efficiently and economically to "diffuse…knowledge of a few elementary branches of education among the poorer classes of the community" (Lancaster, in Reigart, 1916, p. 91). A deeper purpose lay in the assumption that his strict organizational plan would help the children of the poor, immigrants and Native Americans assimilate into a White Anglo-Protestant way of life (Thickstun, 1907, p. 32). The Lancasterian system recruited older students with promise and interest in teaching and gave them additional instruction on Saturdays (for girls) or weekday evenings (for boys) free of charge for six weeks to prepare them as "monitors" in various subjects of study. They worked at first with small group of pupils, then with larger groups, eventually leading classes of hundreds of students and supervising their own monitors. Students practiced first at the "cadet" level by assisting in the lower grades, and after completion were encouraged to open their own schools. The normal program curriculum for monitors-future teachers included the study of grammar, geography, astronomy, arithmetic, and natural philosophy; the boys' curriculum added Latin, to prepare them for positions in the college preparatory schools.

The monitorial system was eventually criticized as undemocratic, militaristic, and shallow in educational effect. By the 1850s the movement had died in New York, unpopular with the poor whom it attempted to serve, whose children were often truant, as well as with parents in the higher social classes who wanted their children exposed to methods that promoted a deeper understanding of subject matter. It also fell out of favor in the Native schools, failing to reach the resistant Native students either academically or socially, leading White supremacist officials to assume these students were "uneducable," sometimes in contrast to their resistant teachers ("Nothing Servile," n.d.; Rayman, 1981; Santee Normal Training and Missionary Association, 1885).

The method had addressed the need to educate the poor at public expense, an unusual goal in early America. But as progressive education entered the imagination of educators and parents in the latter part of the century (described later in this chapter), observers of the monitorial model criticized "[t]he faithful adherence to the manuals or the syllabi prepared by the school authorities rather than adaptation to the interests of the pupils and the community [that] became the prime duty of the teacher...the result of many years of an unquestioning routine... [and] a serious obstacle to the success of progressive administrations" (Reigart, 1916, p. 100).

Normal Schools Move to State Colleges and Universities

According to historian David Tyack, at the end of the nineteenth century, there were 127 public (state-, city-, and county-run) normal schools in the US and approximately the same number of private ones. While they were considered the premier sites for teacher preparation in the country, they still prepared only one-quarter of its teachers. Because they offered high-quality general education at low cost, many normal school students who couldn't afford private college tuition were educating themselves for careers other than teaching (cited in Labaree, 2008, p. 293). But at that time, normal schools were typically three-year programs; short the fourth year that would allow them to convey bachelor's degrees, they were not quite colleges. Looking to grow enrollments (and tuition) and to recognize and satisfy the aspirations of non–teaching-bound students, normal schools successfully lobbied to expand their terms and be called "colleges." Between 1911 and 1930, 88 normal schools had been renamed "teachers' colleges." The new teachers' colleges continued to strengthen and diversify their liberal arts programs – and reduce their teacher preparation programs – until, beginning in 1920, many were reborn yet again, this time as "state colleges." Later, many of these would become universities. The case of Millersville Normal School, founded in 1859 in Pennsylvania, illustrates the diversity of its programs and student pathways. Like many normal schools, it originally offered a variety of programs: a "Model School Course" for teaching observation and practice, a Preparatory Course for students who had not attended high school, an Elementary Course for would-be grade-school teachers, and a Scientific and Classical course strand to prepare high school teachers. Many students had already been teaching elementary school, some only grammar school graduates themselves. Men who graduated and taught school eventually became principals or professors; others left teaching early for medicine, law, the ministry, farming, business, or other work. Female graduates taught, or they chose marriage and family (one could not do both at the time) or became missionaries or took on other work. Millersville became a state teachers' college in 1927, a state college in 1959, and Millersville University in 1983 (Coley & Desmond, 1999).

Paralleling the progression of normal schools to state colleges was the federal re-funding of land-grant universities, many of which competed with normal schools and state colleges for teacher education students or subsumed the smaller institutions. The land-grant universities were a blend of the British liberal arts undergraduate college with the German-specialized and research-oriented graduate school and a very American practical/vocational education. They established professional programs that included both academic study and hands-on practice in the fields of medicine, law, and in education (Kerr, 2001).

This incorporation of teacher education programs into state universities had benefits, and costs. Like the first Morrill Act of 1862, the Second Morrill

Act of 1890 provided funds for endowing and maintaining in each state, "at least one college where the leading object shall be, without excluding other scientific and classical studies...to teach such branches of learning as are related to agriculture and the mechanic arts...in order to promote the liberal and practical education of the industrial classes in the several pursuits and professions in life" ("An Act Donating Public Lands," 1862). This time, however, Congress forbade racial discrimination in admissions, which the state might satisfy by opening enrollment to all, or by establishing separate but "justly" funded institutions:

> No money shall be paid out under this subchapter to any State or Territory for the support or maintenance of a college where a distinction of race or color is made in the admission of students, but the establishment and maintenance of such colleges separately for white and colored students shall be held to be a compliance with the provisions of said sections if the funds received in such State or Territory be equitably divided...
>
> (Racial Discrimination by Colleges Restricted, 1890)

As a result of the 1890 Act, states in the segregated South established 17 of the 100 institutions for "colored students" that are today designated "historically black colleges and universities" (Fast Facts, 2021).

The University of Iowa created the first permanent professorship in pedagogy in 1873. The University of Michigan created an education chair in 1879, followed by Columbia University, Stanford and Harvard, Berkeley, and Ohio State by 1895. By 1920, these individual professorships became departments and then schools or colleges of education. But these new university-based schools and colleges of education were more focused on the academic study of education and in turning out school system administrators, state superintendents, and professors and researchers than in preparing classroom teachers, a mission far different from that of the normal schools (Labaree, 2008, p. 296). According to James Fraser, from the beginning, universities were "ambivalent about their teacher preparation responsibilities" (Fraser, 2007, pp. 138–139). An exception was Henry Barnard, first US Commissioner of Education, whose biographer noted that in his brief (two-year) tenure as president of the University of Wisconsin, he spent far more time uplifting primary and secondary education in the state, supervising teacher institutes in 20 counties, than at the university (Steiner, 1919). Though land-grant university missions included teacher education, in reality their administrators and professors ignored the world of the classroom and the business of preparing its teachers.

One result of the university's ambivalence toward teacher preparation was a gender gap between students and faculty. For a long time the majority of university-based education program students were men working toward careers in administration or policy with a few looking to teach high school. Women preparing for elementary teaching did so in normal schools and teachers' colleges, where, in coeducational programs, they learned alongside men and socialized with them in student organizations, often taking leadership positions in those activities. More than half the normal school and teachers' college faculty were women (Ogren, 1995). Female instructors were called "preceptresses," while their male counterparts were "professors" (Clifford, 1989). But preceptresses were often strong women with new ideas and radical agents for change (Bohan & Null, 2007). They urged students to go South and West and into city slums to undertake work that was often lonely and dangerous, and they went along, as well. Female educators of educators filled the ranks of abolitionist and suffragist organizations. With the incorporation of normal schools into the new universities, there came a decline in the proportion of female faculty and greater inequality in the extracurricular activities open to women, including athletics (Ogren, 2000). The combination of longer school terms and more requirements for teacher licensure – including a high school diploma and some teaching experience before one could even qualify for a certification exam – led to increasing feminization of teaching (Kliebard, 1995). By 1900, 70% of the nation's teachers were women (Woody, 1966 (1929)). Leaders of women's organizations advocated women's pursuit of positions as principalships and superintendencies. But gender-based university culture worked against the professional advancement of women teachers and teacher educators.

Other factors contributed to the belittling of women's suitability for educational positions at any but primary levels. The rapid consolidation and bureaucratization of large schools and districts carried with it the expectation that those who would manage them would be men. And from Freudian psychology, some child development theory, and the general public came the message that too many women teachers were dangerous to boys' "normal" development. This sentiment was voiced in a 1914 article in *Educational Review* by F.E. Chadwick entitled "The Woman Peril in American Education." Chadwick, a Navy man by profession, cited men's general "supineness in municipal affairs...the sitting down of our people and wanting everything done for them, ... [and] the general want of stand-upness" as proof that women teachers have "maimed" men. Boys have been subjected to the "unconsciously destructive influence...of 'emotional, illogical, noncombative' women teachers...No woman, whatever her ability, is able to bring up properly a man child. Men think in terms of steamships, railways, battleships, war, finance, in a word, the great energies of the world which the woman mind never, in a practical way, really concerns itself with, or can it do so" (Chadwick, 1914).

The incorporation of normal schools into state universities did have its benefits: It brought many more students – and tuition income – into the universities. It provided professional education programs with greater academic credibility. But Jurgen Herbst argues that in giving up their separate and distinct status as the major institutions for teacher preparations, normal schools ceded not only institutional status and importance as "people's colleges," but also autonomy in the field of their primary purpose. The move to university campuses, he says, cost professional educators voice in matters of policy and educational management and control over the qualifications for entry into teaching and the content and structure of teacher preparation programs (Herbst, 1989).

New Problems, New Fields, New Ideas: The Teacher Education Curriculum Responds

The late nineteenth and very early twentieth century was a time of great contrasts: it began with a "Gilded Age" when the unchecked wealth of industrial tycoons grew from new markets and manufacturing techniques and on the backs of the grinding poverty of their underpaid workers, including child laborers. It was an age when refugees and people of color had no access to government help or legal standing. New high schools and colleges gave some Americans clear pathways to pursue professional, social, and economic aspirations while Jim Crow laws and White-on-Black violence kept people of color from voting, attending school, and securing basic human and civil rights. It was a period of growing industrialization, urbanization, and immigration. City schools were overrun with new populations of children with critical needs. Teachers needed new strategies and administrative assistance. No longer would textbooks like George Herbert Palmer's *Ethical and Moral Instruction in Schools*, with its emphasis on teacher's role as "master and developed human being," or "spiritualizing influence" help them cope with the number of children in their classes and the variety of those children's critical needs (Palmer, 1909, pp. 39–41).

William Torrey Harris, esteemed superintendent of the St. Louis Public Schools and later US Commissioner of Education from 1889—1906, aimed to reinvent public education in ways that would prepare students for the rapidly changing conditions of American life. Building on the thinking of Hegel, Kant, Froebel, and Pestalozzi, he wanted teachers to move away from rote and discrete "mastery" of "facts" to a deep and critical understanding of subject matter, an awareness of its social and economic rationales, and the ability to help students think about and apply it. Harris saw schools as transcending the family's influence on developing "ungrounded prejudice and unconscious habit" by promoting rational thinking. This schools would accomplish with a curriculum based on Western civilization and culture, through five academic branches: mathematics/logical relationships, geography/natural science, history, the grammatical structure of language, and English literature that addressed universal human themes. As President of the National Education Association and a member of the Committee of 10 charged with reforming high school curricula away from the classics, Harris influenced high school curricula for many years. His popular stance privileged White, Anglo-Saxon Protestant culture and perspectives, defining them as "basic American values." At the same time that pedagogical models in teacher education were beginning to stress "critical thinking," and "the scientific method." Native children were being separated from their families and sent to boarding schools, where their hair was cut and their native language forbidden, so that they could be "Americanized" and "saved" (Harris, 1898).

The field of professional education benefitted from ideas generated within the new disciplines of psychology and sociology and new theory and research in child development and learning. Children were no longer perceived as "mini-adults" but as having their own ways of perceiving and thinking, influenced by their physical development and social circumstances. G. Stanley Hall earned the first Ph.D. in psychology in the US and was most interested in applying the new science to education. As a professor of psychology and "pedagogics" at Johns Hopkins University, he created what was probably the first psychology laboratory, used later by graduate student John Dewey. In 1888, as the founding president of Clark University in Worcester, Massachusetts, he continued developing Child Study as a method of scientifically examining what children know and how they learn it, using questionnaires and observations. Influenced by Charles Darwin and Sigmund Freud, Hall assumed that human development was biologically based and reflected the evolution of humanity and society from primitive to more advanced social forms. School curricula should be modified, thought Hall, for students heading toward different futures. The biological, social, and spiritual roles of boys and girls, for example, were distinctly different. A curriculum for girls should prepare them for their responsibility as wives and mothers, while the "natural" physical, sexual, and social energy of boys needed channeling toward behaviors and values that would grow them into healthy, contributing members of an orderly society. Competitive team sports promoted the "American" values of discipline, control, and moral strength – qualities presumed lacking in immigrant families (Hall, 1883). Hall's thinking on the difference between the sexes fed the idea that the growing preponderance of women teachers was problematic for boys. Though women teachers were fine for the young ones, he worried that, as models of gentleness and passivity, they would try to make older boys into "little gentlemen," robbing them of their natural "roughness," self-reliance, independence, and originality, qualities necessary for their manly roles in society. Boys, he said, were robbers, bandits, and fighters by nature: if not, they weren't "normal." He was in favor of controlled corporal punishment; if teachers were too lenient, if there were no outlet for boys' physical energy and competitiveness, there would be havoc in classroom and society: "I think it is impossible not to connect a certain wildness in boys with the feminization of schools" (Hall, 1908, p. 10239).

Hall's method of collecting information on children's learning and behavior foreshadowed the work of Jean Piaget later in the twentieth century and was copied and contributed to by teacher educators and students in normal schools and universities. State normal schools in New Jersey and in his own adopted city of Worcester partnered with him in comprehensive studies of children's thinking, recording, for example, their daydreams, toy preferences, and questions, as well as their behavior. E. Harlow Russell, president of Worcester Normal School and a friend of Hall's, incorporated child study as an integral part of the normal school curriculum, requiring every student to keep carefully prescribed records of children's behavior under a variety of circumstances. "More than 16,000 observations were collected, organized and studied, a significant contribution to the development of child psychology" (Lewis & Claffey, 2014).

Clark University Pedagogical Museum.
Source: Courtesy of Clark University Archives & Special Collections.
G. Stanley Hall used toys to record children's observations, preferences, and behavior as part of "Child Study."

The Progressive Paradox

"Progressive" educators of the late nineteenth and early twentieth century shared the belief that public education could ameliorate the social, economic, and political unrest caused by rapid economic, demographic, and technological change by preparing American citizens for a reconstructed democratic society. They differed widely, however, in their remedies. Building on the child-focused work of Hall, Freud, and other psychologists and sociologists, one group – "pedagogical progressives" – focused on the needs of the child, the process and conditions of learning, the values and habits of cooperation, social responsibility, and critical thinking to reform both the traditional classical curriculum and pedagogy. Another group, the "administrative progressives," similarly sought to replace outdated curricula, but with an efficient centralized system that differentiated curriculum based on the nation's economic and social needs and on predictions about what work students would be doing in the future and what roles they would occupy in their families and communities. This second group mined science and technology and the ideas of Alfred Binet, Louis Terman, Edward L. Thorndike, and Robert Yerkes, designers of "intelligence" and "aptitude" tests to sort students into "tracks" that would fit them for their presumed futures. Intelligence, they believed, was a single trait informed by race and ethnicity.

Administrative progressives like David Snedden, Charles Prosser, and Ellwood P. Cubberley consolidated small school districts into larger, more efficient units, centralized control in a school committee appointed by local government leaders and created a system of bureaucratic management with levels of administrators: principals, directors, superintendents. They applied the principle of social efficiency to the curriculum. They convinced school committees and state superintendents that it was inefficient and wasteful to put all students through the same curriculum when their futures would diverge, some likely to become doctors, lawyers, scientists, businessmen, etc., and others bound for factories. There should be curriculum pathways that would fit students for their likely futures, not waste their time with information they would never use. Theirs was a view that saw education as utilitarian and "vocational" (Kliebard, 1999). Agreeing with this view, an influential report by a national commission on secondary education entitled *Cardinal Principles of Secondary Education* (Commission on the Reorganization of Secondary Education, 1918) urged high schools to reform their curricula to prepare for the needs of modern society, conceived as seven objectives: (1) Health, (2) Mastery of fundamental processes (e.g., arithmetic), (3) Worthy home membership (e.g., "shop" and "home economics"), (4) Vocation, (5) Citizenship, (6) Worthy use of leisure, and (7) Ethical character. The report, which spurred high school reorganization and programs preparing their teachers, suggested a menu of math, science, history, and English courses modified for the "college-bound" student, the "business student," and the "general" student. Both modern and classical languages disappeared except in the college preparatory "Latin" schools and college "tracks" (Labaree, 2005).

At Stanford University, Cubberley created a new educational subfield: administration. His textbooks were widely read in university departments and schools of education for the first 50 years of the twentieth century (e.g., Cubberley, 1920, 1929). In several editions of *Public School Administration*, published from 1916 to 1947, he advocated the use of tests, measurements, and surveys to assess both educational efficiency and student performance (the "educational product"), a stance familiar to twenty-first century American educators. David Snedden, who had been a teacher, principal, and superintendent in California, Secretary of Education in Massachusetts, and professor at Columbia University's Teachers College, looked at industrial-focused education as democratic. Academic high schools could well prepare the "officers" of society, he thought, but new vocational schools and tracks were best for the "rank and file" who would fill the skilled jobs that society needed. The specialized schools and courses he created in Massachusetts, based on the catalog of skills, habits, and forms of knowledge specific to students' capabilities and vocational interests, listed in his popular text *Educational Sociology,* would help them advance in the struggle of life (Snedden, 1922).

Edward Thorndike's influence on educational policy and teacher education went beyond systems design to the nature and roots of learning itself. He drew attention to the concept of motivation as essential to learning. Anticipating the work of B.F. Skinner on the relationship between behavior and its consequences, he coined the "Law of Effect," to describe the process by which an animal's or a person's response (behavior) that produces a desired effect is more likely to occur again whereas responses that produce an unpleasant effect are less likely to recur

(Thorndike, 1905). Psychologists built on that theory of learning to create the highly influential tradition of behaviorism within the field of psychology. Thorndike used observations, data-gathering, and statistics to develop his theories and apply them to classroom practice. His conclusions were influenced by the assumptions and norms of the racism and sexism of the day. Thorndike believed that intelligence and basic nature were more biological than social, and differed by race (Whites dominating), by ethnicity (Anglo-Saxons dominating) and by gender (males dominating). These differential, inborn, intelligences and natures best fit individuals to particular social and economic roles. "Selective breeding," he claimed, could "alter man's capacity to learn, to keep sane, to cherish justice or to be happy," and was an "economical" way to improve society (Thorndike, 1913).

Columbia University's Teachers College supported Professors Thorndike and Snedden in their social efficiency model of reform but it also embraced the more "child-centered" approach of Professor John Dewey and his colleague William Heard Kilpatrick. These pedagogical progressives directed future educators' attention away from administrative systems to the person at the heart of the educational process: the child. Central to the child's learning, they said, were his interests, her eagerness to learn, his creativity, her welfare, the influence of society and culture on his development, and her own agency in learning. Rather than assuming, like Thorndike, that the child's nature needed improving, Dewey trusted in children's natural desire to learn and experiment, asking teachers to honor their real experience, hone their habits of mind, and improve the social contexts that made up their world. Rather than fitting children to a predicted future, Dewey saw the future as changing in directions no one could predict, but which new generations would need critical thinking skills and scientific modes of practice to handle. The ultimate individual goal of education, thought Dewey, was the ability to think critically. Its overall purpose was the furthering of democracy.

To Dewey, learning was experience mediated by educators and parents. The educator's most important role was to lead students to ask questions about the world around them and use "scientific" thinking and group inquiry to help answer them. For Dewey, there were no dichotomies between experience and education, the child and the curriculum, the intellectual and the vocational. Everything children were taught should be relevant to their experience, and applied, to be meaningful, understood, and tested. As experience had no disciplinary boundaries, neither should the curriculum, which should be organized around problems and projects of social importance. If society imposed conditions harmful to children, families and communities, those conditions should be changed in order for children to learn and grow into socially responsible, thinking citizens. Teacher education should not emphasize the practical details of lesson planning and classroom organization, etc., but rather produce graduates of intelligence and character who have the habit of mind to inquire into subject matter content, the social context, and children's learning and grow their methods accordingly (Dewey, 1902, 1916; Kilpatrick, 1918).

Dewey was part of a community of progressive pedagogues and teacher educators. Early in his career, at the University of Chicago, he created a Laboratory School to test his ideas with Ella Flagg Young, former Chicago teacher and district administrator, who worked with the teachers in deciding how to apply them in a redesigned curriculum. Francis Parker, who had reformed the Quincy, Massachusetts, public schools using progressive methods, was at the time transforming Chicago's Cook County Normal School and its practice school by eliminating rote learning and harsh punishments, replacing them with a broad, interdisciplinary curriculum built on children's interests, curiosity, and energy. In agreement with Parker's practice, Dewey sent his own children to Parker's school. Author of several teacher education books, including *The Practical Teacher* (1884) and *Talks on Pedagogies* (1884), Parker's last project was a private experimental school, the Chicago Institute, which eventually merged with Dewey's Laboratory School (Dewey, 1939; Lagemann, 1996). Later, when Dewey was at Columbia University, his Teachers College colleague, former student William Heard Kilpatrick, created the "project method" to carry out in the classroom Dewey's strategy of giving students practice solving interdisciplinary problems in cooperative ways (Kilpatrick, 1918).

Dewey's view of curriculum as varying with particular individual interests and social needs and his valuing of thinking and learning processes as more important than mastery of particular "facts" generated problems in the implementation of progressive education. Teachers sometimes engaged students in a "hands-on" activity (e.g., building a model Acoma pueblo) absent research or discussion about underlying contexts or broad principles. Too often, schools thought they were being "progressive" but had never read Dewey or fully understood him. Too many instances of project work without substantive learning and too much confusion about how to teach requisite knowledge and skills resulted in fierce criticism and an ultimate rejection of the progressive experiment, especially during and after World War II. The competition to gain scientific, economic, and political ground against the emerging power of the Soviet Union, which beat the United States into outer space in 1957, initiated a period of return to "the basics" and a focus on testing that, except for brief periods in the 1960s and 1970s, have dominated US public schools.

Biographical Sketch

John Dewey (1859–1952). Education for Democracy.
Source: Courtesy of Library of Congress.

Justin Morrill, author of the 1862 Morrill Act, was a Vermonter. His state acted quickly to use the funds to establish the University of Vermont, which 15 years later graduated John Dewey, a local boy from Burlington and the most famous and influential educational philosopher in American history. The philosophy major found a teaching job in a school headed by his cousin in Oil City, Pennsylvania. After a year, he returned to Burlington and continued the study of philosophy with his former professors and corresponded with W.T. Harris, former St. Louis Superintendent, now professor at Johns Hopkins University, whose book Dewey was reading and who invited him to enroll in Hopkins' doctoral program. There he began developing ideas about the "the power exercised by cultural environment in shaping the ideas, beliefs, and intellectual attitudes of individuals," leading to his belief that mind is not separate from matter but is influenced by it. He was increasingly influenced by the pragmatic psychologist Williams James; he took from James the idea that reality is not static, that it changes with time, context, and human perception. Questions of philosophy and psychology, including the philosophy and psychology of education, should not be considered in an intellectual vacuum, but in the context of the social conditions and values dominating everyday life (Dewey, 1897; Hildebrand, 2018). "All education proceeds by the participation of the individual in the social consciousness of the race…[T]he school is a form of community life…[T]he teacher is not in the school to impose certain ideas or to form certain habits in the child, but …to determine…how the discipline of life shall come to the child" (1897, pp. 77, 78, 80). The challenge, to Dewey, was how to live well and responsibly, and how to educate well and responsibly, as individuals and members of society, as reality changes. His answer was to educate for critical thinking, scientific observation, and an understanding that individual fate was tied to the fate of the community and the larger society: "social intelligence." Democracy must be supported, as a consciously collaborative process in which individuals consult with each other to identify and address their common problems and a source of moral values that can guide the development of humane social institutions (Dewey, 1897, 1935a; Hildebrand, 2018).

Dewey first taught philosophy and psychology at the University of Michigan, then in 1894 moved to the University of Chicago, where he was a professor of philosophy and director of the School of Education. At the university, with the help of his wife Alice and Ella Flagg Young, an experienced teacher and administrator, he turned the campus school into a laboratory to test his educational ideas. He considered Mrs. Young the wisest educationist he had met. She'd been the woman to superintend a large city system and first woman President of the National Educational Association, a reflective educator who respected the minds and intentions of both teachers and students. Together, the three created a curriculum that used the child's experience to apply principles, theories, and information to real problems and organized the classroom as practice in democracy (group projects). They were adamantly against rote memorizing without understanding, against isolation, and abstractions without relevance to real situations or objects (Lagemann, 1996).

Dewey's teacher was a mediator of experience, a guide to understanding, a framer of the learning environment, and a coinvestigator of a problem that arose from children's experience and environment. Lab school students learned from their errors, from practice and discussion, using their hands and hearts as well as their heads. The curriculum derived from the investigations, not vice versa. And because problems and questions are not limited to particular fields, the content was interdisciplinary. Everything was new, including the furniture necessary for learning (Dewey, 1902). In *The School and Society*, he told this story:

> [Y]ears ago I was looking about the school supply stores in the city, trying to find desks and chairs which seemed…suitable from all points of view–artistic, hygienic, and educational–to the needs of the children. We had a great deal of difficulty in finding what we needed, and finally one dealer, more intelligent than the rest, made this remark: "I am afraid we have not what you want. You want something at which the children may work; these are all for listening."
>
> (1907, p. 47)

The last years of Dewey's time at the University of Chicago were marred by a difficult relationship between the university and the Laboratory School (Dewey, 1939, p. 34). In 1901 the university subsumed a teacher preparation institute and practice school created by Dewey's colleague and fellow progressive Francis Parker. Unhappy with aspects of the management of the school, whose administrator was Dewey's wife Alice, the university president questioned Dewey's leadership of the merger. Parents and friends of the Laboratory School organized what may have been the first PTA in the nation and, joined by educators from across the country, bombarded the President with letters and private funds. While the President gave Dewey direction of the institute, he continued to underfund and criticize it, and Dewey resigned in 1904. He moved to Teachers College, Columbia University, where he spent the rest of his professional life teaching, writing, speaking, and engaged in social and political activism. He was elected President of the American Philosophical Association in 1905 and cofounded the New School for Social Research, a graduate school promoting the free exchange of ideas in the arts and social sciences. A prolific writer, he published some 700 articles in 140 journals and 40 books; among the books, still read in teacher education programs, are, *The Child and the Curriculum* (1902), *Democracy and Education* (1916), *Experience and Nature* (1925), and *The Public and its Problems* (1927). During the 1930s, the time of the Great Depression, he and colleagues founded *The Social Frontier*, a journal focused on the relationship of politics to education, and the social responsibility of teachers (Dewey, 1935b).

Progressive education taught future teachers that school could not be separate from society and that building a community of teachers and learners was a true educational process. Dewey's ideas moved from university and laboratory schools into public school classrooms and settlement houses established to help the turn-of-the-century immigrants to America. Dewey served as a trustee of Chicago's Hull House, whose founder Jane Addams was a lifelong friend. They borrowed from each other's work and acknowledged their mutual influence (Nieuwejaar, 2015).

Dewey's critics were concerned that his ideas could be interpreted and implemented in ways that engaged students in hands-on projects on "unimportant topics" at the cost of academic depth and breadth. World War II turned the country's attention to the defense effort, and if left in its path a politically divided world, and a race for technological dominance. Progressive education was blamed for the Soviets' early win in the race to space. Other critics noted that his laboratory school students, who were middle-class or upper-middle-class White children, poor children, children of color, immigrant children, had little access to a creative curriculum relevant to their lives.

In Dewey's long life he witnessed major changes in science, technology, national and world politics, from which he concluded that educators could not hope to prepare students for the future by gauging what they needed to learn from the present. The message to prospective teachers issuing from the many programs influenced by his words and ideas was that they needed to prepare students with skills and values that transcended particular times – how to think, how to test for what worked, how to collaborate, so that they could tackle problems and issues that arose with each new decade and make reasoned decisions integral to the welfare and happiness of others at present and in the future. The task of teachers and teacher educators was to educate for democracy, the critical elements being the ability to think critically, and a deep sense of social responsibility (Dewey, 1935b).

David Labaree claims that the administrative progressives won the educational policy battle with the pedagogues. Had pedagogical progressivism won control of public schools, he says, schools today would base instruction on the needs and interests of children, offer an interdisciplinary curriculum, focus on teaching critical thinking skills learned in socially relevant project work, make room for self-directed learning, and encourage values of justice, equality, and community. He sees teacher education as "keeping the faith [of pedagogical progressivism] alive" within the halls of schools of education, but a repository that has little bearing on what actually happens in schools. Labaree sees education professors as caught in a compromise between the need to prepare teachers for industry-led state licensure standards and curriculum frameworks and the desire to promote an approach that is child-centered, "inclusive," flexible, and socially meaningful. But the authors of this book find that in many school districts, the legacy of pedagogical progressivism is still strong. It appears under new names, as "place-based education," "experiential education," "project-based learning," "cooperative learning," "constructivism" and in charter and pilot schools like New York's Central Park East and Mission Hill School in Boston. Teacher educators' persistent advocacy of student choice and voice, collaborative learning, real-world applications, and critical thinking may, however, account for a disjuncture between what prospective teachers learn in their educator preparation programs and what they meet in the school systems that hire them (Labaree, 2005, p. 279).

Preparing Teachers of Color under Jim Crow: Resourcefulness and Resistance

Although it spoke to the goal of an egalitarian and democratic national community, progressive education was largely a White, middle-to-upper-class enterprise. Progressive methods could be found in classrooms across the country, but far more often appeared in schools of the White suburbs of the Northeast and Midwest than in the South or in poor and working-class city neighborhoods. The primary concern of Black parents at the time was whether their children had access to any schools within a reasonable distance from their homes, especially in the segregated South; their second, whether there were qualified teachers. The number of normal programs and schools had grown under the Second Morrill Act, but demand for teacher preparation programs in any form – high school programs, normal schools, colleges, or universities – far outstripped the supply. In the 1930s, the states of Florida, Louisiana, Mississippi, and South Carolina together had a total of 16 accredited high schools that Black students could attend; most had no access to any high school (Irons, 2004, p. 36). Those few schools that existed were understaffed and undersupplied, offered no transportation, and had a limited curriculum taught by teachers who were minimally educated themselves. As late as 1933, only 15.6% of Black teachers had a college degree. Twenty-three percent of Black elementary school teachers had no more than a high school diploma, as compared to 5.7% of White teachers (Caliver, 1933; Fultz, 1995). Organizations like the National Association of Teachers in Colored Schools were important sources of professional development helping teachers pass licensure exams, qualify for higher pay, and improve their skills (Givens, 2016).

To supplement the limited public funds, many educated African Americans opened private schools to prepare others to teach. Perhaps the most famous was Booker T. Washington, founder of the Tuskegee (Alabama) Institute, but he was joined by many others; among them, Mary McCleod Bethune of the Daytona Educational and Industrial Institute in Florida, Charlotte Hawkins Brown at the Palmer Institute in North Carolina, Nannie Helen Burroughs at the National

Trade and Professional School for Women and Girls, Anna Julia Cooper at the M Street School in Washington, D.C., and Lucy Moten at the Miner Normal School in the same city, Fanny Jackson Coppin at the Institute for Colored Youth in Philadelphia, and Eben Blachley and Charles Henry Langston (grandfather of poet Langston Hughes) at the Colored Normal School in Quindaro, Kansas. Some of these schools began as preparatory or high schools, adding normal programs to prepare teachers; others were created as institutes of higher education. Some offered an academic curriculum; others offered a vocational curriculum designed to prepare African Americans for the industrial age as valuable skilled workers and tradespeople. Funding came from Black and White donors and from their founders' pockets. Several of them became colleges or universities (e.g., Bethune-Cookman and Tuskegee).

Within the Black educational community there was a serious argument between those who saw the purpose of higher education as deepening students' knowledge, strengthening their heart and mind, and preparing them as citizens and as leaders; and those who believed its purpose was to prepare them for jobs. The Institute for Colored Youth, the Penn School in South Carolina and others jumped on the vocational/industrial bandwagon of the administrative progressives and dropped their traditional, academic-focused curricula. The normal programs within these schools survived, now, in many cases, graduating teachers bound for vocational high schools. Key players in the debate were Booker T. Washington and W.E.B. DuBois.

Washington had graduated from and taught in the Hampton Normal and Agricultural Institute founded in 1868 by Samuel Armstrong a White former Civil War commander of a "colored regiment." At Hampton, Black and Native students earned their academic tuition by working to maintain the school. Chapman's aim was to prepare Black and Native graduates to teach the Hampton values of self-help and industry at schools in the South. In 1881, Washington opened Tuskegee Normal School, later Institute (now University) in a shack loaned by a Black Church. He raised funds to buy land and his students built the classroom buildings. Their curriculum included carpentry, printing, farming and domestic skills, and academic subjects that were related to their experience (Dr. Booker Taliaferro Washington, 2021; Washington, 1901). Chapter 2 describes the accomplishments of Olivia Davidson, a graduate of Framingham Normal School in Massachusetts who joined Washington in the work of building Tuskegee and later became his wife. Washington spoke nationally, promoting his belief that the road to social acceptance for Blacks began with their economic value to the nation. The idea won him allies among White politicians and philanthropists, including Sears Corporation's Julius Rosenwald, who, in consultation with Washington, provided half the funds needed (matched by local Black communities) to build 5,000 schools for Black children across the South; the DuPonts of Delaware, who built 85 schools in that state; and Anna Jeanes, a White Quaker whose foundation supported Black teacher-supervisors and professional training (Pincham, 2005; Taggart, 1988).

Laboratory at Tuskegee Institute, 1902.
Source: Library of Congress. Reproduction number LC-USZ62-2248.

Washington's primary critic was sociologist and activist W.E.B. DuBois. Rather than focusing on training for jobs needed in the current, racist, economy, Black educators should work with colleges and universities to educate an army of Black intellectuals and educators. This "talented tenth" of the community would then lead the effort to enfranchise and empower the rest of the community with their knowledge of history and culture, the power of their tongues, and their teaching. "The Negro race, like all races," he said, "is going to be saved by its exceptional men." Industrial education was a "faint compromise": "If we make technical skill the object of education, we may possess artisans but not, in nature, men…Men we shall have only as we make manhood the object – intelligence, broad sympathy, knowledge of the world that was and is, and of the relation of men to it…" (Du Bois, 1903, pp. 33–34).

The "Negro college" had accomplished a miracle, its most important product being Black teachers:

> Up from the colleges shot normal schools, and out from the normal schools went teachers, and around the normal teachers clustered other teachers to teach the public schools; the college trained in Greek and Latin and mathematics, 2,000 men; and these men trained full 50,000 others in morals and manners, and they in turn taught thrift and the alphabet to nine millions of men who to-day hold $300,000,000 of property. If was a miracle—the most wonderful peace-battle of the 19th century.
>
> (Du Bois, 1903, p. 47)

The argument between the parties espousing a vocational versus academic education for Blacks was often bitter; Anna Julia Cooper was dismissed as principal of the M Street School in Washington, D.C. when she refused to eliminate the classical college preparatory option as a curriculum choice. Furthermore, there was ample evidence that the industrial education promised to chronically underfunded Black schools in the South was mere manual training and that vocational high schools were a way not only to keep Blacks out of prominent professions but out of the skilled industrial workforce as well (Breitborde, 2019; Keller, 1999).

Biographical Sketch

Fanny Jackson Coppin (1837–1913).
…to Get an Education and Teach My People….
(Reminiscences, 1913, p. 17).
Source: Courtesy of Library of Congress.

Fanny Jackson Coppin's "Reminiscences of School Life, and Hints on Teaching" captures the life of a child born into slavery and raised as a servant, but who, aided by her family and employers who recognized her intelligence and character, obtained an excellent education and worked to do the same for her people. A distinguished student of classical languages and mathematics, she earned a position as principal, then superintendent of the Institute for Colored Youth in Philadelphia (now Cheyney University of Pennsylvania). There she added to its strong academic curriculum a normal program for teaching careers and an industrial education program, carrying the message that African Americans were smart, capable, and entrepreneurial.

An aunt bought Fanny Jackson's freedom from slavery in Washington, D.C., and sent her to New Bedford to live with another aunt who "put her out to work." On days not taken up with washing, ironing, and cleaning, she went to school. At 14 she took a domestic job with the family of George Calvert, great grandson of the founder of Maryland. The family gave her private reading lessons, taught her to sew and darn "beautifully," introduced her to the piano, and took her "bathing in the ocean" at times restricted to Whites. They also sent her to the local public colored school, where she successfully prepared for the Rhode Island State Normal School (now Rhode Island College), which she attended for a year. With her aunt's tuition help, she went to Ohio to attend Oberlin, the only college admitting Black students at the time, "to get an education and to teach my people." There, she took the "gentleman's course," excelling so in Latin, Greek, and mathematics that she was asked to teach a class of (White) high school students "unless they rebelled." She proved to be an effective, and popular, teacher. In her last year, she taught a class of freedmen from the south, and was "deeply touched" to see old men so eager to learn. Graduating in 1865, she was elected class poet and was the second Black woman to earn a bachelor's degree. Proud of her accomplishments, she was also aware of her responsibility to others: "I never rose to recite in my classes at Oberlin but I felt that I had the honor of the whole African race upon my shoulders" (Coppin, 1913, p. 15; Perkins, 1982).

Quakers had established Philadelphia's Institute for Colored Youth in 1837 to contest the proslavery argument that the Blacks were inferior beings. Southern Senator John C. Calhoun dared anyone to find a Black person who could conjugate a Greek verb. The institute was the Quakers' answer. The Board had written to Oberlin, asking for a "colored woman" to teach classic languages and higher mathematics. Fanny Jackson was promised the job and a scholarship to finish her education. In Philadelphia, she delighted in her students' accomplishments, which impressed the school examiners. Within a year, she was named principal of the girls' department; in 1869, principal and superintendent of the entire school, the first Black woman to have these titles. She lived happily with a professor's family but was "sharply minded of my color" by segregated street cars and the absence of Blacks in the city's burgeoning economy ("building after building [is] going up in this city, and not a single colored hand employed in the construction" (Coppin, 1913, p. 28).

The need for teachers in neighboring states of Delaware, Maryland, and New Jersey compelled her to replace her beloved classics curriculum with English studies and a formal normal program. To ground it in teaching realities, Jackson introduced texts on teaching methods and management, and practice teaching in the classes of younger students. Institute graduates included teachers, principals, supervisors, and superintendents of "colored schools" in several states, and college and normal school professors, as well as clergymen, doctors (both male and female), government clerks, foreign ministers, lawyers, newspaper editors, the first Black man admitted to the Philadelphia bar, the first Black student at the University of Pennsylvania, and the first graduates of Howard University's Law School.

The technological advances and economic trends exhibited in the 1876 US Centennial Exhibition in Philadelphia impressed upon Fanny Jackson the need for an industrially trained workforce. "In Philadelphia," she wrote, "the only place where a colored boy could learn a trade, was in the House of Refuge, or the Penitentiary!" (Coppin, 1913, p. 23). The Institute had proved that African Americans were the equals of Whites in academic capability, "but the...education by which the masses must become self-supporting was, to me, a matter of painful anxiety" (1913, p. 24). She spoke in major cities on the necessity of industrial education and the need for funds for expensive industrial school laboratories. To convince the Black community, she used *The Christian Recorder*, edited and printed by Black men in Philadelphia. In it she wrote,

> It is simply astonishing when we consider how many of the common vocations of life colored people are shut out of. Colored men are not admitted to the Printers' Trade Union... We are not employed as salesmen, or pharmacists, or saleswomen, or bank clerks, or merchants' clerks, or tradesmen, or mechanics, or telegraph operators, or to any degree as State or Government officials, and I could keep on with the string of "ors" until tomorrow morning ... I now respectfully submit this matter to the citizens of Philadelphia and cordially invite them to visit us...
>
> (Coppin, 1913, p. 38)

The Institute eventually offered training in bricklaying, plastering, carpentry, shoemaking, printing, tailoring, stenography and typing for boys; and, for girls, dressmaking, millinery, typewriting, stenography, cooking "by the most modern methods" and hosted exhibits and sales of student work. The teachers it graduated were prepared as elementary and industrial educators.

Fanny Jackson's normal students learned to manage a classroom of students working individually or in groups at levels appropriate to their learning; have regular curriculum reviews for children frequently absent for work; invite children to critique each other's work; and use blackboards, bulletin boards, pictures, and diagrams alongside texts. S/he learned to walk among students as they worked to make immediate "cooperative corrections" focusing on principles more than minor details. S/he created rhymes and games to help them memorize grammatical rules. S/he was kind: "Never let the word 'dumb' be mentioned in your class." S/he saw teachers and pupils as partners: "I am always sorry to hear that such and such a person is going to school to be educated. This is a great mistake. If the person is to get the benefit of what we call education, he must educate himself, under the direction of the teacher" (1913, p. 44).

An educator and teacher educator, a columnist advocating for women and African Americans, a founder of homes for women, Fanny Jackson took on missionary work as well in 1881 when she married Rev. Levi Jenkins Coppin, a minister in the African Methodist Episcopal church. In 1902 they traveled to South Africa and founded a missionary school, the Bethel Institute. After a decade of missionary work, Jackson Coppin returned to Philadelphia in ill health, dying in January of 1913. In 1926, the normal department of the Colored Normal and Training School in Baltimore was renamed the Fanny Jackson Coppin Normal School in her memory. It is now Coppin State University (Perkins, 1982).

Just as many formerly enslaved had found a way to teach themselves and others to read despite state bans against literacy, Blacks living under Jim Crow had to "work out" amongst themselves how to get an education. Jarvis Givens uses archived memories of Black students in segregated high schools to illustrate the way teachers acted as agents of change, surreptitiously teaching Black history and undermining the official racist curriculum which made no mention of the history or culture of the students in front of them. Teacher educators providing content for this "fugitive pedagogy" were Black educator-writers of textbooks on Black history, probably self-published; early examples are Edward Johnson's *A School History of the Negro Race in America* (1890) and Leila Amos Pendleton's *A Narrative of the Negro* (1912) (Givens, 2016, pp. 67–68; Johnson, 1890). A later example, who made the greatest impact, was Carter G. Woodson.

Carter Woodson was a Harvard educated historian and veteran teacher. His textbooks, notably the four editions of *The Negro in Our History* (1922), were used in teacher preparation programs in all the Southern states as well as in the North. The book gave rise to Negro history courses in Black high schools, providing Black students with knowledge of their own history and replacing messages of Black inferiority rampant in the larger, White-dominated society with Black identity and pride. In 1915, Woodson founded the Association for the Study of Negro Life and History (ASNLH) to disseminate Black history through Black teachers, the National Association for the Advancement of Colored People (NAACP), and the National Association of Teachers in Colored Schools (NATCS). The ASNLH offered materials, lectures, discussions, and exhibits for its teachers and organized Negro History Week in partnership with national teacher associations, state/city departments of education, colleges and universities, and educational leaders like Nannie Helen Burroughs and NATCS President Mary McLeod Bethune. To carry Woodson's message of identity and pride into print, Bethune used the *Negro History Bulletin* read by Black teachers as a vehicle for exchanging of stories, lesson plans, and assignments (Givens, 2016, p. 103; 2021, Chapter 5).

Givens recounts a story told by Jerry Moore, an alumnus of the segregated Webster Parish Training School in Louisiana. On the desk of his teacher, Tessie McGee, lay the official outline for the history and social studies curriculum approved by the Louisiana State Department of Education. Instead of reading from this outline, however, she read to them from a book in her lap: Woodson's *The Negro in Our History.* Moore remembers that when anyone entered the room, Ms. McGee would stop reading from the book in her lap and begin reading from the outline on her desk. When that person left, "her eyes went back to the book in her lap." In this way, Moore learned about civilizations in Africa; Toussaint L'Ouverture; Black and White antebellum abolitionists; Blacks soldiers in the Union Army; and Black writers, inventors, physicians, lawyers, orators, educators, and intellectuals, and their White allies. Ms. McGee's fugitive pedagogy, says Givens, was an example of the subversive, instructional strategies and creative responses to White opposition that Black teachers used from the time of slavery to teach Black students their own history and culture (Givens, 2021, pp. 1–2).

Conclusion

In the latter part of the nineteenth century, the United States was still largely rural; by the turn of the twentieth century, the country was changing via the forces of industrialization, urbanization, and immigration. In the transition, those seeking teaching jobs prepared in a wide variety of ways. In the rural Midwest and South, to secure their first job, they may have completed the eight grades of grammar school and then passed a county test of content knowledge. In the urban Northeast, they were often high school graduates who had attended a normal school or college. Committed teachers typically continued their training and strengthened professional bonds in summer institutes and conventions or additional terms at normal schools or colleges. Many became teacher educators, especially as the nation expanded and, with it, the need for more schools and teachers. And as the number of schools and teachers grew, so did the desire for professional renewal and connection. The latter nineteenth and early twentieth century saw the creation of national professional associations: the National Teachers Association in 1857 (with men only until 1866), which became the National Education Association in 1870 and a fully representative assembly in 1920; the National Colored Teachers Association in 1906, a year later renamed the National Association of Teachers in Colored Schools to include the many White teachers working in segregated schools for Black students; and the American Federation of Teachers in 1916 as a union affiliate of the American Federation of Labor. As the country weathered critical periods of social upheaval, war, and industrial, economic and demographic change, the role of schools in society moved nearer to the center of concern for political and economic leaders. Where the problem a century earlier had been one of numbers – how to educate enough teachers, including those of limited means, well enough to pass on their knowledge to increasing numbers of children, the new century saw arguments arise about the best way to prepare teachers, given arguments about the purpose of public education in general. An industrializing economy and scientific advancements required more time in school and a more complex curriculum, and higher standards for teaching licensure. When a high school diploma became a prerequisite to licensure, the door to teaching opened wider to young women, who were attending high school in greater numbers than boys who, in many areas of the country, could begin learning a trade at age 14.

New research into children's learning and development and new attention to what might account for differences among them led to varied ideas about what, if anything, should be done to "differentiate" what, and how, we teach them. Universities took on the role of teacher preparation, creating departments for academic "educationists" – philosophers, psychologists, sociologists, and pedagogues. Normal schools either moved into these universities or transformed themselves into four-year, ultimately multipurpose, colleges. Some argue that the loss of the normal schools robbed the field of education of special institutions that could have been the sources of professional standards and purveyors of professional training and reduced the field to second-class status in arts-and-sciences–focused universities. University-based education programs, however, enlisted faculty in those arts and sciences to design new ways of engaging students in learning: This era spawned the Progressive Education movement, which left a continuing legacy of "project-based," "place-based," and "experiential" learning, vocational-industrial programs leading to skilled trades, and the discovery that young children think and learn differently from adults.

The innovations did not reach all students. Hard lines were drawn around students of different races, social classes, and genders, offering them an education tailored to someone else's assumptions about their futures, determined by tests purporting to measure their "aptitude" or their imagined contribution to the economy, rather than the present inequities they might have been facing. Their schooling was also limited by the amount of funds states and localities were willing to provide to their particular group, and, in the case of the Southern states, limited by legal segregation that hardly reflected the premise of "separate but equal." Students of color had limited access to teacher institutes, normal schools, colleges, and universities; in many cases, their limited access to basic elementary education derailed any hopes of any advanced education. There are, however, myriad examples of teachers of color who found ways to bring relevant and important curricula to their students and who created normal programs and colleges to prepare many of them to carry on the work.

References

An Act donating public lands to the several states and territories which may provide colleges for the benefit of agriculture and mechanic arts [Morrill Act]. (1862). Washington, DC: National Archives and Records Administration, Chapter CXXX. Retrieved from http://www.ourdocuments.gov/doc.php?doc=33&page=transcript

Bohan, C. H., & Null, J. W. (2007, Summer-Fall). Gender and the evolution of normal school education: A historical analysis of teacher education institutions. *Educational Foundations*, 21(3–4), 3–26. Retrieved from https://files.eric.ed.gov/fulltext/EJ831197.pdf

Breitborde, M.-L. (2019). "Fitted for their community": Race, power and the transition to vocational education at Penn School. In G. Lauzon (Ed.), *Educating a working society* (pp. 33–58). Charlotte, NC: Information Age Publishing.

Caliver, A. (1933). *Education of Negro teachers*. Bulletin, No. 10. 4. Office of Education, U.S. Dept. of the Interior. U.S. Government Printing Office, Washington, DC. ERIC No. ED543652. Retrieved from https://files.eric.ed.gov/fulltext/ED543652.pdf

Chadwick, F. E. (1914). The Woman Peril in American education. *Educational Review*, 47(9), 109–119.

Clifford, G. J. (1989). Introduction. In G. J. Clifford (Ed.), *Lone Voyagers: Academic women in coeducational institutions* (pp. 18–20). New York, NY: Feminist Press.

Coley, R. E., & Desmond, C. T. (1999, April 23). Parallel lives: The relationship between the sexes at Millersville state normal school, 1855–1927. ERIC ED433274. Paper presented at the national conference of the American Educational Research Association, Montreal. Retrieved from https://files.eric.ed.gov/fulltext/ED433274.pdf

Commission on the Reorganization of Secondary Education. (1918). *Cardinal principles of secondary education: A report of the commission on the reorganization of secondary education*. Bulletin 35. Bureau of Education, U.S. Department of the Interior. U.S. Government Printing Office, Washington, DC. ERIC Number: ED541063. Retrieved from https://files.eric.ed.gov/fulltext/ED541063.pdf

Coppin, F. J. (1913). *Reminiscences of school life, and hints on teaching*. Philadelphia, PA: A.M.E. Book Concern. Retrieved from https://docsouth.unc.edu/neh/jacksonc/jackson.html

Cordier, M. H. (1997). *Schoolwomen of the prairies and plains: Personal narratives from Iowa, Kansas, and Nebraska, 1860s–1920s*. Albuquerque, NM: University of New Mexico Press.

Cubberley, E. P. (1920). *The history of education*. Cambridge, MA: Riverside Press.

Cubberley, E. P. (1929). *Public school administration*. Cambridge, MA: Riverside Press.

Dewey, J. (1897, January). My pedagogical creed. *School Journal*, 54, 77–80. Retrieved from http://dewey.pragmatism.org/creed.htm

Dewey, J. (1902). *The child and the curriculum*. Chicago, IL: University of Chicago Press.

Dewey, J. (1907). *The school and society*. Chicago: University of Chicago Press.

Dewey, J. (1916). *Democracy and education*. New York, NY: Macmillan.

Dewey, J. (1935a). *Liberalism and social action*. New York, NY: G. P. Putnam's Sons. Retrieved from https://archive.org/stream/dewey_liberalism/dewey_liberalism_djvu.txt

Dewey, J. (1935b). The teacher and his world. *The Social Frontier*, 1(4), 7.

Dewey, J. M. (1939). Biography of John Dewey. In P. A. Schilpp (Ed.), *The philosophy of John Dewey* (pp. 3–45). New York, NY: Tudor Publishing Company. Retrieved from https://brocku.ca/MeadProject/Dewey/Dewey_1939.html

Dr. Booker Taliaferro Washington, Founder and First President of Tuskegee Normal and Industrial Institution. (2021). Tuskegee, AL: Tuskegee University. Retrieved from https://www.tuskegee.edu/discover-tu/tu-presidents/booker-t-washington

Du Bois, W. E. B. (1903). The talented tenth. In *The Negro problem: A series of articles by representative Negroes of to-day*. New York, NY: Teachers College Press. Retrieved from http://moses.law.umn.edu/darrow/documents/Talented_Tenth.pdf

Fast Facts: Historically Black Colleges and Universities. (2021). Institute for Education Sciences, National Center for Educational Statistics, U.S. Department of Education. Retrieved from https://nces.ed.gov/fastfacts/display.asp?id=667

Fraser, J. W. (2007). *Preparing America's teachers: A history*. New York, NY: Teachers College Press.

Fultz, M. (1995). Teacher training and African American education in the south, 1900–1940. *The Journal of Negro Education*, 64(2), 196–210. doi:10.2307/2967242

Givens, J. R. (2016). *Culture, curriculum, and consciousness: Resurrecting the educational praxis of Dr. Carter G. Woodson, 1875–1950*. Ph.D. Dissertation, University of California, Berkeley. Retrieved from https://escholarship.org/uc/item/38h233rw

Givens, J. R. (2021). *Fugitive pedagogy: Carter G. Woodson and the art of Black teaching*. Cambridge, MA: Harvard University Press.

Hall, G. S. (1883). The contents of children's minds. *Princeton Review*, 2, 249–272.

Dr. Hall on Sissifying the Schools. (1908, January 7). *Evening Gazette*, Worcester, MA, p. 439.

Harris, W. T. (1898). *Psychological foundations of education.* New York, NY: D. Appleton & Co.

Herbst, J. (1989). *And sadly teach: Teacher education and professionalization in American culture.* Madison, WI: University of Wisconsin Press.

Hildebrand, D. (2018, Winter). John Dewey. In E. N. Zalta (Ed.), *The Stanford encyclopaedia of philosophy.* Retrieved from https://plato.stanford.edu/archives/fall2021/entries/dewey/

Irons, P. (2004, Summer). *Jim Crow's schools.* American Educator. American Federation of Teachers. Retrieved from https://www.aft.org/periodical/american-educator/summer-2004/jim-crows-schools

Johnson, E. A. (1890). *A school history of the Negro race in America, from 1619 to 1890, with a short introduction as to the origin of the race; Also a short sketch of Liberia.* Raleigh, NC: Edwards & Broughton, Printers and Binders. Retrieved from https://docsouth.unc.edu/church/johnson/johnson.html

Kaufman, P. W. (1984). *Women teaching on the frontier.* New Haven, CT: Yale University Press.

Keller, F. R. (1999, Autumn). An educational controversy: Anna Julia Cooper's vision of resolution. *NWSA Journal*, 11(3), 49–67. Retrieved from https://www.jstor.org/stable/4316681

Kerr, C. (2001). *The uses of the university* (5th ed.). Cambridge, MA: Harvard University Press.

Kilpatrick, W. H. (1918, September). The project method: Child-centeredness in progressive education. *Teachers College Record*, 19, 319–334. Retrieved from https://archive.org/details/projectmethodus00kilpgoog

Kliebard, H. (1995). The feminization of teaching on the American frontier: Keeping school in Otsego, Wisconsin, 1867–1880. *Journal of Curriculum Studies*, 27(5), 545–561.

Kliebard, H. (1999). *Schooled to work: Vocationalism and the American curriculum 1876–1946.* New York, NY: Teachers College Press.

Labaree, D. F. (2005, February). Progressivism, schools and schools of education: An American romance. *Paedagogica Historica*, 41(1&2), 275–288.

Labaree, D. F. (2008). An uneasy relationship: The history of teacher education in the university. In M. Cochran-Smith, S. M. Nemser, & J. McIntyre (Eds.), *Handbook of research on teacher education: Enduring issues in changing contexts* (3rd ed., pp. 290–306). Washington, DC: Association of Teacher Educators.

Lagemann, E. C. (1996, May). Experimenting with education: John Dewey and Ella Flagg young at the university of Chicago. *American Journal of Education*, 10(3), 171–185.

Lewis, L., & Claffey, R. L. (2014). Worcester normal school. In M.-L. Breitborde & K. Kolodny (Eds.), *Remembering Massachusetts state normal schools: Pioneers in teacher education* (pp. 98–107). Westfield, MA: Institute for Massachusetts Studies.

Nieuwejaar, K. (2015). *Learning through living together: The educational philosophy of Jane Addams.* Ph.D. Dissertation, Columbia University. Retrieved from https://academiccommons.columbia.edu/doi/10.7916/D84J0CXF

"Nothing Servile": Native Resistance at the Santee Normal Training School. (n.d.). Beloit, WI: Beloit College Logan Museum of Anthropology Online Exhibition, Beloit College. Retrieved from https://www.loganmuseumexhibits.com/preserving-the-dakota-language

Ogren, C. A. (1995, Spring). Where coeds were coeducated: Normal schools in Wisconsin, 1879–1920. *History of Education Quarterly*, 35(1), 1–26.

Ogren, C. A. (2000). "A large measure of self-control and personal power": Women students at state normal schools during the late-nineteenth and early-twentieth centuries. *Women's Studies Quarterly*, 28(3/4), 211–232. Retrieved from http://www.jstor.org/stable/40005486

Palmer, G. H. (1909). *Ethical and moral instruction in schools*. Boston, MA: Houghton Mifflin. Retrieved from https://www.google.com/books/edition/Ethical_and_Moral_Instruction_in_Schools/42pIsDmeHZEC?hl=en&gbpv=1&dq=Palmer,+Ethical+and+Moral+Instruction&printsec=frontcover

Perkins, L. M. (1982). "Heed life's demands": The educational philosophy of Fanny Jackson Coppin. *The Journal of Negro Education*, 51(3), 181–190. Retrieved from https://www.jstor.org/stable/2294688

Pincham, L. B. (2005, Spring). A league of willing workers: The impact of northern philanthropy, Virginia Estelle Randolph and the Jeanes teachers in early twentieth-century Virginia. *The Journal of Negro Education*, 74(2), 112–123. Retrieved from https://www.jstor.org/stable/40034537

Racial Discrimination by Colleges Restricted. (1890, August 30). U.S. code, title 7, agriculture, Chapter 13, agricultural and mechanical colleges, subchapter II. College aid annual appropriation, section 323. Retrieved from https://www.law.cornell.edu/uscode/text/7/323

Rayman, R. (1981, Winter). Joseph Lancaster's monitorial system of instruction and American Indian education, 1815–1838. *History of Education Quarterly*, 21(4), 395–409. Retrieved from https://www.jstor.org/stable/367922

Reid, D. (2015). People's colleges for other citizens: Black land-grant institutions and the politics of educational expansion in the post-Civil-War South (2015). In A. Marcus (Ed.), *Science as service: Establishing and reformulating American land-grant universities, 1865–1930* (pp. 141–174). Tuscaloosa, AL: University of Alabama Press.

Reigart, J. F. (1916). *The Lancasterian system of instruction in the schools of New York City*. Ph.D. Dissertation, Columbia University. Retrieved from http://www.columbia.edu/cu/lweb/digital/collections/cul/texts/ldpd_6316626_000/ldpd_6316626_000.pdf

Santee Normal Training and Missionary Association, American. (1885). Santee normal training school. 4. Santee Agency, Nebraska, for the year ending 1885. Santee normal training school. Retrieved from https://digitalcommons.unomaha.edu/santee_school/4

Snedden, S. (1922). *Educational sociology*. New York, NY: Century Press.

Steiner, B. C. (1919). *The life of Henry Barnard: The first United States Commissioner of Education, 1867–1870*. Bulletin No. 8 (pp. 89–93). U.S. Department of the Interior, Bureau of Education, Washington, DC. Retrieved from https://files.eric.ed.gov/fulltext/ED541144.pdf

Taggart, R. J. (1988). *Private philanthropy and public education: Pierre S. Du Pont and the Delaware schools, 1890–1940*. Newark, DE: University of Delaware Press.

Thickstun, E. (1907, October). Education department. *The Indian School Journal*, 7(32), 33–41. Retrieved from https://catalog.archives.gov/OpaAPI/media/2745460/content/nrf/chilocco/the_indian_school_journal_october_1907.pdf

Thorndike, E. L. (1905). *The elements of psychology*. New York, NY: A. G. Seiler.

Thorndike, E. L. (1913, July–December). Eugenics: With special reference to intellect and character. *Popular Science Monthly*, 83, 125–138. Retrieved from https://archive.org/details/popularsciencemo8313newy

Washington, B. T. (1901). *Up from slavery: An autobiography*. Garden City, NY: Doubleday & Company.

Woodson, C. (1922). *The Negro in our history*. Washington, DC: Associated Publishers. Retrieved from https://archive.org/details/negroinourhisto01woodgoog/page/n12/mode/2up

Woody, T. (1966/1929). *A history of women's education in the United States*. New York, NY: Farrar, Strauss & Giroux.

Zimmerman, J. (2009). *Small wonder: The little red schoolhouse in history and memory*. New Haven, CT: Yale University Press.

Chapter 4

Preparing Teachers in the Mid-to-Late Twentieth Century: National and Global Influences

The second half of the twentieth century in the United States was shaped by the contexts of the Civil Rights Movement, the War on Poverty, and wide-ranging appeals for social justice. On a global level, the threat of arms competition and nuclear conflict stemming from the Cold War with the Soviet Union, coupled with the tensions of the race to outer space, also influenced the landscape. These different and complex contexts not only shaped the lives of children and families during this period, but also the work of specialists, including teachers and other school professionals, who provided services to these groups. These circumstances affected how these individuals prepared for their professional responsibilities.

This chapter explores the contexts surrounding teacher education during the second half of the twentieth century in the United States, and how these frameworks influenced the structure, curricula, and pedagogy of teacher preparation programs and the experiences of their participants. At this time, most teacher preparation programs were situated squarely in four-year college and university settings. The normal school model had phased out. Standards for teaching rose and tightened, with set requirements for certification/licensure. By September 1960, a total of 42 states and territories enforced the minimum requirement of a baccalaureate degree for the certification of elementary school teachers. All states required a baccalaureate degree for high school teachers (Stinnett, 1960). By the end of the twentieth century, a baccalaureate degree was required for all certified/licensed early childhood, elementary, and secondary education public school teachers.

Social and Political Contexts in the Latter Half of the Twentieth Century United States

In the 1950s, most schools in southern US states were legally segregated by race ("de jure"). Others elsewhere in the country were segregated "de facto," by racially separated neighborhoods or by tradition. These schools did not receive equal resources. Children who attended schools for African Americans, for example, often found themselves in overcrowded buildings which lacked enough desks, chairs, and school books for the students. In some areas of southern states, there

Teacher Preparation in the United States, 91–116

Published under exclusive licence by Emerald Publishing Limited
doi:10.1108/978-1-80071-687-220221005

also were only elementary schools for African American children. High schools were not available. The Supreme Court case Brown v the Board of Education in 1954 ruled that the "separate but equal" rationale that had been used in justifying segregation in 1896 with the Plessy v Ferguson case was untenable and unjust, and ordered public school districts to desegregate "with all deliberate speed" (Lowe, 2004). Though a small number of districts desegregated in a timely manner, most refused to integrate for decades following this ruling. Overt racism resulted in educational inequities for hundreds of thousands of African American children which profoundly shaped their lives. Many argue that segregation continues in the contemporary context and that desegregation is not possible within urban borders. Though the outcomes of Brown v Board of Education have taken time to unfold, this landmark case was influential in moving toward educational equity for various groups, including those with disabilities rights, limited English, and for LGBTQ students. The case set a precedent which created change in the field of education in critical ways (Lengyel & Vanbergeijk, 2021).

Brown v Board of Education 1954

Brown v Board of Education was a supreme court case in which the justices unanimously ruled that racial segregation of children in public schools was unconstitutional. There were five consolidated cases under Brown v Board of Education. This number of different cases was significant because it presented school segregation as a national issue. One of the plaintiffs was Oliver Brown who filed a class action suit against the Board of Education of Topeka, Kansas. In 1951, his daughter, Linda Brown, was denied entrance to the all-White elementary schools in Topeka. In Brown v Board of Education, it was argued that segregation violated the equal protection laws of the 14th amendment (Tushnet, 1995). The case was argued by Thurgood Marshall, who would become the first African American Supreme Court Justice in 1967.

Psychological research was cited in the Brown v Board of Education case, including a study by Kenneth Clark, who was at that time an assistant professor at the City College in New York City (Benjamin & Crouse, 2002). Kenneth Clark, in collaboration with his wife Mamie Clark, had conducted a doll experiment with African American children. The findings of the experiment highlighted the internalized racism in African American children and the self-abasement that was pronounced among children attending segregated schools. This experiment was cited in the 11th footnote of the Brown decision (Benjamin & Crouse, 2002).

With the case of Brown v Board of Education, "the Court claimed, 'to separate them [African American children] from others of similar age and qualifications solely because of their race generates a feeling of inferiority as to their status in the community that may affect their hearts and minds in a way unlikely ever to be undone'" (Wraga, 2006, p. 425). One of the justices, Earl Warren, wrote that "in the field of public education the doctrine of separate but equal has no place as segregated schools are inherently unequal" (Wraga, 2006, p. 425). As a result of this case, school segregation was legally ended.

Following Brown v Board of Education, the Civil Rights Movement, in concert with the War on Poverty, gained momentum. Along with basic human rights, these initiatives addressed the need of learners for equitable educational experiences. The Civil Rights Movement, for example, resulted in Congress enacting civil rights statutes which prohibited discrimination in educational programs that received federal assistance. These statutes included Title VI of the Civil Rights Act of 1964 prohibiting race, color, and national origin discrimination. This was followed by the Title IX of the Education Amendments of 1972 prohibiting sex discrimination and Section 504 of the Rehabilitation Act of 1973 prohibiting disability discrimination. The Bilingual Education Act of 1968 also was passed during this time. Prior to the Bilingual Education Act, children who did not speak English were immersed in English language classes and at times punished for speaking their native languages (Stewner-Manzanares, 1988). In the early 1970s in San Francisco, for example, there were approximately 2,900 non-English speaking students of Chinese ancestry in the public school district. Only 1,000 of these students received supplemental language services. With support of a public interest lawyer, Kinney Kinmon Lau and other students subsequently challenged the San Francisco Unified School District regarding this practice. Their case went before the Supreme Court which ruled that the lack of supplemental language instruction for public school students with limited English proficiency violated the Civil Rights Act of 1964.

Group of Chinese Children Posing on the Steps of Immigrants Development Center of San Francisco at 843 Stockton Street in the early 1970s. *Source:* Courtesy of San Francisco History Center, San Francisco Public Library.

Following these new laws, curricula began to emphasize diversity. Bilingual education classes proliferated. A small number of bilingual schools also opened to serve Mexican American and Puerto Rican communities (Nieto, 2004). Over the decades that followed, the education of students with disabilities also was addressed in the learning process. One strong and influential leader in the Civil Rights Movement, who has dedicated her life to promoting the general well-being and educational rights of children, was Marian Wright Edelman, who founded the Children's Defense Fund in 1973.

Biographical Sketch

Marian Wright Edelman.
Source: Courtesy of Children's Defense Fund.

Marian Wright Edelman was born on June 6, 1939 in Bennettsville, South Carolina. One of five siblings, she grew up in a segregated town. She remembers that as a Black child, she could never "take anything for granted and never for a moment lacked a purpose worth fighting, living, and dying for" (Edelman, 1999). Edelman graduated from Spelman College, established for Black women in 1881, and Yale Law School. After graduating from law school, she directed the NAACP legal defense and educational fund in Jackson, Mississippi. She later moved to Washington, D.C. in 1968 and served as a counsel for the Poor People's Campaign that Dr Martin Luther King organized before his death. In 1973, she began the Children's Defense Fund, whose "Leave No Child Behind" mission is to ensure every child a "*Healthy Start*, a *Head Start*, a *Fair Start*, a *Safe Start*, and a *Moral Start* in life and successful passage to adulthood with the help of caring families and communities" (Children's Defense Fund, 2021).

Throughout her life, Edelman has received hundreds of honorary degrees and awards for her work. She is the author of nine books, as well as numerous academic articles and columns. In one of Edelman's columns, published by the Children's Defense Fund on September 9, 2016, – "Teaching for Success: Welcoming and Respecting Every Child," she wrote, "You can have the best curriculum in the world and as many degrees as you can pay for from the best schools but the foundation for building strong children is respecting and remembering the specialness of every individual child. Educating each of our children is a sacred trust and a noble undertaking. I am so grateful to all those who go into school buildings across our nation every day to build strong educated citizens to ensure the competitiveness and security of our nation." Edelman's work has influenced educators throughout the United States, including aspiring teachers.

Source: Courtesy of Swarthmore College Special Collections. Button, Pin, and Ribbon Collection – Identifier 1497.

The War on Poverty declared by President Lyndon Johnson in 1964 resulted in the Economic Opportunity Act of 1964, which also impacted the field of education in that it created a Job Corps, the VISTA project, a federal work-study program, and the national Head Start initiative for preschool age children. The War on Poverty also produced the Elementary and Secondary Education Act (ESEA), signed into law in 1965. This act established the Title I program subsidizing school districts with a large share of impoverished students.

Elementary and Secondary Education Act

In launching the War on Poverty and the ESEA, President Johnson reflected on a year he spent teaching students in Cotulla, Texas, a small border town between Texas and Mexico. He saw that many of his students faced great hardships connected to poverty. This experience deeply influenced his motivation in launching this initiative.

The ESEA marked the beginning of the federal government involvement in the day-to-day operations of public schools (Jennings, 2015). One goal of the ESEA was to reduce the achievement gap between P-12 students from school districts in economically disadvantaged and wealthy districts (Standefer, 2006). The law specifically "directed the attention of teachers and administrators toward better serving economically and educationally disadvantaged children" (Jennings, 2015, p. 42).

Through the ESEA, books and audiovisual equipment were provided to both public and private schools for libraries. There were funds available for research and training for teachers. State governments were pushed to take stronger roles in improving all of their schools. The ESEA also provided funds for free and reduced lunches for students. The ESEA has been reviewed by Congress every four to five years and renewed (Jennings, 2015). Since ESEA was first established, it has been reauthorized a number of times. For example, ESEA was reauthorized as the No Child Left Behind Act (NCLB) in 2001 under President George W. Bush. In 2015, it was reauthorized and renamed the Every Student Succeeds Act (ESSA) in President Barack Obama's administration.

Educational plans and programs that unfolded during the second half of the twentieth century also were affected by global contexts. The Cold War with the Soviet Union, from the late 1940s to the 1990s, resulted in an arms race and perceived threats of nuclear conflict. In the public school settings, children often practiced bomb drills – hiding beneath desks in their classrooms in case of an attack. These were called "duck-and-cover" drills. The simultaneous race to outer space engaged these two "cold-warring" nations in fierce competition. In 1957, the Soviet Union shocked the United States by launching Sputnik, the first earth-orbiting satellite. This created new fear regarding national security, as satellites could monitor and take pictures of other countries. The Cold War and space race not only resulted in trepidation, tension, and competition between these countries, but also drew attention to the need to educate children with the knowledge, skills, and values required to build strong nations. In the United States, there was amplified interest in strengthening education in mathematics, sciences, and foreign languages. The National Defense Education Act, implemented in 1958, provided an increased number of pathways to colleges and universities for a larger number of students (Pruitt, 2019).

National Defense Education Act of 1958

The National Defense Education Act (NDEA) established federal funding for higher education. It made low-cost student loans available for public and private colleges and universities. "In 1960 there were 3.6 million students in college, and by 1970 there were 7.5 million. Many of them received their college education only because of the availability of NDEA loans" (United States Senate, 2021). Since the enactment of NDEA, there has been additional aid added for teacher training and instructional improvement (Harden, 1981).

During this time, the Equality of Educational Opportunity Survey (EEOS) also opened the door for national testing of public school students in grades 1, 3, 6, 9, and 12. This connected to the initiatives to prepare academically strong children to support the country. The testing allowed for regional and national reporting of test scores for White and Black students, and national reporting for Hispanic, American Indian, Asian, and other groups. Though it did not allow for reporting in individual states, some achievement gaps could be identified (Beaton et al., 2011). The National Assessment of Educational Progress (NAEP), a national testing program, was introduced in the 1960s and the first data were collected in 1969 (Beaton et al., 2011). Though embraced by some, objections to the NAEP and national testing in general focused on the encroachment of the federal government on states' rights to govern public education. Federal oversight began to increase during the second part of the twentieth century. The United States Department of Education, which set uniform rules and standards that are applied nation-wide, became a cabinet-level department of the United States government in 1980.

The United States Department of Education

Between 1908 and 1975, there were more than 130 bills introduced to Congress to form a national department of education (Stallings, 2002). It wasn't until the 1960s, however, that this idea gained traction when Senator Abraham Ribicoff began to consistently work on the formation of a Cabinet-level department of education. The National Education Association (NEA) also supported this pursuit, providing additional backing. When President Jimmy Carter was elected in 1976, he endorsed Cabinet level status for education. In October 1979, Congress passed the Department of Education Organization Act (Public Law 96-88) (United States Department of Education, 2010). Once the United States Department of Education was established, the Honorable Shirley Hufstedler was selected to begin work on the Department of Education. When President Ronald Reagan was elected in 1980, he appointed Terrell Bell to succeed Hufstedler (Stallings, 2002). New presidential administrations subsequently have influenced who leads the United States Department of Education, as well as its goals and policies.

Prior to the endorsement of Cabinet level status for education, there was an Office of Education. In 1867, President Andrew Johnson created a Department of Education to collect statistical data. It was renamed "Office of Education" in 1868. The operations of the Office of Education were fairly small. In the years that followed, this office was housed in different agencies including the United States Department of Health Education and Welfare (United States Department of Education, 2010).

In the contemporary context, the United States Department of Education has a budget that is over 68 billion dollars. It employs approximately 4,400 employees (United States Department of Education, 2021). "ED's mission is to promote student achievement and preparation for global competitiveness by fostering educational excellence and ensuring equal access" (United States Department of Education, 2021).

Building on concerns connected to the academic skills of students, in 1983 the US National Commission on Excellence in Education released *A Nation at Risk: The Imperative for Educational Reform*. The widely distributed report listed reasons why the country's educational system was failing to meet the national need for a competitive workforce (Mehta, 2015). The report resulted in an assessment of the quality of teaching in the United States and the learning that took place at the primary and secondary levels. With regard to the preparation of teachers, the committee recommended that aspiring educators demonstrate competence in a specific academic discipline, to remedy their perception that students graduating from public schools lacked important content knowledge. The eighteen members of the commission who wrote and released this report included a former governor, business professionals, administrators from institutions of higher education (college and university presidents), a few university faculty members, school board members, a superintendent, principals, and one practicing teacher.

Structure and Curriculum of College and University Teacher Education Programs

The national and international contexts affecting life in the US in the second half of the twentieth century shaped the lives of children and families. It further influenced the work of teachers and other school professionals, and how they were prepared for their careers. In the mid-to-late twentieth century, for example, most public school teachers were required to complete an undergraduate baccalaureate degree with coursework in education and a student teaching practicum experience. Alternatively, students could complete a postbaccalaureate certification-only program, or a graduate school degree, such as a Master of Arts in Teaching (M.A.T.). The requirements of these programs, if met, resulted in teacher certification. As mentioned in Chapter III, teacher preparation programs housed in colleges and universities, however, had "ambivalent relationships" with their arts and science academic counterparts. In these "marriages of convenience," the universities provided "status and academic credibility" to education participants, while teacher education programs provided "students and social utility," as well as income, to colleges and universities (Labaree, 2008, p. 290).

Master of Arts in Teaching

The Master of Arts in Teaching (M.A.T.) degree was established in 1936 at Harvard University "to prepare liberal arts college graduates for teaching in the secondary schools" (Cogan, 1955, p. 1). When first administered at Harvard, the degree was not awarded and administered by the Graduate School of Education, but rather by "an Administrative Board drawn from the University at large" (Cogan, 1955, p. 1). The degree highlighted the idea that the education of secondary school teachers was strongly linked to their subject area field, in addition to professional education. Yale University also began an M.A.T. in 1951. Similar to the Harvard program, Yale's M.A.T. required extensive undergraduate preparation in the subject area in which the candidate desired to teach (Holden, 1959). In 1968, educators Roger Harrell, William Graves, and James Foster from Texas A&M University also advocated for an M.A.T. program at their institution as a way to help fill vacancies in teaching, noting that a national shortage had emerged in 1957. They presented plans to implement the M.A.T. programs in both elementary and secondary education at their university. In the 1950s and 1960s, the Ford Foundation began to provide significant support to 50 colleges and universities for the development of M.A.T programs, to address teacher shortages (Shuman, 1981). Most of these programs required an initial summer of coursework, sometimes including a practicum in a campus school or summer enrichment school. "The intensive program was followed by a teaching internship, usually salaried, which essentially took one of three forms (1) teach full time for one semester either the fall or spring and spend one full semester on campus taking courses; (2) teach half a day for an entire school year while carrying a reduced load of coursework during the fall and spring semesters; or (3) teach full time for a full year, carrying one evening course during each semester and taking a full summer of work" (Shuman, 1981, pp. 9–10).

Today, the M.A.T is a degree for individuals seeking their initial certification or licensure. The degree takes different forms. Many are full-time graduate degrees. Some function as fifth year programs in which a student spends a year beyond the bachelor degree to obtain the teaching license. There also are part-time evening and weekend M.A.T. programs for people moving from other careers into teaching.

The required coursework for certification varied from state to state during the second half of the twentieth century – and continues into the current day. State departments or state boards of education have held the authority for fixing the requirements, issuing, and reissuing teacher certificates (Stinnett, 1960). In the beginning of the twentieth century, the use of teacher examinations grew as a requirement for certification/licensure. The National Committee on Teacher Examinations, for example, was appointed by the American Council on Education in 1939 at the request of a group of superintendents (Flanagan, 1941). The task of the committee was to develop a series of teacher exams. The group of superintendents who requested this work believed that these exams could provide information about certain aspects of the training and professional preparation of teachers. This information then could assist administrators with teacher selection (Flanagan, 1941). The Carnegie Foundation for the Advancement of Teaching provided funds for the project. In 1960, 22 states used teacher exams for certification. Of these states, 13 had exams connected directly to the state certification office (Slaughter, 1960). The teacher-testing movement, thereafter, grew explosively in the 1980s and 1990s and today almost all states have some sort of teacher-testing requirement (Latham, Gitomer, & Ziomek, 1999).

At the college level, there historically have been differences in required coursework in teacher preparation programs, which have usually reflected state requirements that were sometimes minimal. This coursework has been developed and overseen by college professors. In 1965, for example, students at Swarthmore College in Pennsylvania who were interested in secondary education teaching took courses in the Psychology and Education Department. To obtain a secondary education teaching certification, these students completed coursework in: Introduction to Psychology, Educational Psychology, Introduction to Teaching, Principles and Methods of Secondary Education, History of Education, and Student Teaching (Swarthmore College, 1965). This was in addition to their subject area work.

In the University of California at Irvine's course catalog in 1965, it was noted that "the faculty assumes as one of its responsibilities the education of teachers for elementary and secondary schools and junior colleges. Those responsibilities are to be met through curricula combining subject matter concentration in teaching fields, studies seeking to relate theory and practice, and supervised internships designed to test educational theory in teaching and to develop professional attitudes" (University of California at Irvine, 1965, p. 85).

In 1970 Massachusetts required only four courses for an elementary teaching license: a "foundations" course in philosophy of education, a course in child development, a "methods" course in any subject area that was part of the elementary education, and student teaching. A student at a liberal arts college could receive certification after taking Child Development (often a Psychology course), History and Philosophy of Education, Methods of Teaching Science, and Student Teaching (which could be two days each week).

In 1975, Kansas State University required aspiring candidates to complete general education requirements, a subject area concentration, and professional and specialized courses for a baccalaureate degree in elementary education. In the field of secondary education, candidates completed general education requirements, a subject area major, and a professional semester (Kansas State University, 1975).

In some rural areas of the country, access to different types of teacher preparation programs was limited. Educators Belva Collins and John Schuster (2001), for example, wrote that in places such as rural Kentucky in the early 1960s "there was no personnel preparation program in special education" (p. 23). "The first faculty in special education at the University of Kentucky was not hired until 1968" (p. 23). By the 1970s, however, advocacy groups, such as the Association for Retarded Citizens, increasingly lobbied Congress to ensure that children with disabilities could receive a free and appropriate education which increasingly pushed teacher preparation programs to address this area. When special education was introduced in teacher preparation programs, some of the courses and majors addressed "the trainable mentally handicapped" (Collins & Schuster, 2001). Student teaching often took place in separate and specialized schools serving students with moderate to severe disabilities. Since special education courses were not available in some rural parts of the country, interested students took correspondence courses or they took part in distance learning initiatives. A professor, for example, might have driven six hours to deliver the connected courses on a Friday night and Saturday (Collins & Schuster, 2001). By the 1980s, coursework in special education had expanded in teacher preparation programs throughout the United States. Educators Feden and Clabaugh (1986), as well as many other educators, reflected on the outcome of the new special education laws which was that public school children were to be educated in the least restrictive environment – in inclusion settings. In teacher preparation programs, a subsequent result was the cross categorical certification of special education teachers.

At this point in the twentieth century, some universities also developed multiple departments within the field of education. In the 1980s, for example, the University of Illinois at Urbana-Champaign had an Education School which included an Educational Policy Studies Department and an Education Practice Department for elementary and secondary education, special education, physical education, and other fields. An Educational Psychology Department provided coursework in child development for elementary teachers, psychology of learning for teachers, construction and use of tests in teaching, and anthropology of education (University of Illinois at Urbana-Champaign, 1980).

As teacher preparation expanded in the college and university settings, faculty also influenced the wider profession as they introduced new theories and teaching approaches. Eleanor Duckworth, of the Harvard Graduate School of Education, developed a teaching approach that was titled *Critical Exploration in the Classroom*. Duckworth, a former student of Jean Piaget at the Institut des Sciences de l'Education in Geneva, Switzerland, drew from his work. She also connected with the work of Brazilian educator Paulo Freire, who practiced a political and liberationist approach to education. Freire believed it was important to understand and value the learner's experiences and insights in the classroom. He also understood that schooling could either oppress or liberate students.

Duckworth (1987) published several books that were widely read. One of these books was *The Having of Wonderful Ideas* which was first published in 1987 with Teachers College Press. In this book, Duckworth argued that the process of testing out their own ideas is critical to children's cognitive development. She also noted that this process is important for teachers as well.

> It is just as necessary for teachers as for children to feel confidence in their own ideas. It is important for them as people and it is important in order for them to feel free to acknowledge the children's ideas. If teachers feel that their class must do things just as the book says, and that their excellence as teachers depend on this, they cannot possibly accept children's divergence and creations.
>
> (Duckworth, 2006, p. 15)

Prior to her work at Harvard, Duckworth had been an elementary school teacher. In addition, she had participated in the Elementary Science Study (ESS) in 1962, which was a curriculum development and science education reform project that grew out of MIT. Duckworth's subsequent influence in curriculum development grew throughout the United States and with several other countries.

Other faculty in teacher preparation programs were influential with the growing field of multicultural education. One of these educators was James Banks, born in 1941 in Arkansas. Banks earned degrees from Chicago Teachers College and Michigan State University before he assumed a faculty position with the College of Education at the University of Washington from 1969 to 2019. During his career, Banks became a president of the American Educational Research Association (AERA) and the National Council for the Social Studies (NCSS). A prolific author, Banks' books included *An Introduction to Multicultural Education* (2008); *Teaching Strategies for Ethnic Studies* (1979); and *Cultural Diversity and Education: Foundations, Curriculum, and Teaching* (1981) among others. Banks believed that "continuing education about diversity is especially important for teachers" (Banks, 2001, p. 197). He advocated for professional development programs that would help educators uncover attitudes toward racial, ethnic, language, and cultural groups, acquire knowledge about diverse groups, become acquainted with diverse perspectives, and understand how institutionalized knowledge in schools can perpetuate stereotypes (Banks, 2001, p. 197). A strong promoter of multicultural education, he recognized that the field also had its critics. In an article he wrote for Phi Delta Kappan in 1993, he debunked some of the myths surrounding multicultural education. One of these myths was that multicultural education was for others. He wrote,

> The major theorists and researchers in multicultural education agree that the movement is designed to restructure educational institutions so that all students, including middle-class white males, will acquire the knowledge, skills, and attitudes needed to function effectively in a culturally and ethnically diverse nation and world.
> (Banks, 1993, p. 23)

Banks often has been referred to as the father of multicultural education. (University of Washington, 2021). His work shaped teacher preparation with regard to curriculum development, pedagogical methods, and approaches to relationships.

Sonia Nieto was another teacher education faculty member who contributed to the growing field of multicultural education. Raised in Brooklyn, New York, Nieto received her baccalaureate degree in Elementary Education from St. John's University. In Madrid, Spain, she earned a master's degree in Spanish and Hispanic Literature. She thereafter earned her doctorate from the University of Massachusetts Amherst in curriculum studies with concentrations in multicultural education and bilingual education. One of Nieto's first teaching positions was at an elementary school in Brooklyn where she taught Puerto Rican and African American children. She recalled:

> I'm Puerto Rican, and I grew up in Brooklyn with kids who were a lot like the Puerto Rican and African American kids I was teaching. But it was a rough, under-resourced school, and I hadn't really been prepared for the assignment. In college, I had learned how to design units and write lesson plans. But all of our teacher education books had pictures of White kids and White teachers on the cover, and they described a very different reality from the one that I was experiencing. My program hadn't taught me much about the history of public education, the sociopolitical contexts of urban schooling, the challenges facing students from low-income and immigrant backgrounds. . . So it was a difficult start to my career.
>
> (Heller, 2020, p. 32)

Sonia Nieto subsequently has written numerous influential articles and books throughout her career. One of her groundbreaking books was *Affirming diversity: The Sociopolitical Context of Multicultural Education* that was first published in 1992. Reflecting on multicultural education, she wrote:

> Multicultural education cannot be understood in a vacuum but rather must be seen in its personal, social, historical and political context. Assuming that multicultural education is "the answer" to school failure is simplistic at best for it overlooks important social and education issues that affect daily the lives of students... However, if broadly conceptualized and implemented, multicultural education can have a substantive and positive impact on the educational experiences of most students.
>
> (Nieto, 1992, pp. xxiii–xxiv)

Educator Diane Ravitch, in contrast, took a more conservative approach to the teaching of culture in the twentieth century. She believed in teaching a "culture in common" (Ravtich, 1991, p. 8). As Assistant Secretary of Education from 1991 to 1993, her positions about schooling shaped teacher preparation programs from a conformist lens. However, after leaving her position with the federal government in 1993, Ravitch would rethink her views about schooling and publicly apologize, including for conflating a strong curriculum with standardized testing. Ravitch subsequently worked as a research professor at New York University's Steinhardt School of Culture, Education, and Human Development from 1994 to 2020. She started a blog (dianeravitch.net), viewed by millions, that is focused on discussions about education.

During the second half of the twentieth century, social activism was promoted by other teacher education faculty. Maxine Greene, for example, from Teachers College, explored living in awareness and "wide awakeness" in connection to advancing social justice. Greene believed that individuals should live deliberately with full attention to life. Individuals should search for meaning in life. Greene connected her beliefs about "wide awakeness" to studying curriculum, including interdisciplinary studies, and in particular, the arts and aesthetic education (Greene, 1977). Greene went on to become the president of several professional organizations including the AERA, the Philosophy of Education Society, the American Educational Studies Association (AESA), and the Middle Atlantic States Philosophy of Education Society (The Maxine Greene Institute, 2021). Her educational theory was considered hopeful as it enabled teachers and students to envision what might be. Through her writing and professional roles, Greene influenced teacher preparation in compelling ways.

Source: Courtesy of Swarthmore College Special Collections. Button, Pin, and Ribbon Collection – Identifier 104.

Ian Harris from the University of Wisconsin Milwaukee also promoted social activism through peace education courses that he began to teach at his university in 1985. He subsequently published a number of important and prominent books about peace education (Harris, 1988). Educator and philosopher Nel Noddings (2008) connected ideas about peace education to care education, an influential area of thought that she helped to developed in the 1980s and 1990s.

> Care theory and peace education go well together…In every facet of life, we encounter the living other…. Care theory describes caring encounters and caring relations, and gives us some guidance on how to establish, maintain, and enhance such relations. To teach for caring relations is to teach for peace in communities, in individual lives, and in the world.
>
> (Noddings, 2008, p. 87)

Some of Noddings' notable books included *Caring: A Relational Approach to Ethics and Moral Education* (1984); *The Challenge to Care in Schools: An Alternative Approach to Education* (1992); *Happiness and Education* (2003); *Peace Education: How We Come to Love and Hate War* (2012). Prior to her work as an education professor at Stanford University from 1977 to 1998, Noddings taught elementary and high school mathematics and was a school administrator. Noddings was influential for promoting an understanding of an ethic of care in teaching and in connected relationships.

In 1984, educator Ted Sizer started the Coalition for Essential Schools. A goal of the Essential Schools was for each student to master a limited number of essential skills and areas of knowledge. Sizer also believed that there was no fixed blueprint for the Essential Schools. "It is rather, a set of ideas, ideas and conditions and convictions. We call them principles, which, on the basis of substantial experience and research, strike many of us as an essential part of life in a worthy school. It's ideas, not specific practices, which drive your and my work" (Sizer, 2009). When Sizer started the Coalition for Essential Schools, he was chair of the Education Department at Brown University. His work became widely known in teacher preparation programs. Notable educator Deborah Meier, with assistance from Ted Sizer's Coalition of Essential Schools, thereafter started a small school movement.

Biographical Sketch

Deborah Meier
Small School Movement.
Source: Courtesy of Deborah Meier.

Deborah Meier was born in 1931. She attended Antioch College and then received her MA in History from the University of Chicago (National Academy of Education, 2021). Meier started teaching in a kindergarten classroom in Chicago (Dykman, 1997). In the 1960s, she and her family moved to New York where she worked as a kindergarten teacher in Central Harlem (Meier, 2021). In the East Harlem District 4, she also helped to revitalize the public schools.

In 1974, Meier was approached by Anthony Alvarado, superintendent of New York City's Community School District, who asked her to start a school in East Harlem. Meier accepted and with a small group of colleagues started the Central Park East Elementary School. They had no start-up funds, but enough money to cover the salaries of five teachers and one aide. They borrowed books, found free furniture, and gathered supplies from various sources so they could run the school. In 1978, Meier and her colleagues started a second school. Reflecting on small schools, Meier (1996) wrote that they "come as close to being a panacea for America's educational ills as we're likely to get. Smallness is a prerequisite for the climate and culture that we need to develop the habits of heart and mind essential to a democracy" (p. 12).

Meier received the MacArthur Fellowship in 1987 (Dykman, 1997). Her books have included *The Power of Their Ideas; Lessons to America from a Small School in Harlem* (2002); *In Schools We Trust* (2014) and others. In 1995, Meier moved to Boston and started Mission Hill which is a K-8 school in Roxbury.

Several prominent psychologists, who worked in university schools of education, also introduced new theories of development and learning styles which shaped teacher preparation programs in the second half of the twentieth century. Lawrence Kohlberg, for example, who was a faculty member in Harvard's Graduate School of Education, introduced groundbreaking work focused on the stages of moral development. He believed school professionals should approach classroom management, as well as the hidden curriculum of schools, from a theory of moral education (Kohlberg, 1975).

Howard Gardner, also a faculty member at Harvard's Graduate School of Education, developed the theory of multiple intelligences (MI). In an article that Gardner wrote for Educational Leadership in 1997, he shared that "From my perspective, MI can be an extremely useful tool - or better, partner – in the process of creating excellent schools" (p. 20). He further wrote, "It can aid in a variety of missions from engaging more children to encouraging deeper understanding to preparing students for work" (Gardner, 1997, p. 20).

Educator Anthony Gregorc, who taught educational administration and curriculum and instruction at the University of Illinois at Urbana-Champaign and at the University of Connecticut, in contrast, developed a mind styles model (concrete sequential, concrete random, abstract sequential, and abstract random). In an article that he wrote for the NASSP Bulletin, Gregorc suggested that teachers would best achieve professional growth in programs designed to fit the individual (1975). Each of the theories developed by these aforementioned psychologists shaped the learning of candidates in teacher preparation programs – and how they prepared to work with their students, as well as their colleagues.

Responding to national and global contexts, teacher education grew and expanded during the second half of the twentieth century in colleges and universities. Though this expansion took place, there were antagonistic and hostile efforts aimed at reforming these programs (Martin, 1994). For example, there were some strong attempts to dissolve teacher education departments so more liberal arts graduates could enter the field. There were calls to strengthen the standards connected to teaching so teachers could better support US students. Alternative certification programs also were created (Martin, 1994). In 1990, for example, Teach for America (TFA) was launched (Teach for America, 2021). In response to wide-ranging efforts to reform college and university teacher preparation programs, the American Association of Colleges of Teacher Education (AACTE), which emerged in 1948 as the successor to the American Association of Teacher Colleges (AATC), strengthened energies aimed at searching for best practices, fostered exchange of information, promoted various programs, and worked on accreditation (Ducharme & Ducharme, 1998). The National Council for the Accreditation of Teacher Education (NCATE), for example, was created in 1954 to assume the responsibilities of accreditation for college and university programs. During this time, the AACTE also worked diligently in Washington, DC to influence policy and action to benefit education schools (Ducharme & Ducharme, 1998).

National Council for the Accreditation of Teacher Education

The National Council of the Accreditation of Teacher Education (NCATE) was established in 1954 and recognized as an accreditor of teacher preparation programs, largely at the college and university setting, by the US Department of Education. The American Association of Colleges of Teacher Education, the National Association of State Directors of Teacher Education and Certification, the Council of Chief State School Officers, and the National School Boards Association assisted in the establishment of NCATE (Wang & Chen, 2009). Starting with its inception, NCATE set standards for the appraisal of institutions of teacher education. These standards were reviewed, updated, and changed approximately every five years. Some of these standards related to the knowledge and dispositions of aspiring teachers, assessments, field experiences and clinical practices, diversity, and the qualifications of teacher preparation faculty. A primary goal of NCATE was to improve the quality of teacher education (Wang & Chen, 2009). Some criticisms of NCATE centered on the question of internal versus external accountability; for example, whether external accountability detracts from the right of institutions to determine their own internal standards and design processes to assess whether they have met their own standards (Tamir & Wilson, 2005). Other criticisms have addressed the time and costs spent on achieving accreditation.

Participants in College and University Teacher Education Programs

In 1955, there were 1,141,000 public school teachers in the United States. Since a baccalaureate degree was required to become a certified/licensed teacher at this time, this meant that a large percentage of these educators met this requirement by participating in a formal teacher preparation program at the college or university level. By 1975, there were 2,198,000 public school teachers in the United States and by 1995 this number increased to 2,598,000 (National Center for Education Statistics, 2014). These numbers reflected not only the growth in the number of teachers employed in the public school setting in the United States, but also increased enrollment in college and university teacher preparation programs.

Though enrollment in teacher preparation programs expanded during the second half of the twentieth century, their candidates reflected a homogenous group. Participants in teacher education programs largely were White females. The public school teaching force, likewise, reflected this demographic. In 1987, for example, there were 2,323,000 practicing teachers in the United States. Seventy percent of these teachers were female and 30 percent were male. Eighty-seven percent of these teachers identified as White (National Center for Education Statistics, 2019). In light of the racial and cultural diversity in the US student population, the lack of diversity of participants in teacher preparation programs was and continues to be an issue of significant concern in the twenty-first century. This will be discussed in more depth in the last two chapters of this book.

Following completion of teacher preparation programs, most graduates went on to work with children in the public school settings, teaching at various levels. Many achieved significant accomplishments and successes. One of these individuals was Jaime Escalante, who graduated in 1973 from California State University in Los Angeles with a mathematics degree and teaching credentials. After graduating from this university, Escalante began to teach at Garfield High School in Los Angeles in 1974 – a school whose accreditation had been threatened due to the extremely low performance of students. Escalante offered to teach an Advanced Placement (AP) calculus class at this school. An immigrant from Bolivia, he had previously taught math and physics there and was energetic to share his enthusiasm for teaching similar classes in Los Angeles. Though Escalante did not receive strong support from the school administration, he pursued the AP calculus class. In 1981, 18 of his students passed the AP calculus exam. In 1983, 30 students passed the exam. These numbers continued to grow in the years that followed. Though this was a significant achievement, the lack of support that Escalante encountered from his school administration grew into opposition. There were complaints from the administration that he arrived to school too early and worked too late. In 1989, Jay Matthews wrote a book about him titled, *Escalante: The Best Teacher in America*. Other books followed, as well as a movie *Stand and Deliver*. In 1988, Escalante was awarded the Presidential Medal for Excellence in Education by President Ronald Reagan.

Jaime Escalante. AP Photo.

Geoffrey Canada, another notable graduate of an education program, was born in 1952 in the South Bronx in New York. There he was raised in poverty by a single mother in an area of high crime rates and violence. When he was a teenager, he went to live with his grandparents in Wyandanch, New York. Canada received his baccalaureate degree in psychology and sociology from Bowdoin College in Maine in 1974, then a master's degree in education from the Harvard Graduate School of Education. Canada is best known for his work in the 1990s with the Harlem Children's Zone, a nonprofit organization whose goal is "to provide comprehensive, critical support to children and families in order to re-weave the very fabric of community life" (Harlem Children's Zone, 2021). The Harlem Children's Zone includes charter schools, a preschool program, health programs, and other community-based services. Reflecting on schools, Canada believes that they "offer us our best hope of reaching millions of children in desperate need for after school, evening, and weekend activities" (2001, p. 54). Canada has written and spoken extensively about his comprehensive approach to working with children and families (Canada, 2000, 2001). His work has been studied in many types of academic settings, including teacher preparation programs.

Another graduate of a twentieth century teacher preparation program was Christa Corrigan McAuliffe, who completed her studies at Framingham State College in Massachusetts in 1970. She became known for her participation in the Teacher in Space Program.

Biographical Sketch

Christa McAuliffe. Teacher in Space Program.
Source: Courtesy of NASA.

Christa Corrigan McAuliffe was born on September 2, 1948 in Boston, Massachusetts. She was one of five children born to Edward and Grace Corrigan. When she was five, she moved to Framingham, Massachusetts. After completing Catholic high school in Framingham, she enrolled at Framingham State College as a commuter student. The tuition was affordable at $200 a year. There she studied education and history, receiving her bachelor degree in 1970. McAuliffe described herself as an average student, earning As and Bs (Cook, 2021). She was an activist and involved in protests of the Vietnam War. After college, she married Steven McAuliffe whom she had met in high school. Thereafter, she moved to the Washington, D.C. area with her new husband where he was pursuing his law degree (Cook, 2021).

While in the Washington D.C. area, McAuliffe earned a master's degree with secondary education certification from Bowie State College, a historically Black college in Maryland, which she attended part-time during the evenings. She taught History and English to junior high school students in Maryland. Later, after moving to New Hampshire, she taught at Bow Memorial, a middle school near Concord, New Hampshire. In 1983, she began to teach at Concord High School. During this time, McAuliffe served on the executive board of the New Hampshire Council for Social Studies. In addition, she was president of her local teacher association (Cook, 2021) McAuliffe had two children (Corrigan, 1993).

In the early 1980s, President Ronald Reagan and the National Aeronautics and Space Administration (NASA) announced plans for a Teacher in Space Project. This project was to send a teacher in space on the Challenger shuttle. Author Kevin Cook (2021) wrote that "Christa...grew up with the space program. Her favorite TV hero was Superman, the man who flew faster than rockets. Her political hero was President Kennedy, who announced the United States would put a man on the moon before the decade was out" (p. 5). McAuliffe applied for the Teacher in Space project and was selected from more than 11,000 applicants.

In September 1985, McAuliffe went to the Johnson Space Center in Houston, Texas to train for this mission. While in space, Christa McAuliffe planned to conduct a series of live lessons that she would share with school-aged children. For example, she planned to show major areas of the space shuttle and describe their functions. (NASA Teacher in Space Project) On January 28, 1986, the Challenger space shuttle took off from the Kennedy Space Center in Cape Canaveral, Florida. It was a very cold day and ice had to be scraped off of the shuttle (Cook, 201). Less than two minutes after take-off, the shuttle exploded and the astronauts, including Christa McAuliffe, died. McAuliffe's mother, Grace Corrigan, recalled,

> Christa saw the year of her space experience as a grand and welcome opportunity for education – an opportunity to draw our attention in a positive way to schools, to our children, and to community involvement in improving ... our educational system. This would be the year of awareness, a year to elevate the role of teachers to the height it should have.
>
> (Corrigan, 1993, p. xii)

After this tragic accident, Challenger Centers throughout the United States were established. Connected science programs expanded. Framingham State established the Christa McAuliffe Challenger Center. The NCSS established the Christa McAuliffe Reach for the Stars Award in 1986 (National Council for the Social Studies, 2021). The US Congress also approved the Christa McAuliffe Fellowship program in 1986. This Program awarded "a one-year sabbatical to one classroom teacher in each of the 50 states and US territories for study, research, or academic improvement" (Burkhalter, McLean, & Jones, 2004, p. 49).

Conclusion

The context of the second half of the twentieth century in the United States was one that was marked by activism, calls for social justice, and political movements that resulted in new educational laws and acts. At the same time, increased tensions and fears due to the international arms race, space race, and Cold War with the Soviet Union pushed forward new educational standards and higher academic outcomes. These contexts and tensions not only shaped P-12 learners, but also the candidates who participated in teacher preparation programs. One outcome was an increase in the requirements for certification/licensure in teacher preparation programs. These requirements included courses in specific areas of content and professional studies, and prepracticum and practicum experiences. The county certification exams that largely disappeared with the advent of college- and university-based programs returned in the form of state licensure exams linked to new state standards. While candidates in teacher preparation programs strived to meet these standards, they also were exposed to new theories centered on the learning styles and needs of individual children, on multicultural education and the education of students with disabilities. They learned new innovative approaches to curriculum development. In addition, they were introduced to ideas about social justice, activism, and peace education, either embedded in curriculum courses and in stand-alone classes.

The contexts that shaped teacher preparation programs in the twentieth century provided a path forward into twenty-first century teacher preparation initiatives which are discussed in the next chapter. As seen with teacher preparation in previous centuries, the work of educators would continue to be viewed as a powerful conduit to changing lives and wider communities.

References

Banks, J. (1979). *Teaching strategies for ethnic studies*. New York, NY: Pearson.

Banks, J. (1981). *Cultural diversity and education: Foundations, curriculum, and teaching*. New York, NY: Routledge.

Banks, J. (1993). Multicultural education: Development. *Phi Delta Kappan*, *75*(1), 22–28.

Banks, J. (2001). Diversity within unity: Essential principles for teaching and learning in a multicultural society. *Phil Delta Kappan*, *83*(3), 196–198.

Banks, J. (2008). *An introduction to multicultural education*. New York, NY: Pearson.

Beaton, A. E., Rogers, A. M., Gonzalez, E., Hanly, M. B., Kolstad, A., Rust, K. F., … Jia, Y. (2011). *The NAEP primer*. Washington, DC: U.S. Department of Education, National Center for Educational Statistics.

Benjamin, L., & Crouse, E. (2002). The American Psychological Association's response to Brown v. Board of Education: The case of Kenneth B. Clark. *American Psychologist*, *57*(1), 38–50.

Burkhalter, B., McLean, J., & Jones, M. (2004). Recipients' views of the role of Christa McAuliffe fellowships in science education. *Science Educator*, *13*(1), 49–57.

Canada, G. (2000). Raising better boys. *Educational Leadership*, *57*(4), 14–17.

Canada, G. (2001). The best way we know how. *Reclaiming Children and Youth*, *10*(1), 54–56.

Children's Defense Fund. (2021). *Mission*. Retrieved from https://www.childrensdefense.org/about/who-we-are/our-mission/

Cogan, M. (1955). "Master of arts in teaching" at Harvard University. *Journal of Teacher Education*, *6*(2), 135–142.

Collins, B., & Schuster, J. (2001). Some thoughts on the history of rural special education: A first hand account. *Rural Special Education Quarterly*, *2*(1/2), 22–29.

Cook, K. (2021). *The burning blue: The untold story of Christa McAuliffe and NASA's Challenger disaster*. New York, NY: Henry Holt and Company.

Corrigan, G. (1993). *A journal for Christa: Christa McAuliffe, teacher in space*. Lincoln, NE: University of Nebraska Press.

Ducharme, E. R., & Ducharme, M. K. (1998). *The American Association of Colleges for Teacher Education: A history*. Washington, DC: AACTE Publications.

Duckworth, E. (1987). *The having of wonderful ideas & other essays on teaching & learning*. New York, NY: Teachers College Press.

Duckworth, E. (2006). *The having of wonderful ideas and other essays on teaching and learning* (3rd ed.). New York, NY: Teachers College Press.

Dykman, A. (1997). Interview with Deborah Meier. *Techniques: Making Education and Career Connections*, *72*(2), 30–35.

Edelman, M. (1999). *Lanterns: A memoir of mentors*. Boston, MA: Beacon Press.

Feden, P., & Clabaugh, G. (1986). The 'new breed' educator: A rationale and program for combining elementary and special education teacher preparation. *Teacher Education and Special Education*, *9*(4), 180–189.

Flanagan, J. (1941). An analysis of the results from the first annual edition of the national teacher examinations. *The Journal of Experimental Education*, *93*(3), 237–250.

Gardner, H. (1997). Multiple intelligences as a partner in school improvement. *Educational Leadership*, *55*(1), 20–21.

Greene, M. (1977). Toward wide-awakeness: An argument for the arts and humanities in education. *Teachers College Record*, *79*(1), 119–125.

Gregorc, A. (1975). Matching inservice activities with teacher personalities. *NASSP Bulletin*, *59*(395), 24–28.

Harden, T. (1981). The national defense education act: A turning point in federal aid. Accession number ED212084.

Harlem Children's Zone. (2021). Our history and zone map. Retrieved from https://hcz.org/our-purpose/our-history-zone-map/

Harrell, R., Graves, W., & Foster, J. (1968). *Master of arts in teaching program*. Texas A&M University.

Harris, I. (1988). *Peace education*. Jefferson, NC: McFarland & Co.

Heller, R. (2020). Why we teach: A conversation with Sonia Nieto. *Phi Delta Kappan*, *101*(8), 31–36.

Holden, W. (1959). The master of arts in teaching at Yale, 1951–1958. *Journal of Teacher Education*, *10*(4), 393–400.

Jennings, J. (2015). ESEA at 50. *Phi Delta Kappan*, *96*(7), 41–46.

Kansas State University. (1975). Kansas State University bulletin. Kansas State University. Retrieved from https://archive.org/details/generalcatalo197576kans/mode/2up

Kohlberg, L. (1975). Moral education for a society in moral transition. *Educational Leadership*, *33*(1), 46–54.

Labaree, D. (2008). An uneasy relationship: The history of teacher education in the university. In M. Cochran-Smith, S. Feiman Nemser, & D. J. McIntyre (Eds.),

Handbook of research on teacher education: Enduring issues in changing contexts (3rd ed., pp. 290–306). Washington, DC: Association of Teacher Educators.

Latham, A., Gitomer, D., & Ziomek, R. (1999). What the tests tell us about new teachers. *Educational Leadership*, *56*(8), 23–26.

Lengyel, L. S., & Vanbergeijk, E. (2021). A brief history of special education: Milestones in the first fifty years (part I of II). Retrieved from https://www.epmagazine.com/blog/a-brief-history-of-special-education-milestones-in-the-first-50-years-part-i-of-ii

Lowe, R. (2004). The strange history of school desegregation. *Rethinking Schools*, *18*(3). Retrieved from https://rethinkingschools.org/articles/the-strange-history-of-school-desegregation/

Martin, R. J. (1994). Multicultural social reconstructionist education: Design for diversity in teacher education. *Teacher Education Quarterly*, *21*(3), 77–89.

Matthews, J. (1989). *Escalante: The best teacher in America*. New York, NY: Henry Holt.

Mehta, J. (2015). Escaping the shadow: 'A nation at risk' and its far-reaching influence. *American Educator*, *39*(2), 20–26.

Meier, D. (1996). The big benefits of smallness. *Educational Leadership*, *54*(1), 12–15.

Meier, D. (2002). *The power of their ideas: Lessons for America from a small school in Harlem*. Boston, MA: Beacon Press.

Meier, D. (2014). *In schools we trust: Creating communities of learning in an era of testing and standardization*. Boston, MA: Beacon Press.

Meier, D. (2021). Deborah Meier on education. Retrieved from https://deborahmeier.com/about/

NASA. (n.d.). The teacher in space project. Retrieved from https://digitalcommons.framingham.edu/uncategorized/SO_496d86d0-e150-4319-9c93-08893d32df7b/

National Academy of Education. (2021). Deborah Meier. Retrieved from https://naeducation.org/our-members/deborah-meier/

National Center for Education Statistics. (2014). Digest of education statistics: Public and private elementary and secondary teachers, enrollment, pupil/teacher ratios, and new teacher hires: Selected years, fall 1955 through fall 2024. Retrieved from https://nces.ed.gov/programs/digest/d14/tables/dt14_208.20.asp

National Center for Education Statistics. (2019). Digest of education statistics: Number and percentage distribution of teachers in public and private elementary and secondary schools, by selected teacher characteristics: Selected years, 1987–88 through 2017–18. Retrieved from https://nces.ed.gov/programs/digest/d19/tables/dt19_209.10.asp

National Council for the Social Studies. (2021). *Christa McAuliffe reach for the stars award*. Retrieved from https://www.socialstudies.org/membership/christa-mcauliffe-reach-stars-award#:~:text=The%20purpose%20of%20the%20fund,innovative%20social%20studies%20a%20reality

Nieto, S. (1992). *Affirming diversity: The sociopolitical context of multicultural education*. Boston, MA: Allyn & Bacon.

Nieto, S. (2004). Black, white, and us: The meaning of Brown v Board of Education for Latinos. *Multicultural Perspectives*, *6*(4), 22–25.

Noddings, N. (1984). *Caring: A relational approach to ethics and moral education*. Berkeley, CA: University of California Press.

Noddings, N. (1992). *The challenge to care in schools: An alternative approach to education*. New York, NY: Teachers College Press.

Noddings, N. (2003). *Happiness and education*. New York, NY: Cambridge University Press.

Noddings, N. (2008). Caring and peace education. In M. Bajaj (Ed.), *Encyclopedia of peace education* (pp. 87–92). Charlotte, NC: Information Age Publishing, Inc.

Noddings, N. (2012). *Peace education: How we come to love and hate war*. New York, NY: Cambridge University Press.

Pruitt, S. (2019). How 'duck-and-cover' drills channeled America's cold war anxiety. *History*. Retrieved from https://www.history.com/news/duck-cover-drills-cold-war-arms-race

Ravtich, D. (1991). A culture in common. *Educational Leadership*, *49*(4), 8–11.

Shuman, B. (1981). An MAT program to meet future needs. *Improving College and University Teaching*, *29*(1), 9–11.

Sizer, T. (2009). Ted Sizer's opening remarks. *Horace Feature*, *25*(2–3), 1–3.

Slaughter, E. (1960). The use of examinations for state certification of teachers. *Journal of Teacher Education*, *11*(2), 231–238.

Stallings, D. T. (2002). A brief history of the U.S. Department of Education, 1979–2002. *Phi Delta Kappan*, *83*(9), 677–683.

Standerfer, L. (2006). Before NCLB: The history of ESEA. *Principal Leadership*, *6*(8), 26–27.

Stewner-Manzanares, G. (1988). *The bilingual education act: Twenty years later. The national clearinghouse for bilingual education: Occasional papers in bilingual education. Number 6* (pp. 1–8).

Stinnett, T. M. (1960). Certification requirements and procedures among the states in 1960. *Journal of Teacher Education*, *11*(2), 173–184.

Swarthmore College. (1965). *Swarthmore College bulletin: 1965–1966* (*Volume LXIII*, Number 1). Swarthmore, PA: Swarthmore College. Retrieved from https://digitalcollections.tricolib.brynmawr.edu/object/sc11979

Tamir, E., & Wilson, S. (2005). Who should guard the gates? Evidentiary and professional warrants for claiming jurisdiction. *Journal of Teacher Education*, *56*(4), 332–342.

Teach for America. (2021). History. Retrieved from https://www.teachforamerica.org/what-we-do/history

The Maxine Greene Institute. (2021). *Biography*. Retrieved from https://maxinegreene.org/about/maxine-%20%20greene/biography

The National Commission on Excellence in Education. (1983). *A nation at risk: The imperative for educational reform*. Washington, DC: U. S. Department of Education.

Tushnet, M. (1995). *Brown v. Board of Education: The battle for integration*. New York, NY: Franklin Watts.

United States Department of Education. (2010). An overview of the U.S. Department of Education. Retrieved from https://www2.ed.gov/about/overview/focus/what.html

United States Department of Education. (2021). About ED. Retrieved from https://www2.ed.gov/about/landing.jhtml

United States Senate. (2021). Sputnik spurs passage of the national defense education act. Retrieved from https://www.senate.gov/artandhistory/history/minute/Sputnik_Spurs_Passage_of_National_Defense_Education_Act.htm

University of California at Irvine. (1965). University of California at Irvine initial bulletin: 1965–1966 catalogue. Retrieved from https://www.reg.uci.edu/catalogue/1965-1966Catalogue.pdf

University of Illinois at Urbana-Champaign. (1980). Courses catalog 1980–82 at the University of Illinois at Urbana-Champaign. Retrieved from https://archive.org/details/coursescatalog198082univ/page/n5/mode/2up?view=theater

University of Washington. (2021). James A. Banks home. Emeritus professor. Retrieved from https://education.uw.edu/people/faculty/jbanks/

Wang, C., & Chen, X. (2009). The characteristics and enlightening of NCATE. *International Education Studies*, *2*(2), 72–76.

Wraga, W. (2006). The heightened significance of Brown v. Board of Education in our time. *Phi Delta Kappan*, *87*(6), 425–428.

Chapter 5

Transitioning into the 21st Century

The beginning of the twenty-first century in the United States, following the 9/11 terrorist attacks, was a period marked by tragedy, pain, and some breakdown in relationships. The 9/11 attacks resulted in thousands of deaths in the United States, triggering the formation of the USA Patriot Act of 2001, the Homeland Security Act of 2002, as well as the invasion of Afghanistan by United States troops. Though Muslim organizations in the United States were quick to condemn the 9/11 attacks, harassment and hate crimes against Muslims and South Asians took place. Discrimination and profiling subsequently occurred, including in the school setting.

While the start of the twenty-first century was one that was marked by tragedy, it also was a period which led to some advancements in equity and human rights issues. The United States citizens elected the country's first African American president, Barack Obama, in 2008. The Supreme Court legalized same sex marriage across the nation in 2015 (Liptak, 2015). Climate change and global warming began to be addressed, including in communities most at risk for climate change effects. In 2021, the first African American woman and Asian American Vice President, Kamala Harris, began her term of office.

Political organizing, aimed at creating change, led to a wide variety of movements. Some addressed an alarming number of opioid addictions and deaths among young people and their families, resulting in an increase in the number of children placed in the foster care system. Gun violence in and out of the school setting was targeted. Racial injustices, and violence targeting African Americans, were challenged. The Black Lives Matter movement took hold. Women's rights, immigration laws, and the rights of LGBTQ youth and families also were tackled. Demonstrations on behalf of Native Americans led to a proclamation from President Joseph Biden establishing Indigenous Peoples' Day, in recognition and celebration of the invaluable contributions and resilience of Indigenous peoples.

Teacher Preparation in the United States, 117–138

Published under exclusive licence by Emerald Publishing Limited
doi:10.1108/978-1-80071-687-220221006

Creative Commons. *Source*: Lorie Shaull.

> The demonstration was organized by Teens For Gun Reform, an organization created by students in the Washington DC area, in the wake of the shooting at Marjory Stoneman Douglas High School in Parkland, Florida. This demonstration was covered by various news outlets, including NPR.
>
> (Romo, 2018)

Far from being a unified front, however, the residents of the United States became more splintered and pronounced in their viewpoints in the twenty-first century. As progressive groups rallied for more openness and justice, others in the United States demonstrated for more conservative, and at times racist and xenophobic, positions. Disparate outlooks resulted in many peaceful interactions between groups and communities, but at other times brought about threats, violence, and even deadly encounters. An insurrection at the US Capitol Building, the seat of our Congress, took place on January 6, 2021 when supporters of Donald Trump, the 45th president of the Unites States, sought to overturn the 2020 presidential election, which ended his term of service. During the Capitol insurrection, bombs were discovered in the area, and violent clashes resulted in many injuries and some deaths. Events such as this one showed the United States as a deeply divided and polarized country as it proceeded through the first part of the twenty-first century. The onset of the COVID pandemic in 2019, taking more than 950,000 lives in the United States and millions across the world, and the deep differences of opinion on how to fight it, has not ended this polarization.

As depicted in the first section of this book, teachers have long been charged with the challenge of navigating and making sense of the diverse and sometimes difficult social, economic, and political contexts in which children and families live. The start of the twenty-first century certainly has continued to be this case. Teachers have been responsible for recognizing that their students and families have different needs, experiences, and enormously contrasting perspectives on many issues. This responsibility and connected challenges have filtered into teacher preparation programs. In these programs, teacher candidates have been introduced to new courses to prepare them to work with the children and families of diverse backgrounds. Teacher educators and their students have dialogued about appropriate and effective roles teachers should play in crisis situations and about ways to draw support from wider communities. At the same time, aspiring teachers continue to be required to meet standards set at the state level and influenced deeply by the federal government. The regulation of teacher preparation programs has become more pronounced. This chapter explores how both state and federal regulations and human contexts have shaped teacher preparation programs at the start of the twenty-first century.

Federal Acts That Shaped Twenty-First Century Teacher Preparation Programs

The Goals 2000 Educate America Act developed by the Administration of President Bill Clinton in 1994 amended the Elementary and Secondary Education Act of 1965 (ESEA) (Anderson & Welsh, 2000). This Act had specific goals which shaped the educational experiences of those preparing to teach. First, Goals 2000 supported standards aimed at raising the academic achievement of all P-12 students. It drew attention to students' unequal access to equitable educational experiences and subsequent academic growth. In particular, the Goals 2000 Act acknowledged that "the achievement gap between poor and non-poor students and between White and minority students is not inevitable, but reflects many kinds of inequity in educational opportunity" (Independent Review Panel of the Federal Education Legislation, 1999, p. 7).

The Goals 2000 Educate America Act also held public schools across the United States accountable for learning outcomes. An independent panel reviewing federal education legislation in 1994 wrote,

> Increased attention has been placed at all levels of government on holding schools and districts and even federal agencies accountable for results. We find this attention to results appropriate and desirable, but we stress that it must be based on legitimate and coherent criteria, adequate support for improvement, and appropriate authority if it is to be effective.
> (Independent Review Panel of the Federal Education Legislation, 1999, p. 3)

Annual report cards subsequently were required of public schools. These report cards included information on student achievement, class size, school safety, attendance, graduation rates, and teacher qualifications (The White House Office of the Press Secretary, 1999).

As a result of the Goals 2000 Educate America Act, states developed curriculum standards that had to be taught and mastered at each grade level. States were encouraged to utilize subject-based national organizations (e.g., National Council of Teachers of Mathematics, National Council of Teachers of English) as a template for their own state standards (Wakeman, Browder, Meier, & McColl, 2007). Massachusetts, for example, developed the Massachusetts Curriculum Standards in 1994. These frameworks focused on the arts, history and social sciences, English language arts, mathematics, science and technology, digital literacy and computer science, vocational technical education, and foreign languages (subsequently renamed world languages). The work in developing the state standards later would evolve into national curriculum standards. In 2007, the state leaders of public education (chief state school officers) began the work to develop common standards to be utilized by all states. The idea was that students in Idaho should learn material similar to that learned by students in New York. With support from the National Governors Association (NGA), the development of national standards commenced in 2009 and the final version of the Common Core State Standards was released in 2010. In 2011 states began the process of reviewing and adopting the common standards. In the states that adopted the standards, teachers were required to incorporate them into their lessons and curriculum plans. Candidates in teacher preparation programs subsequently were responsible for learning these standards, as well as developing, implementing and assessing standards-connected lessons and units of study during their pre-practicum and practicum (student teaching) experiences.

State Adoption of Common Core Standards

Forty-one states, the District of Columbia, four territories, and the Department of Defense Education Activity (DoDEA) had adopted the Common Core State Standards as of 2021. Nine states did not adopt the Common Core State Standards, including Alaska, Florida, Indiana, Minnesota (adopted ELA standards only), Nebraska, Oklahoma, South Carolina, Texas, and Virginia. Puerto Rico also did not adopt the standards (Common Core State Standards Initiative, 2021).

Accompanying the Goals 2000 Educate America Act was the Improving America's Schools Act (IASA) which emphasized that improvements in the quality of teachers and teaching were urgently needed throughout all areas of the United States. Specifically:

- Greater investment in both preservice teacher education and high-quality professional development for teachers was vitally needed.

- Because high-poverty schools needed and deserved the best teachers, states and districts were required to ensure that teachers and instructional aides in these schools had to be at least as qualified as those in non-Title I schools.
- Congress did not allow districts to spend federal funds to hire paraprofessionals to provide instruction, since it was assumed that they lacked adequate training for that role. Congress sought to phase out districts' use of paraprofessionals in Title I instruction altogether during the reauthorization. Districts were encouraged to use paraprofessionals in non-instructional roles. They were to be commended for placing bilingual paraprofessionals in classrooms with high concentrations of students with limited proficiency in English (Independent Review Panel of the Federal Education Legislation, 1999, pp. 3–4).

Teacher preparation programs across the country responded to increased federal surveillance of the quality of teachers. Participants in these programs were required to complete designated content and pedagogical coursework. During the practicum (student teaching) experience, teacher candidates demonstrated proficiency on professional standards set at the state level.

With the implementation of IASA, faculty in teacher preparation programs reflected on the requirements of effective programs. Education professor emeritus and researcher Linda Darling-Hammond from Stanford University became a vocal advocate for strong teacher preparation programs in the twenty-first century, as she felt this encouraged teachers to stay in the profession long-term. Strong teacher preparation programs resulted in less turnover of teachers who chose to leave the field for other careers. Darling-Hammond suggested that the education community needed to think critically about specific elements that help to build model teacher preparation programs (Scherer, 2012).

Biographical Sketch

Linda Darling-Hammond. *Source*: Courtesy of Learning Policy Institute.

Linda Darling-Hammond earned her BA from Yale University and her Ed.D. from Temple University. She began her career in education as a public school teacher. She co-founded both a preschool and a public high school. Throughout her career, she has consulted widely with federal, state, and local officials and educators on strategies for improving education practices and policies (Stanford University Graduate School of Education, 2021). From 1994–2001, Darling-Hammond was executive director of the National Commission on Teaching and America's Future. In 2006, she was named one of the nation's most influential people affecting educational policy, and in 2008 she directed President Obama's Education Policy Transition Team. In 2019, she was asked to serve as the president of the California State Board of Education by Governor Gavin Newsom (Freedberg, 2019). She also served as the leader of President Biden's education transition team (Gomez, 2021). Darling-Hammond is the Charles E. Ducommun Professor of Education Emeritus at Stanford University (Stanford University Graduate School of Education, 2021). She also is the current president and CEO of the Learning Policy Institute which conducts independent research to improve education policy and practice.

Darling-Hammond believes that many teacher preparation programs have strengthened participants' readiness for curriculum development, assessment, and differentiated instruction (Scherer, 2012, p. 18). She credits many teacher education programs with offering strong clinical experiences connected to coursework. She thinks that the core value of every profession is that everyone in the profession has a common body of knowledge and skills needed to be responsible and effective. "When you have a lot of people coming in with very little training, confidence in the profession goes down. Lowering standards also drives salaries down, which then makes it hard to recruit and keep good people in the profession. The whole enterprise of teaching is seriously undermined" (cited in Scherer, 2012, p. 18).

The Eisenhower Professional Development Program, an investment effort of the US government focused on developing the knowledge and skills of classroom teachers, also expanded during this time. Developed in the twentieth century, the program supported the US Department of Education's objective of ensuring that a talented and dedicated teacher was in every classroom in America. In 1995, nine projects were funded to explore if partnerships could be a source of improvement in teacher education and teacher induction. In California, this was the California Consortium for Teacher Development, while in Kansas it was the State of Kansas Teacher Education Systemic Reform Initiative. In Massachusetts, the Massachusetts Consortium for Initial Teacher Professional Development was formed, and in Oregon the partnership was named the Standards-based Teacher Education Project (Blackwell, 2002). New Mexico's program was funded through a school system and named the New Mexico Teacher Learning Community Program. Each of these nine projects subsequently evaluated the (1) impact of partnership; (2) models of teacher education; (3) engagement of arts and science faculty; (4) teacher education curriculum; (5) clinical experiences; (6) standards;

(7) recruitment and retention; and (8) professional development. In fiscal year 1999, $335 million was appropriated for state and local activities. Through increased regulation from the federal level, the Eisenhower Professional Development Program shaped those entering teaching at the start of the twenty-first century and their experiences in teacher preparation programs (The American Institutes for Research, 1999). Teaching was identified as a high stakes profession that would yield critical outcomes for P-12 students and the roles that they would undertake in their futures when they entered the workforce.

In 2001, federal legislation further influenced the field of education with the No Child Left Behind Act (NCLB). NCLB was a US Act of Congress passed with bipartisan support under President George W. Bush's administration. NCLB scaled up the role of the federal government in education by holding schools accountable for student test outcomes (Klein, 2015). In teacher preparation programs, candidates were introduced to NCLB and its attendant expectations. As students in public schools were required to meet standards, candidates in teacher preparation programs continued to be expected to be competent in both content and pedagogical knowledge. An emphasis was placed on using scientifically based research in teacher preparation. The NCLB also introduced the term "highly qualified" teachers with Title II of the Act which was Preparing, Training, and Recruiting High Quality Teachers and Principals. The goal was to have a highly qualified teacher in every classroom by 2005. This meant that teachers needed to hold a bachelor's degree and knowledge of the content of their field, and full certification.

No Child Left Behind Act

The NCLB Act increased accountability of schools and teachers as determined by student outcomes on standardized tests, as well as required schools to rely on scientifically based research for the materials and teaching methods used. P-12 schools were required to demonstrate Adequate Yearly Progress (AYP) under NCLB (RAND, 2007). Under NCLB, standards based reform continued and increased (Jennings & Rentner, 2006). Test scores were used to gauge how well schools progressed with raising student achievement. To ensure that students and teachers took the annual state tests seriously, many states made the tests "high-stakes," requiring a passing score for high school graduation. Under provisions of the Act referred to as Supplemental Education Services (SES) – NCLB also "mandated that if schools and districts did not make test score targets, then they had to provide needy students with tutoring, paid for out of a federal pot of money" (Burch, 2020, p. 16). Importantly, NCLB provided options for school choice. Parents could remove their children from "low-performing schools" and send them to another school in the district.

The Center on Education Policy (CEP) conducted a continuous and comprehensive review of NCLB. The CEP found that as a result of NCLB, state and district officials reported that student achievement on state tests rose. Schools spent a majority of time on reading and mathematics, at times at the expense of other subjects. Schools paid close attention to the alignment of curriculum, instruction, and test scores. Students took increased numbers of tests. Schools also paid increased attention to achievement gaps among students (Jennings & Rentner, 2006).

At the same time, a research brief from RAND Education (2009), reported that in 2006–2007 only 1% of the public participated in school choice allowed under NCLB. Only 43% of the school districts that were required to offer school choice notified the parents/families before the start of the school year of this option. In 2006–2007, 6.9 million children were eligible for Supplemental Education Services allowed under NCLB. However, only 17% of eligible students participated. Parents chose not to enroll their children in SES services because they did not feel that they needed the extra help or they found that these services were offered at inconvenient times. In addition, though 75% of the nation's schools made Adequate Yearly Progress in 2003–2004, 25% did not. "About one-third of schools that did not make AYP was because of their work with students with disabilities or LEP student groups. About two-thirds of those schools reported needing technical assistance to improve instruction for these subgroups" (RAND, 2007, p. xvii). States also varied greatly in making AYP. The percentage of schools that made AYP in 2003–2004 ranged from 95% in Wisconsin to 23% of schools in Alabama and Florida (RAND, 2007, p. xxi).

Some questions and challenges about NCLB subsequently were raised by educators. For example, questions were cultivated about the extent to which NCLB shaped curriculum and student learning. In the elementary school setting, some educators questioned if phonics (reinforced by some educators under NCLB) improved children's reading in terms of meaning, construction, and comprehension (Altwerger et al., 2004). Others questioned the extensive testing required by NCLB and what the standardized tests really measured. Research fellow Jon Valant (2020) suggested that testing whether students know how to multiply, from his perspective, is easy. However, "testing whether students are assembling the knowledge, skills, and dispositions that will allow them to listen and respond carefully to each other's ideas, or to identify and reject propaganda 15 years after they graduate, is hard" (29). How do we measure if students are able to navigate real world complexity and ambiguity?

In December 2015, under President Barack Obama, Congress passed the Every Student Succeeds Act (ESSA). The law that Obama signed preserved many components of NCLB, but allowed for a more flexible approach to student testing and school accountability. A difference with ESSA was that it shifted many education decisions and rules from the US Department of Education back to states and school districts (Institute of Education Sciences, 2020). Under ESSA, teacher preparation programs continued to require that participants meet standards and pass related licensure exams. One example of a teacher licensure exam is the Praxis which has been administered by Educational Testing Services (ETS) (ETS, 2021).

President Barack Obama appointed Arne Starkey Duncan as the United States Secretary of Education in 2009. As the US Secretary of Education, Duncan set up the $4 billion Race to the Top initiative. This initiative allowed states to apply for federal funding for reform efforts. The reforms could include expanding charter schools and/or evaluating teachers based on how well their P-12 students performed on standardized tests. Though Duncan received substantial opposition to his support of the use of P-12 student test scores in teacher evaluations, many states moved forward with this method of teacher assessment (Burris & Welner, 2011). Some states such as Massachusetts began the process of connecting P-12 student exam scores back to their classroom teachers and then back to the teacher preparation programs where these teachers received their licensure. This process began to be used in evaluating teacher preparation programs. Education journalist Michelle MacNeil wrote that Duncan pushed to overhaul teacher and principal preparation.

> His department … proposed several initiatives that [did not receive] much traction. And he counts that as one of the weaknesses in his service so far. In his two postelection speeches, Mr. Duncan … said that teacher education programs are "part of the problem" and that the Education Department is looking at a competitive initiative to foster innovation in schools of education, though he didn't get specific.
>
> (McNeil, 2012)

Former president of Columbia University's Teachers College, Arthur Levine, also became a vocal critic of traditional college and university teacher preparation programs in the United States. In an interview with *The New York Times*, he noted that "the problem is not that higher ed isn't capable of preparing teachers well, it's just that it hasn't done it, and it needs to. These programs need serious repair, but it can be done" (Firestone, 2013). He suggested that the United States is underpreparing educators to teach in STEM areas, in particular. While serving as president of the Woodrow Wilson National Fellowship Foundation, Levine worked on a STEM initiative, which from his perspective, resulted in teacher preparation programs making positive changes.

> Our foundation created a scholarship program in five states, Indiana, Michigan, Ohio, New Jersey and Georgia, where we form a coalition with the governor, the state education officers, legislators, and unions. We recruit teachers with STEM backgrounds and ask them to take a one-year master's degree. At a participating university, we give them a fellowship of $30,000, and they agree to teach in-state for a minimum of three years.

> Then we tell the universities that we want them to replace their existing STEM teacher education program with one that is highly selective and focused on learning in the classroom where their graduates are going to teach. The end result is 23 universities that have changed their teacher education programs in the way we've asked them to do. They've created very effective programs.
> (Firestone, 2013)

Controversial groups such as the National Council on Teacher Quality (NCTQ) latched onto Levine's rhetoric and position about teacher preparation programs to support their own work. NCTQ, for example, began a process of rating teacher preparation programs across the country. In response, some researchers raised significant concerns about the research methodology utilized in this process. Educator Edward Fuller wrote that the research had a number of serious flaws that included "narrow focus on inputs, lack of a strong research base, missing standards, omitted research, incorrect application of research findings, poor methodology, exclusion of alternative certification programs, failure to conduct member checks, and failure to use existing evidence to validate the report's rankings" (Fuller, 2014). The American Association of Colleges of Teacher Education also released to their membership, their reactions of NCTQ's work. "AACTE is committed to meeting members' needs and serving as a national voice and resource on behalf of the educator preparation profession. We recently released a letter to all members that refutes the National Council on Teacher Quality (NCTQ) Teacher Prep Review" (AACTE, 2021).

During the first part of the twenty-first century, deans of teacher preparation programs, department chairs, and faculty often sought support in understanding changes in federal and state requirements, as well as guidance about how to respond to criticisms. In response, the American Association of Colleges of Teacher Education (AACTE) provided annual conferences to bring professionals together to learn about changing landscapes shaping teacher preparation. The AACTE also has helped to coordinate topical action groups focused on accreditation, diversifying the teacher workforce, LBTQ advocacy and inclusion in teacher education, HBCU teacher education, preparing teachers for rural schools and communities, and other. States also have developed chapters of the larger AACTE organization. These chapters have brought together faculty and staff from teacher preparation programs in specific states for dialogues and professional development.

Curriculum Content of Early Twenty-First Century Teacher Preparation Programs

Responsive to these new mandates, participants in teacher preparation programs in the early twenty-first century have completed programs that have included courses in content and pedagogy, along with pre-practicum and practicum field experiences. Because curriculum in US colleges is typically the province of college and university faculty, there have been differences in the particular content of teacher preparation programs across states and the country. To meet state program certification requirements, however, all of these programs have had to be approved by their respective state departments of education in order to be able to recommend teacher candidates for licensure. Some states also have worked in close collaboration with the national accrediting agencies such as the National Council for the Accreditation of Teacher Education (NCATE) which was founded in 1954 and the Teacher Education Accreditation Council (TEAC) which was founded in 1997. Some of these states have made it mandatory for college and university teacher preparation programs to achieve national accreditation, whereas in other states national accreditation has been optional. In some states where national accreditation is mandatory, the process may assist states which lack resources (staffing in the state education departments) to review all teacher preparation programs in its borders. NCATE and TEAC merged in 2013 under the new name of the Council for the Accreditation of Educator Preparation (CAEP).

Some teacher preparation programs in early childhood and elementary education have required participants to complete a double major with a content area. Others have required participants to complete a number of diverse art and science courses, without declaring a formal double major. At some college and universities, students could pursue a double major in early childhood or elementary education, along with special education. Students pursuing a teaching license in secondary education at the middle or high school level, in most cases, have been required to major in a subject area in which they want to teach, along with required education courses. Given the expanding range of standards and requirements and the increasingly complex work of teaching, some colleges and universities have required an additional "fifth" year for licensure completion – a five-year program organized in a variety of ways, sometimes including a master's degree.

While candidates in teacher preparation programs have met increased standards, they simultaneously have been exposed to course work that has reflected the larger human contexts of the lives of the children and families with whom they work. Participants in these programs have learned how poverty and fragile economic circumstances shape the learning experiences of children, a circumstance that almost all teachers confront during their careers. Aspiring teachers learn that "nearly one in seven children – 10.5 million – were poor in 2019. Nearly 71% of poor children were children of color. More than one in four Black children and more than one in five Hispanic and American Indian/Alaska Native children were poor compared with one in 12 white children" (The Children's Defense Fund, 2021, p. 6). In addition, "more than 1.5 million children enrolled in public schools experienced homelessness during the 2017–2018 school year" (The Children's Defense Fund, 2021, p. 6).

Participants in teacher preparation programs have studied how trauma shapes the experiences of P-12 children, described by some as a public health epidemic (Craig, 2016). Trauma may result in behaviors such as defiance, shutting down, becoming overly self-reliant, struggling with boundaries, and/or becoming too reliant on others (Pawlo, Lorenzo, Eichert, & Elias, 2019). Long-term exposure to chronic stress from trauma also affects brain development and has negative effects on learning (Sciaraffia, Zeanah, & Zeanah, 2018). There subsequently have been practices developed and shared about how to best respond to young people who have experienced trauma. It is understood that "the issues facing children and families are complex, systemic and multi-layered and acknowledging that complexity is crucial in thinking about the role of schools" (Quinn, Mollet, & Dawson, 2021, p. 24).

Participants in teacher preparation programs have studied ableism and how it shapes the lives of students and families with disabilities. Ableism is discrimination in favor of able-bodied people. It can take the form of ableist language. It may mean that "the world is unwelcoming and inaccessible for people with disabilities" (Hehir, 2007, p. 9). It may unfold as a focus on a disability to the exclusion of all else. In teacher preparation programs, aspiring teachers have learned about the harm and damage that ableism can cause. They have learned how to give students "the supports, skills, and opportunities needed to live as full a life as possible with their disability" (Hehir, 2007, p. 11).

Aspiring teachers also have learned about school safety and how to keep young people protected in their classrooms. In 2019, 7% of all students in grades 9–12 reported that they had been threatened (or injured) with a weapon on school property. In 2019, 5% of students between the ages of 12–18 reported that they avoided certain areas of the school grounds for fear that they might be harmed. During the 2017–2018 school year, there were 56 school associated violent deaths (Institute of Education Sciences, 2020). The Children's Defense Fund (2021) reports that "gun violence was the leading cause of death for children and teens ages 1–19 in 2018, surpassing motor vehicle accidents for the first time" (8). In addition, "in 2019, 3,371 children and teens were killed with guns – one every 2 hours and 36 minutes" (8).

In response to wider contexts, social emotional learning programs and initiatives have proliferated in P-12 schools. Social emotional learning (SEL) is a teaching practice that attempts to help students better comprehend their emotions, to feel emotions fully, and demonstrate empathy for the feelings and experiences of others. A large number of grants have been available to support these programs. When reflecting on the social and emotional needs of children, educator Johnson (2020) has written that educators also need to be aware of compassion fatigue – weariness that comes from caring. It is important for educators to practice self-care.

Some educators have written that there must be more to social emotional learning. Educators can be well-versed in social emotional learning and still inflict harm on their students. Educator Dena Simmons has written that we cannot be emotionally intelligent without also being culturally responsive. Simmons has advocated for a community-generated, student-centered approach to SEL, racial justice, and healing. Otherwise, social emotional learning could become white supremacy with a hug, as described by Simmons (2021).

Those pursuing teacher preparation programs have studied anti-racist pedagogy as part of their course work. Gloria Ladson-Billings' work, for example, has been studied extensively in these programs. Her books include *The Dreamkeepers: Successful Teachers of African American Children* (1994) and *Crossing Over to Canaan: The Journey of New Teachers in Diverse Classrooms* (2001). Bettina Love's book, *We Want to Do More Than Survive: Abolitionist Teaching and the Pursuit of Educational Freedom* (2019), also has become a common read for some teacher preparation programs. In her book, Bettina Love (2019) writes "abolitionist teaching is built on the creativity, imagination, boldness, ingenuity, and rebellious spirit and methods of abolitionists to demand and fight for an education system where all students are thriving, not simply surviving" (11). In her book, Love also discussed the importance of promoting awareness of intersectionality, the interconnected nature of social categorizations or markers such as race, class, gender, and disability, as they apply to a given individual or group. Educators Carl Grant and Elisabeth Zwier (2011) likewise have reflected on the importance of preservice teachers understanding intersectionality.

> They [preservice teachers] are beginning to realize that contrary to what they have always believed, socially-constructed categories of difference (such as gender, race, ability) rather than merit alone, do matter and contribute significantly to students' experiences, outcomes for success, and future life opportunities. To prepare intersectionally aware teachers, we argue preservice teacher education programs can reframe curricula and pedagogies, foster critical consciousness, counter problematic ideologies, and engage with diverse communities (183).

Many twenty-first century faculty in teacher preparation programs also have engaged participants in critical pedagogy in response to neoliberalism. Neoliberalism is the dominant ideology that covers different areas of life, often resulting in conformity and adherence to the status quo. Critical pedagogy, in contrast, is a philosophy that invites educators to encourage students to critique structures of power and oppression. It encourages emancipation from oppression. This is a philosophical approach that grew from the work of Brazilian educator Paulo Freire whose work has been influential in the United States and throughout the world. Educators Cutri, Whiting, and Bybee (2020), for example, have explored how critical pedagogy could be utilized in their online multicultural education course. They wrote, "critical pedagogy is foundational to critical multicultural teacher education, and an emergent body of research has begun to examine how critical pedagogy can be implemented online" (54–55). In their course, they aimed to "relationally engage students intellectually and emotionally to promote systematic self- and societal-critique regarding issues of equity and social justice" (55).

Biographical Sketch

Paulo Freire
Brazilian Educator and Philosopher

Paulo Freire was born on September 19, 1921 to a middle-class family in Recife, the capital of the state of Pernambuco in Brazil. His mother was a devout Catholic, and his father was a Spiritist (Shugurensky, 2011). Though his father worked as an army officer, Freire experienced poverty and hunger as a child as a result of the Great Depression. He believed that this affected his ability to learn (Gadotti, 1994). The economic uncertainty of his household was further affected by his father's death in 1934. Initially taught to read by his parents, Freire attended a small private school as a child. Though it was unlikely that Freire would be able to enroll in secondary school, his mother convinced the director of a private high school to accept Freire and to waive the fees (Shugurensky, 2011). His older brother also helped the family financially.

In 1943, Freire was admitted to the University of Pernambuco law school. He graduated and became a lawyer, but his heart was in teaching. Freire married and had children which strengthened his interest in education. He taught high school (Shugurensky, 2011). In 1946, he began to work for the Department of Education and Culture of the Social Service of Industry (SESI). In this position, Freire assisted the working class and came to understand their way of learning about the world (Gadotti, 1994). He made a transition toward a radical understanding of education. At SESI, he developed workers' clubs in which members could explore their problems and seek collective solutions (Shugurensky, 2011). In his work with adults, Freire argued that learning should begin with the day-to-day experiences of learners. In 1960, Freire founded Recife's Popular Culture Movement (Shugurensky, 2011). He believed that traditional education domesticated learners into accepting oppressive approaches. In response, he started to develop an alternative approach to education aimed at liberation (Shugurensky, 2011). In 1962, Freire took a leading role in a literacy program where he and his team pioneered a psychosocial approach to education. With this work, 300 sugarcane workers learned to read and write in 45 days. A Brazilian coup subsequently ended Freire's literacy efforts and imprisoned him for 70 days. Freire was exiled from Brazil in 1964 for 10 years, eventually returning in 1980. He thereafter was a supervisor in an adult literacy project in Brazil from 1980 to 1986. He then became a municipal Secretary of Education in Sao Paulo in 1988.

Paulo Freire wrote *Education as the Practice of* Freedom (1967), *Pedagogy of the* Oppressed (1968), and other books. In 1969, he spent a year at Harvard University in Massachusetts, sharing and teaching about his pedagogical theories. Freire's work has sparked widespread ethical considerations of curriculum and instruction (Barros, 2020). These considerations often have been studied in teacher preparation programs. Freire is the third most cited education scholar in the world (Barros, 152).

Understanding the contexts and needs of children also has resulted in state-defined coursework in some teacher preparation programs. In Massachusetts, a state with a large population of immigrants, it was learned that a significant percentage of English Language Learners (ELL) were not meeting academic success in the public school setting due to a lack of teachers trained in English language learning. Specifically, a joint investigation of Boston's ELL programs with the US Department of Education revealed that there were serious shortages of qualified Sheltered English Immersion (SEI) teachers and thousands of ELL students without SEI services. This violation of equal rights was referred to the Department of Justice, which on September 27, 2011 published the following outcome in *Justice News*.

> Today, in response to a letter from the Justice Department, the Massachusetts Board of Elementary and Secondary Education voted to grant the Commissioner of Education authority to draft state regulations that will require training of all Sheltered English Immersion (SEI) teachers who instruct English Language Learner (ELL) students. The department's letter notified Massachusetts that it has violated the Equal Educational Opportunities Act (EEOA) by not mandating adequate training for SEI teachers. The resolution passed by the board today specifically directs the Commissioner to present the proposed regulations to the board by February 2012.
>
> (Department of Justice, 2011)

With regard to teacher preparation programs, it was noted that "the proposed regulation will define the preparation and training that teachers must have in order to instruct ELL students in academic content, along with a plan for implementing the new regulations" (Department of Justice, 2011). In a relatively short period of time, most in-service teachers completed a sheltered English immersion course. Teacher preparation programs throughout Massachusetts added a sheltered English immersion course (or equivalent) to the curricula.

In recognition of how diverse contexts shape children's learning, teacher preparation program participants also have dialogued about the importance of developing and promoting partnerships among families, communities, and schools. The significance of these collaborations was an idea that grew in the late twentieth century and into the twenty-first century. The thought was that the groups of people in a child's life could better support his/her/their development by working together, sharing ideas, and promoting understanding. One key individual who shaped this work was Dr James Comer from Yale University Medical School.

Biographical Sketch

Dr James Comer. Yale University Medical School - Child Study Center. *Source*: Medical Historical Library, Harvey Cushing/John Hay Whitney Medical Library, Yale University.

Dr James Comer was born on September 25, 1934 in East Chicago, Indiana. His father worked in a steel mill, and his mother was a stay-at-home mom. Dr Comer earned his bachelor degree at Indiana University and his medical degree from Howard University School of Medicine. Thereafter, he earned a master degree in public health from the University of Michigan.

Dr Comer is the Maurice Falk Professor of Child Psychiatry at the Yale Child Study Center. He also served as an associate dean at the Yale School of Medicine. He is a co-founder and past president of the Black Psychiatrists of America (Yale University School of Medicine, 2021). Dr Comer recognized that a child's overall development makes academic learning possible. He became known for his work on the Comer School Development Program in the New Haven Public Schools in Connecticut in 1968. The Comer School Development Program contained essential elements of school-based management which fostered strong collaboration with families and communities. Parents, for example, served on the governance and management team of the school, and they also had their own parent team. "The parents helped design a program to support the academic and social program that the school planning and management team came up with. The parents and the teachers worked together on those activities" (O'Neill, 1997, p. 8). As a result of implementing the School Development Program, the academic achievement of students in these schools grew significantly. Since Dr Comer worked with his first schools in 1968, the Comer School Development Program expanded. "Over the past nearly 50 years numerous schools have used SDP similarly to close the achievement gap. The SDP model has been implemented in more than 1,000 schools in 26 US states, the District of Columbia, Trinidad and Tobago, South Africa, England, and Ireland" (Yale University Child Study Center, 2021).

Dr Comer reflected on how his childhood shaped his work as a child psychiatrist. "My interest developed from the fact that the friends I grew up with – poor. African American youngsters who were just as bright as I – went on a downhill course in life. When I looked back at this, I realized that the only difference was that I received support for my emotional and social development that my friends did not receive. My mother and father taught me respect and gave me the social skills to solve problems and promote well-being" (O'Neil, 1997, p. 6).

Several other educators and researchers have studied and advocated for strong educational partnerships. Dr Joyce Epstein from Johns Hopkins University, for example, established the National Network of Partnership Schools in the 1990s. She currently serves as the director of the Center on School, Family, and Community Partnerships at Johns Hopkins (Johns Hopkins School of Education, 2021). Sociologist of education Sara Lawrence Lightfoot from the Harvard Graduate School of Education wrote influential books on the relationships between families and schools including *The Essential Conversation: What Parents and Teachers Can Learn from Each Other* (2004) and *Worlds Apart: Relationships between Families and Schools* (1978). Researcher Joy Dryfoos from Columbia University is credited with coining the term "full-service schools." Her seminal book, *Full-Service Schools: A Revolution in Health and Social Services for Children, Youth and Families*, published in 1994, inspired politicians like Congressman Steny Hoyer to support funding for comprehensive services for schoolchildren. Karen Mapp from the Harvard Graduate School of Education and her colleagues also published *Powerful Partnerships: A Teacher's Guide to Engaging Families for Student Success* in 2017. While studying educational collaborations, aspiring educators have been asked to attend school board meetings, PTO meetings, and community meetings – and observe and practice in schools linked to community organizations providing comprehensive services to students and their families.

The COVID Pandemic

Unexpectedly, the COVID-19 Pandemic unfolded in 2019 with the World Health Organization (WHO) declaring it a public emergency of international concern on January 30, 2020. The COVID pandemic has affected many areas of an individual's life including health, employment, residency, community interactions, and schooling experiences. At the onset of the pandemic, P-12 schools moved to remote learning, as did institutions of higher education. When this happened, the first priority of schools (at all levels) was to reach out to students and families to check-in on them and try to support them holistically. Another significant priority was to continue to provide academic support.

Participants in teacher preparation programs witnessed the outcomes of the COVID-19 pandemic in distinct ways. Course work moved to a remote learning or online format for a period of time. Pre-practicum and practicum experiences in the public school settings transitioned to a remote format, if these placements could be secured at all. The move to remote learning highlighted the digital divide that exists in the United States. In some rural communities, for example, more than 50% of the P-12 students had no internet at home. This was the situation for some teacher candidates, as well. Given the need for social distancing, P-12 students could not board buses. If someone was able to drive P-12 students to a mobile hot spot, the students then needed to sit in their car while connecting with their teachers and downloading lessons (Berry, 2020). While learning about how to use technology to strengthen P-12 student learning, teacher candidates recognized that one's economic circumstances significantly impacts access to technology.

Participants in teacher preparation programs also saw how the pandemic resulted in increased anxiety and depression for some P-12 students. Students with preexisting mental health issues were at greater risk because school was disrupted. By examining emergency room visits for mental health, the Children's Defense Fund found increases of between 24 and 31% for people under the age of 18, compared to the same period in 2019 (Children's Defense Fund, 2021). Early treatment is important, yet many services for struggling kids were not accessed or delayed during the COVID pandemic because they often were provided in school (Minihan, 2020). When families faced unemployment, this too exasperated emotional stress. In response, teachers and school professionals engaged in wellness calls with children and families (Center on Reinventing Public Education, 2020). Some educators visited with children and families outside their homes while socially distancing, so they could provide them with in-person support. Other educators delivered cards and meals. Participants in teacher preparation programs witnessed how P-12 schools responded to the COVID crisis.

Students of Twenty-First Century Teacher Preparation Programs

In 2015–2016, there were slightly more than 2,300 postsecondary institutions (colleges and universities) that awarded degrees and/or certificates in education in the United States. This was approximately 300,000 degrees and certificates in education in 2015–2016. Thirty-one percent of awarded degrees and certificates were at the undergraduate baccalaureate level. Fifty-six percent were at the master degree level. The remainder of the degrees were at the associate and doctoral levels. The majority of degrees and certificates awarded by Colleges of Education were and continue to be at the graduate level (American Association of Colleges for Teacher Education, 2018).

In 2018, women earned 81% of undergraduate degrees and certificates conferred by Colleges of Education. They also made up 76% of the total number of participants enrolled in undergraduate teacher preparation programs. In 2018, students who earned bachelor's degrees in education were traditional age, financially dependent on their parents, and came from families in which one or both parents attended college. At the bachelor's degree level, colleges of education were and continue to be less diverse than higher education as a whole. Similar to the undergraduate population, students who earned master's degrees and graduate certificates in education also have been disproportionately White and female (AACTE, 2018). "Despite concerted efforts to recruit diverse students, colleges of education are not nearly as racially and ethnically diverse as the P-12 schools where they prepare students to work" (AACTE, 2018, p. 9). Alternative teacher preparation programs have proven to be more diverse than those at the college and university setting.

According to the AACTE (2018), colleges of education face declining enrollment, difficulty recruiting diverse students and faculty, difficulty filling teacher shortages in key subject areas, and rapid attrition among new teachers (AACTE, 2018). In many parts of the United States, there is a significant teacher shortage. "Exacerbating the challenge of supplying an adequate number of teachers is a significant long-term decline in undergraduate interest in education as a field of study" (AACTE, 2018, p. 28). Some of the reasons for this decline include the pay associated with teaching, work conditions, and greater opportunities for women to pursue other careers. Nonetheless, others enter teaching and view it as a profession connected to incredible intrinsic rewards and professional and personal growth. They see that their work can help create positive changes for individuals and the larger world.

In the twenty-first century, teacher preparation programs have new and unique challenges and visions to consider as they reflect on ways to strengthen their programs of study. They need to think about how to best reinvigorate interest in this worthy and influential profession. The last chapter of this book explores an array of policies and practices that teacher preparation programs may adopt and pursue.

References

Altwerger, B., Arya, P., Jin, L., Jordan, N., Laster, B., Martens, P., … Wiltz, N. (2004). When research and mandates collide: The challenges and dilemmas of teacher education in the era of NCLB. *English Education*, *36*(2), 119–133.

American Association of Colleges for Teacher Education. (2018). *Colleges of education: A national portrait*. Washington, DC: American Association of Colleges for Teacher Education.

Anderson, L., & Welsh, M. (2000). *Making progress: An update on state implementation of federal education laws enacted in 1994*. Washington, DC: Policy Studies Associates prepared for U.S. Department of Education.

Barros, S. (2020). Paulo Freire in a hall of mirrors. *Educational Theory*, *70*(2), 151–169.

Berry, B. (2020). Teaching, learning, and caring in the post-COVID era. *Phi Delta Kappan*, *102*(1), 14–17.

Blackwell, P. (2002, April). Putting the pieces of teacher education together lessons learned by the Eisenhower initial teacher professional development programs. In Paper Presented at the Annual Meeting of the American Educational Research Association. New Orleans, LA. Retrieved from https://www.govinfo.gov/content/pkg/ERIC-ED465745/pdf/ERIC-ED465745.pdf

Burch, P. (2020). Federal policy and the push to privatize education. *Phi Delta Kappan*, *102*(2), 14–20.
Burris, C., & Welner, K. (2011). Conversations with Arne Duncan: Offering advice on educator evaluations. *Phi Delta Kappan*, *93*(2), 38–41.
Center on Reinventing Public Education. (2020). *Our families need us. This is what we do: Lessons from learn charter school network's COVID-19 response*. Seattle and Washington, DC: Center on Reinventing Public Education.
Children's Defense Fund. (2021). *The state of America's children 2021*. Washington, DC: Children's Defense Fund.
Common Core State Standards Initiative. (2021). *Standards in your state*. Retrieved from http://www.corestandards.org/standards-in-your-state/
Craig, S. (2016). The trauma-sensitive teacher. *Educational Leadership*, *74*(1), 28–32.
Cutri, R., Whiting, E., & Bybee, E. (2020). Knowledge production and power in an online critical multicultural teacher education course. *Educational Studies*, *56*(1), 54–65.
Department of Justice. (2011, September 27). Massachusetts takes steps to require sheltered English immersion training in response to justice department's letter. Retrieved from https://www.justice.gov/opa/pr/massachusetts-takes-steps-require-sheltered-english-immersion-training-response-justice
ETS Praxis. (2021). *Praxis*. Retrieved from https://www.ets.org/praxis
Firestone, D. (2013, December 17). Q. & A. with Arthur Levine. *The New York Times*. Retrieved from https://www.nytimes.com/2013/12/18/opinion/q-a-with-arthur-levine.html
Freedberg, L. (2019, February 12). Gov. Newsom names new head of state board of education in California. Retrieved from https://edsource.org/2019/newsom-names-new-head-of-state-board-of-education-in-california/608484
Freire, P. (1967/1976). *Education as the practice of freedom*. Danbury, CT: Writers and Readers Publishing Cooperative.
Freire, P. (1968/2000). *Pedagogy of the oppressed*. New York, NY: Bloomsbury.
Fuller, E. (2014). Shaky methods, shaky motives: A critique of the national council of teacher quality's review of teacher preparation programs. *Journal of Teacher Education*, *65*(1), 63–77.
Gadotti, M. (1994). *Reading Paulo Freire: His life and work* (John Milton, Trans.). Albany, NY: State University of New York Press.
Gomez, M. (2021, January 14). Will California students have to take standardized tests at home? Educators are wary. *Los Angeles Times*. Retrieved from https://www.latimes.com/california/story/2021-01-14/will-california-students-take-standardized-tests-at-home
Grant, C., & Zwier, E. (2011). Intersectionality and student outcomes: Sharpening the struggle against racism, sexism, classism, ableism, heterosexism, nationalism, and linguistic, religious, and geographical discrimination in teaching and learning. *Multicultural Perspectives*, *13*(4), 181–188.
Hehir, T. (2007). Confronting ableism. *Educational Leadership*, *64*(5), 8–14.
Institute of Education Sciences. (2020). *The transition to ESSA: State and district approaches to implementing title I and title II-A in 2017–2018*. Washington, DC: U.S. Department of Education; Institute of Education Sciences. *Report on indicators of school crime and safety: 2020*. Washington, DC: U.S. Department of Education.

Jennings, J., & Rentner, D. (2006). Ten big effects of the No Child Left Behind act on public schools. *Phi Delta Kappan*, *72*(4), 4–9.

Johns Hopkins School of Education. (2021). Joyce L. Epstein. Retrieved from https://education.jhu.edu/directory/joyce-l-epstein-phd/

Johnson, M. (2020). Self-care: The antidote to compassion fatigue. *Educational Leadership*, *78*(2), 46–51.

Klein, A. (2015, April 10). No Child Left Behind: An overview. *Education Week*.

Ladson-Billings, G. (1994). *The dreamkeepers: Successful teachers of African American children*. Hoboken, NJ: Jossey-Bass.

Ladson-Billings, G. (2001). *Crossing over to Canaan: The journey of new teachers in diverse classrooms*. Hoboken, NJ: Jossey-Bass.

Lightfoot, S. L. (1978). *Worlds apart: Relationships between families and schools*. New York, NY: Basic Books.

Lightfoot, S. L. (2004). *The essential conversation: What parents and teachers can learn from each other*. New York, NY: Ballantine Books.

Liptak, A. (2015, June 26). Supreme Court ruling makes same-sex marriage a right nationwide. *The New York Times*. Retrieved from https://www.nytimes.com/2015/06/27/us/supreme-court-same-sex-marriage.html

Love, B. (2019). *We want to do more than survive: Abolitionist teaching and the pursuit of educational freedom.* Boston, MA: Beacon Press.

Mapp, K., Carver, I., & Lander, J. (2017). *Powerful partnerships: A teacher's guide to engaging families for student success*. New York, NY: Scholastic Professional.

McNeil, M. (2012). Duncan sketches out 'long haul' agenda. *Education Week*, *32*(12), 1–31.

Minihan, J. (2020). Maintaining relationships, reducing anxiety during remote learning. *Educational Leadership*, *78*(2), 20–27.

O'Neil, J. (1997). Building schools as community: A conversation with James Comer. *Educational Leadership*, *54*(8), 6–10.

Pawlo, E., Lorenzo, A., Eichert, B., & Elias, M. (2019). All SEL should be trauma-informed. *Phi Delta Kappan*, *101*(3), 37–41.

Quinn, K., Mollet, N., & Dawson, F. (2021). The compassionate schools framework: Exploring a values-driven, hope-filled, relational approach with school leaders. *Educational and Child Psychology*, *38*(1), 24–36.

RAND Education. (2007). *State and local implementation of the No Child Left Behind Act: Volume III–Accountability under NCLB: Interim report*. Santa Monica, CA: RAND.

RAND Education. (2009). *No Child Left Behind educational options: Availability expands, but participation remains low*. Santa Monica, CA: RAND.

Romo, V. (2018, February 19). Teens 'lie in' at White House to push for stronger gun control. NPR. Retrieved from https://www.npr.org/sections/thetwo-way/2018/02/19/587089773/teens-lie-in-at-white-house-to-protest-for-stronger-gun-control

Scherer, M. (2012). A conversation with Linda Darling-Hammond. *Educational Leadership*, *69*(8), 18–23.

Sciaraffia, M., Zeanah, P., & Zeanah, C. (2018). Understanding and promoting resilience in the context of adverse childhood experiences. *Early Childhood Education Journal*, *46*(3), 343–353.

Shugurensky, D. (2011). *Paulo Freire*. London: Bloomsbury Academic.

Simmons, D. (2021). Why SEL alone isn't enough. *Educational Leadership*, *78*(6), 30–34.

Stanford University Graduate School of Education. (2021). *Linda Darling Hammond.* Retrieved from https://ed.stanford.edu/faculty/ldh

The American Institutes for Research. (1999). *Designing effective professional development: Lessons from the Eisenhower program.* Washington, DC: U. S. Department of Education.

The Independent Review Panel on the Evaluation of Federal Education Legislation. (1999). *Measured progress: An evaluation of the impact of federal education legislation enacted in 1994.* Washington, DC: U. S. Department of Education.

The White House Office of the Press Secretary. (1999). Educational accountability and excellence. Retrieved from https://clintonwhitehouse6.archives.gov/1999/05/1999-05-19-fact-sheet-on-educational-accountability-and-excellence.html

Valant, J. (2020). Good schools for a troubled democracy. *Phi Delta Kappan*, *102*(3), 28–31.

Wakeman, S., Browder, D., Meier, I., & McColl, A. (2007). The implications of No Child Left Behind for students with developmental disabilities. *Mental Retardation and Developmental Studies*, *13*(2), 143–150.

Yale University Child Study Center. (2021). Comer school development program. Retrieved from https://medicine.yale.edu/childstudy/communitypartnerships/comer/

Yale University School of Medicine. (2021). James Comer, MD, MPH. Retrieved from https://medicine.yale.edu/profile/james_comer/

Chapter 6

Moving Forward: Recommendations for Teacher Preparation in the Twenty-First Century United States

Introduction

In this final chapter, we survey current conditions and concerns in US teacher education and offer recommendations for policy and practice given its history of purpose and promise. We conduct this analysis in a time of great challenges that are both daunting and propitious. In the twenty-first century United States we are facing the pressures of new waves of immigrants and refugees; medical, social, economic, and educational crises brought on by the COVID pandemic; environmental crises related to climate change; and threats to our unity and our government principles and institutions fanned by a dangerous fomenting of political dissension. The fact that these challenges are shared by people all over the world means that our institutions – including public education and the preparation of our teachers – are directly affected by what happens elsewhere, and the reverse is also true.

We are also, however, experiencing challenges that offer opportunities to advance the well-being of our people and the education of our children in ways that improve life in the US and the world. The Black Lives Matter movement, here and abroad, challenges us to confront and correct systemic racism and to uncover areas of history long hidden, including the history of people whose lives and stories have been marginalized. It offers educators the challenge of measuring "inclusion" not quantitatively but in the quality of students' and teachers' feelings of belonging. In many places the COVID crisis has brought together, families, teachers and school administrators, nonprofit organizations, museums, libraries, and businesses who have partnered to share resources, in online and hybrid formats, for communities who need them for teaching, learning, and professional development. The challenge of finding ways to work, learn, and teach given the need for "social distancing" has led us to invent new ways to find and evaluate sources of information (and ferret out "disinformation") that provide more flexibility in content, form, and delivery.

Psychologist Gil Noam agrees that the COVID pandemic, besides being deadly and devastating, offers us opportunities to learn how to cope and build resilience in difficult times and how to educate children to prepare them for a

Teacher Preparation in the United States, 139–162

Published under exclusive licence by Emerald Publishing Limited
doi:10.1108/978-1-80071-687-220221007

different world (Noam, 2020a). He points out that during the pandemic, we adults have found ways to communicate, work, balance our lives, and create community; lessons that should apply to the ways we educate our children and their teachers. Noam urges us to understand that education in "the new normal" should be flexible, and should be aimed at students' active engagement, belonging, assertiveness (voice), and reflection. Schools have been far too rigid, too focused on academic achievement as measured by numbers, depersonalized, and unequal, while what young people facing the future need are the skills and habits of problem-solving, analyzing, asking questions, and thinking differently. Schools should also be concerned with the basic physical, social, and emotional needs of children, conditions basic to their learning: the need for connection, belonging, voice, movement, and reflection. The greatest challenge facing educators, he says, is the challenge of social equality. If schools and teaching are not radically transformed, the educational disparity evident in the pandemic will continue. In many school districts, education was actively withheld from children in the name of educational equality; for example, they sent workbooks home to be used as the primary materials of instruction because many children had limited access to technology. Many schools have not been as concerned with children's new learning as they have with their not forgetting what was already learned. Without significant change, children of the upper and upper-middle classes, benefitting from greater personal and outside resources, will learn to navigate and analyze and use data and information, and continue to be the societal, economic, and political winners.

Noam looks at teachers as key to the changes he proposes. He presumes that the content of most teacher preparation programs includes a holistic concern with children's well-being. Programs teach prospective teachers how to encourage children to move their bodies, voice their thoughts, choose, analyze, and reflect on what they're learning. It's when these newly licensed teachers arrive in real schools that they find not enough space or time or opportunity to carry out what they learn in their preparation programs; e.g., to be creative and to connect with students or each other. Noam sees schools as so focused on roles, authority, pressure, and test scores that they have lost focus on the humanity of the learner and the teacher. While many critics of university-based teacher preparation decry the gap between the theories and ideals propounded in those programs and the practicalities of real classrooms (see this discussion in Chapter 3) in Noam's opinion, it is current classroom reality that must change (Noam, 2020b). We believe that the change should include strong voices for teachers in policy-making so that they may help move public education in the direction of what's right and good for the twenty-first century world.

Educators in institutions of higher education, research organizations, and professional associations continue to refine what needs to be learned in twenty-first century classrooms and how to prepare teachers to teach to those ends. This chapter makes recommendations for the structure, content, and purpose of teacher preparation in the United States, given the challenges of our time, what students need to know and be able to do in the present and in the future, and how their teachers can best be prepared to help them. In making these recommendations, we will draw from the thinking of influential teacher educators in our history and at present, and from the conditions, events and purposes that have shaped US teacher preparation over time.

Current Challenges in Teacher Preparation

US public education is today imbued with problems that influence the work of teachers and the business of preparing them. We describe the impact of these challenges on teacher education and the ways that teacher preparation policy and practice contribute as a source or a solution.

1. *Pervasive educational inequity*. There is continuing disparity between the quality, quantity, and appropriateness of resources and services provided to white students versus students of color, to economically secure students versus students living in poverty, and, in some areas, urban versus rural students, resulting in differential and unequal educational experiences and outcomes (Morgan & Amerikaner, 2018). Among the factors contributing to educational inequity include,

- The rising percentage of children in public schools with critical needs affecting learning: immigrants, refugees, and English learners, and children living in conditions of housing instability, food insecurity and without adequate health or mental health services.
- Budget limitations that deprive poor communities of the resources (staff, materials, space) needed to provide an equitable education for their children.
- An overfocus on standardized, quantitative tests whose content reflects the knowledge base of dominant white Anglo culture and presumes that everyone will answer the same question in the same way.
- An underfocus on the ways in which race affects the experience of children in schools, including the effect of the dearth of BIPOC (Black, Indigenous, and People of Color) teachers. In 2018–2019 school year, 24% of US public schools were deemed "high-poverty" (at least 75% students were eligible for free or reduced-price school lunches). Forty-five percent of students in high-poverty schools were Black, 44% Hispanic, 37% Native. Another 29% of Black students and Hispanic students, and another 36% of Native students, were enrolled in mid-high-poverty schools (where 50%–75% were eligible for free/reduced-price lunches) (Irwin et al., 2021). These students were undoubtedly affected by food and housing insecurity family stress, and the fear and anxiety that psychologist Abraham Maslow (1954) included in his "hierarchy of needs" that are barriers to learning.

Maslow also posited a sense of belonging as prerequisite to learning. Neither federal or state departments of education nor teacher preparation programs have adequately addressed how race affects school learning. Though the No Child Left Behind Act (see Chapter 5) mandated that states report achievement test results by subgroups, including racial groups, neither state nor federal leaders have looked at how race might operate in students' experience of school and in test outcomes, nor how race might inform a proposed solution. Only recently have states begun to look at how race affects curriculum content and the testing of subject matter knowledge, as well as how it affects whether a child feels comfortable and included, conditions basic to their ability to attend and learn (see Current Challenges #2 below). State control of the standards and content of public schools may, in fact, limit attention to race as a factor in the educational inequity/disparity or as a factor to consider in the solution. In some states (e.g., Idaho, Oklahoma, Tennessee, Texas, Iowa, New Hampshire, Arizona, and South Carolina), state representatives have enacted legislation banning critical race theory as a mode of analysis or a part of the curriculum, or any consideration of racism as problematic and central to American history and society (Ray & Gibbons, 2021). Many school districts within states have established their own similar bans.

Some 80% of elementary and secondary teachers in the US today identify as white (non-Hispanic); 9% identify as Hispanic, 7% as non-Hispanic Black, and 2% as non-Hispanic Asian (U.S. Department of Education, 2016; Partelow, 2019) In the 2018–2019 school year, their students were 47% white, 27% Hispanic, 15% Black, 5% Asian (Fast Facts, 2021). The disparity between teacher and student demographics matters. Research supports the contention that closer demographic parity between teachers and their students results in greater achievement, higher educational aspirations, and persistence to graduation and beyond (Gershenson, Hart, Lindsay, & Papageorge, 2017, March). Christine Sleeter and others criticize teacher education programs that enroll predominantly white students in programs that promote norms of color-blindness, absent attention to the experience and the voice of their students of color (Milner, Pearman, McGee, 2013; Sleeter, 2017). Crowley and Smith (2015) found that many white social studies teachers avoid discussions of the ways that structural racism has operated in US history and society. The landmark 1,619 Project compiled by journalist Nikole Hannah-Jones in collaboration with leading historians (Hannah-Jones, Elliot, Hughes, & Silverstein, 2019; Hannah-Jones, Roper, Silverman & Silverstein, 2021) presents US history not as a history of national unity but of dissension based on the irresolvable contradiction in our original Constitution – freedom and slavery. Hannah-Jones' *New York Times* editor Jake Silverstein suggests that the arguments now roiling state legislatures, local school board meetings, and policy-making rooms over the uncovering of the negative past – the stories of those left out – "means we've finally arrived" at a place where we can begin to carry out our great experiment in "true, sustained multicultural democracy" (Silverstein, 2021, p. 52).

We are heartened by the Biden administration's plans to prioritize educational equity by securing resources to "shore up schools struggling with the aftermath of COVID-19, tackle inter-generational educational disparities, address the holistic needs of children, and incentivize states to help our schools rebuild on a stronger and more equitable foundation," by providing for example, universal preschool, affordable childcare, wraparound services (after-school programs and social/psychological supports), more funds for teacher preparation and stronger pipelines for teachers of color (Fact Sheet: How the Biden Administration is

Advancing Educational Equity, 2021, n.p.). The proposed funding is necessary but, without attention to the quality of the experience of children and their teachers, it is insufficient for solving long-term systemic reasons for educational inequities.

2. *Declining interest in teaching as a career*. According to the Center for American Progress (Partelow, 2019), the national enrollment in teacher preparation programs has declined by more than one-third since 2010, despite the growth in bachelor's degree programs in the same period. Of note is that fact that when only traditional preparation programs (i.e., university-based undergraduate or graduate programs offering licensure) are considered, the decline in enrollment for that period is 43%. In fact, enrollment in alternative programs (typically non-university-based programs, of relatively short duration, and wherein prospective teachers can teach before they complete the program) have risen since 2016. The number of students completing teacher preparation programs declined by 28%. States are reporting teacher shortages in all areas, especially mathematics, science, English-language instruction, and special education (Sutcher, Darling-Hammond, & Carver-Thomas, 2016; Teacher Shortage Areas, 2021). Declining interest in teaching appears to be due to a perception that teachers' pay is relatively low, that the work is increasingly too difficult, and the work conditions are inadequate to teachers', and students', needs. But pay also varies greatly by region and school district and the strength of teachers' unions, and many would-be teachers are motivated more by a sense of mission than by the level of remuneration. Though the demand for ESL teachers is understandable given US immigration trends, for example, the number of teacher candidates enrolled in ESL preparation programs has in fact climbed 30% from 2012–2018 (Partelow, 2019). Teacher shortages also vary with geography, with some regions – for example, rural Maine, Tennessee, and Oklahoma – experiencing or anticipating more serious shortages than others.

The COVID pandemic has made declining program enrollment more critical, as teachers are leaving the workforce; in the face of the hardship of teaching online, their concern for their own health and safety, the constraints on teaching approaches, the continuing pressure of high-stakes tests, they are resigning, retiring, taking leaves of absence, or moving to other districts. California has been especially hard hit, with shortages across the state, in cities and in rural towns. According to The Learning Policy Institute, California's teacher pipeline problems are exacerbated by state testing policies for licensure and inadequate financial aid for those wanting to complete preparation programs; teachers are "burning out" on increased workloads. To recruit and prepare new teachers, the Institute suggests that the state support teacher–school district partnerships and teacher residency programs that place candidates with bachelor's degrees in internships in schools with support from school staff, university supervisors, and graduate-level courses. These options are discussed below under recommendations and models (Carver-Thomas, Leung, & Burns, 2021).

3. *Declining faith in public schools*. The popularity of charter schools, including those operating for profit, government support of vouchers, have moved parents away from public schools to private and quasiprivate options, taking funds away

from those public schools in the process. The Trump administration and social-media rhetoric have created a false narrative that presents public schools as having failed, that test scores have worsened over the years. In an article entitled, "Americans Have Given Up on Public Schools. That's a Mistake," early childhood educator Erika Christakis reminds us that colonial settlers in Massachusetts learned quickly that leaving schooling in private hands was naïve and ineffective: the 1642 law requiring that parents teach their children was ignored, and five years later another was passed requiring every town to hire a teacher and establish a school for its children, at public expense. The current debate over public education underestimates its successes; for example, ignoring significant rises in test scores of Black and brown children. It also forgets its purpose, says Christakis. Lately, many Americans and politicians tend to "talk about education…as a private consumable," rather than as a "public good." Their stance is false, she says, and dangerous (Christakis, 2017, pp. 1–2).

The COVID pandemic is responsible for some return to the American public's faith in their schools, at least in their local schools. As in the past, people give much higher marks to their own schools than they do the schools of the nation as a whole. In 2021, according to Education Next, 55% of adults graded their local schools as "A" or "B," while only 23% gave US public schools those marks. Tellingly, 60% of Latinx and 46% of Black respondents graded their local schools as "A" or "B." But these figures represent a rise of 20 points since 2008. Data showed declining support for charter schools (down seven points to 41%) and support for voucher plans dropped 10 points to 45% (Henderson et al., 2021). The overall trend in the past 10 years as wealthier students – with easier access and more knowledge of private schools, charters, and vouchers – exit public schools, they leave behind poorer children with more ancillary needs in fewer schools with lower budgets.

4. *Lack of agreement on essential elements in teacher preparation and clear standards for program content or form.* The US Constitution makes no provision for education; standards for the preparation and licensing of teachers, as for K-12 curriculum, are technically set by the separate states. Since the Civil War, the federal government has weighed in on state standards but only on issues that relate to Constitutional questions (for example, the Supreme Court's Plessy v. Ferguson ruling in 1896 allowing "separate but equal" facilities for Blacks and white [by extension, including higher education institutions that prepare teachers] and then reversing that decision in Brown v. Board of Education in 1954, discussed in Chapter 4) and by withholding substantial federal funding from programs that are out of compliance with federal reporting requirements; e.g., those mandated by the No Child Left Behind and ESSA legislation (see Chapter 5). The profession itself has established national guidelines for teachers in various fields through their specialized associations – e.g., the National Council of Teachers of English, the National Council for the Social Studies and the Council for Exceptional Children – but these standards apply only if individual states or individual institutions choose to partner with the national agencies or their conglomerate organization, the Council for the Accreditation of Educator Preparation (CAEP), to approve programs (see Chapter 5 for a discussion of these options).

Nationwide, US teacher preparation is an assembly of a variety of types of programs with related but sometimes disparate standards of subject matter knowledge and classroom experience. In most states, would-be teachers have multiple pathways to licensure. These include undergraduate, postgraduate, and graduate school "traditional" programs, and, in some states, "alternative programs" offered by nonprofit and/or for-profit organizations, including teacher residencies and six-week intensive programs that purport to prepare neophyte teachers for the classroom. Traditional programs typically require core courses in curriculum content, courses in pedagogy, prepracticum field experiences, and a full-time supervised student-teaching practicum before students are hired as teachers of record. Alternative programs typically enroll candidates who already have a bachelor's degree and are relatively hired as teachers while they continue with coursework and program support.

Enrollment in non-university-based alternative programs increased 42% from 2008–2015 (Partelow, 2019). The most prominent of the nonprofit alternative programs is Teach for America (TFA). In search of well-educated teachers for schools that served poor children of color, it appealed to students in elite private colleges looking for a way to do public service work without a long-term commitment. TFA's founders assumed that college graduates with strong academic performance in the liberal arts and having undergone a 6–8-week summer institute in teaching techniques would do a better job of teaching in schools that were failing than traditionally prepared students whose own educational background was less academically superior. Formal professional education, they felt, had not worked and was not necessary. Many TFA recruits who taught for the required year or two, or who left before that requirement, have reported that their preparation was inadequate, particularly with regard to guided practice, lesson planning and assessment, classroom management, strategies for students with disabilities and emotional problems, and understanding the ways in which politics, economics, and family life affect students, their schools, and communities. They felt that their students had suffered as a result (Blumenreich & Rogers, 2021; Brewer & deMarrais, 2015). New York teacher educators and researchers Blumereich and Rogers concluded that neither traditional university-based teacher preparation programs nor alternatives like TFA that adhere to a "best and brightest" narrative have proved sufficient for developing high-quality teachers. However well-educated, well-intentioned, and enthusiastic teachers are, they cannot overcome larger systemic issues like poverty, racism, and insufficient funding in the drive to educate children of poverty.

For-profit teacher preparation programs, many of them large and unaffiliated with higher education, have proliferated in the past few years. Students enrolled in for-profit higher education institutions/organizations in general have low rates of program completion, are less likely to be hired, more often default on federal loans, and have lower earnings than graduates of nonprofit programs. Because the US Department of Education does not require that teacher preparation programs report their nonprofit or for-profit status in their annual report of program completers, it is difficult to discover whether these general outcomes apply to students enrolled in for-profit alternative teacher education programs

(Partelow, 2019). Marilyn Cochran-Smith and others decry the dearth of research on the experiences of alternatively prepared teachers:

> Teachers who enter the profession through alternative routes in the U.S. are placed in classrooms based largely on the assumption that their knowledge of subject matter, prior professional and life experiences, and tightly compressed preparation equips them to teach students. However, our review found very little examination of the nature or quality of their clinical preparation as teachers. Clearly, more research is needed on the nature and impact of alternatively certified teachers' preprofessional preparation for teaching and on the in-class mentoring support most states require them to receive upon assuming responsibility as teachers of record.
>
> (Cochran-Smith et al., 2015, pp. 113–114)

Absent required national standards, the curriculum of teacher preparation programs reflects state education standards, influenced by the content of the high-stakes tests required of K-12 students. The onus of raising scores on standardized tests of literacy, mathematics, and science, dominates the K-12 curriculum and thus, teacher preparation. There is little room for broadening a prospective teacher's knowledge of global issues or civic education, or for ways to integrate social and emotional learning into classroom life and curriculum. Moreover, free to develop their own standards, states legislatures, and boards of education can politicize the teacher education curriculum; as we write, several states have passed laws banning references to critical race theory in both K-12 schools and in public universities, including those that prepare teachers. There is legislation pending in Kentucky that bans mandatory diversity training in its public universities (Ray & Gibbons, 2021). In other states, cultural proficiency and structural racism are central to what prospective teachers learn with regard to their prospective students' learning and experience of school.

5. *Lack of consensus on what the "problem" of teacher education is.* In an article on teacher preparation at "new graduate schools of education" (state-authorized postbaccalaureate teacher preparation programs not housed in universities), Marilyn Cochran-Smith, a 40-year veteran professor and dean/director at two major American universities, lays out the long history of complaints about university-based teacher education. She frames three versions of "the problem": teacher education as a problem of regulation, a problem of accountability, and as a problem of theory-vs-practice.

While some argue for flexibility in program content and form, most researchers and practitioners of teacher education argue that there is a clear knowledge base that should guide teaching and inform professional standards for preparing teachers and approving programs, and cite research indicating that knowledgeable, well-prepared, and licensed teachers were the most important factor in students' learning (Darling-Hammond, 2000; Sykes, 1999). Their solution to the problem, therefore, is that all teacher candidates complete programs that adhere to a set of common professional standards. Those who see the problem of teacher education as one of accountability complain that both standards of programs and outcomes (measured as their pupils' test scores) are too low. Their solution to the problem is to gather and monitor data on teacher performance and program outcomes, to ensure that only effective teachers are in the classroom and that only effective programs are allowed to continue. Those who see the problem as a disconnect between university preparation and program graduates' ability to teach and manage classrooms effectively call for less theory and more clinical experience in preparation programs. While there is wide divergence in the meaning of "practice," and "good teaching," there is a general call for performance assessments for teacher candidates, for longer and more supported classrooms experience in their programs, and for in-school teacher residency programs (Cochran-Smith et al., 2020).

Recommendations, Suggestions, and Some Models for Practice

In view of the current challenges to teacher education as well as its pathways of purpose and place in American history, and mindful of our own experience as teachers, teacher educators, and educational researchers, we argue below for some changes in policy, practice, and direction. We present these recommendations in three groups: recommendations related to the content of teacher education programs, recommendations related to the structure and form of formal teacher preparation, and recommendations regarding ways our national government can help guide the preparation of excellent teachers for US public schools.

Recommendations Related to Program Content

1. *Program purpose, design, and operation should be infused with intentional social and ethical purpose and should prepare teachers and leaders who teach to values of democracy, social justice, and inclusion; who use culturally sustaining pedagogy; and who are actively antiracist.*

"Teaching is an interpretive practice that requires knowledge of the community where students grow and develop, and where they are socialized" (Hollins, 2015). While professional development school models that partner university programs with local schools have helped to introduce prospective teachers to the life of a school, the community around the school – the way that community informs the experience of students and the place and role of the school within that community – have been neglected. Program content and experiences should lead students to recognize, understand, and interact with the community, including recognizing and responding to social problems. A 2019 report from more than 350 school of education, current and former deans, directors and program heads ("Deans for Equity and Justice") called for replacing the typically "thin" understanding of equity that grounds most educator preparation programs (i.e., as a problem of individual rights and liberties, solutions targeting student achievement and teacher accountability) with a new "strong equity" framework (i.e., as a legacy of systemic injustices that threaten participatory democracy) that accepts teaching and teacher education as necessarily political and ideological (Education Deans for Equity and Justice, 2019; see also; Dewey, 1935).

In their statement, the Deans describe trends in teacher education that purport to focus on equity but which merely target the "thin" version; among these trends are, program marketing, external regulation, candidate assessment, and the teaching of "best" practices. They see schools of education as perpetuating the inequities caused by broader societal injustices that hurt children and weaken democracy: "intentionally or not, [schools of education] have perpetuated injustices, discriminated, and exercised subtler forms of bias" (Education Deans for Justice and Equity, 2019, p. 6). They have ignored – or supported – the negative assumptions, perceptions, and predictions about students' futures, that teacher and teacher candidates carry, and that are felt by students. The Deans' statement is more than a call for "cultural proficiency"; it asks that teacher candidates learn the community from which the students make their way to school and that community's history. It asks that programs identify their legacies in that community and change those legacies in ways that advance democracy (Education Deans for Justice and Equity, 2019, p. 6).

The multiauthored book *Transforming Teacher Education for Social Justice* (Zygmunt & Clark, 2015) offers strategies that teacher preparation programs can use to increase teacher candidates' knowledge of who their students are and what their communities offer and might need: among their suggestions are the building of a cadre of "host families" to welcome teacher candidates and invite to community activities, and community-oriented service-learning projects. The American Association of Colleges of Teacher Education (AACTE) has established a Community-Engaged Teacher Preparation Topical Action Group to "build and sustain a collaborative network of teacher educators committed to preparing socially just, equity-focused, community teachers…and to create a space for dissemination and sharing of innovative and best practices in community-engaged teacher preparation from colleges and universities throughout the world" (https://aacte.org/professional-development-events/topical-action-groups/community-engaged-teacher-preparation/).

We call also for programs to prepare teachers in ways that respect and use multiple modalities of teaching, learning, and assessment, including making use of culture-based materials and forms of expression. We agree with Dorinda Carter Andrews that the typical models of presenting information, assessing knowledge, and judging teacher candidates serve to impede candidates' learning and performance as well as their ability to reach and teach their future students. Program content – including course assignments, field-based models of teaching, candidate assessments, etc. – should be delivered in multiple modalities. Using cultural referents and multiple modalities will move both teacher educators and their students away from the negative mindsets that compromise candidates' ability to know themselves and their students. Carter Andrews offers some ideas; for example, she asks teacher candidates to develop autobiographies using artifacts to investigate life stories and encourages them to offer their students multiple ways of responding to required readings, including illustrations, photo essays, and video (Carter Andrews, Brown, Castillo, Jackson, & Vellanki, 2019). For similar reasons, Bettina Love uses storyboarding, moviemaking, zine-creating, and hip-hop to engage students in an English class and to exercise their critical voices (Love, 2014).

Finally, we agree with Meira Levinson (Levinson & Fay, 2019) that the field of education is imbued with ethical decisions at every level; classroom/school dilemmas relating, for example, to questions about grading, admitting students to "advanced work classes," modifying assignments for particular students, distributing their attention in crowded classrooms – and policy dilemmas: the limits on free speech and "hate speech" in schools, or the problem of differential access to curriculum and technology during a pandemic. Levinson is building a field of educational ethics that she intends will be interdisciplinary, philosophically rigorous, and focused on educational policy and practice. Meanwhile, teacher preparation programs should give educational ethics a prominent place in their curriculum, to help new teachers develop their stances and their voices as advocates.

2. *Programs should facilitate teacher candidates' personal growth, including their powers of reflection, psychological flexibility, creativity, and their use of new ways of communicating and learning.*

In addition to "outward-facing" strategies, engaging teacher candidates in the project of social justice and critical consciousness requires "inner-facing" reflection. Dorinda Carter Andrews urges "humanizing pedagogy" for preservice teachers and their teacher-educator professors that cultivates critical self-reflection, resistance to binary thinking (e.g., Black/white; immigrant/citizen), and ontological and epistemological pluralism. Rather than allow, or promote, "color-blindness" (an unwillingness to acknowledge race or ethnicity as significant to teaching and learning), "color-muteness" (an unwillingness to engage in conversations about race) or "cultural incompetence" (a lack of awareness of how power and privilege operate in teaching and learning), programs should teach candidates about their own cultural history and those of others. Carter Andrews reminds us that "becoming" is an ongoing process; because culture is dynamic, we can never at any point be fully culturally competent. Teacher educators should help teacher candidates develop mindsets and learning environments that address the whole student by modeling the kind of self-reflection and pedagogy that they hope future teachers will employ (Carter Andrews et al., 2019). In a similar vein, and of special concern in this time of pandemic crisis, developmental psychologist Gil Noam (2020a) wants teachers to help their students learn resilience, He suggests that teachers – and teacher educators – build into their lives and workplaces time for reflection, mindfulness, and practice using their voices, as well as for physical movement, social connectedness, and new ways of thinking, communicating, and learning.

3. *Teacher preparation programs, and national standards, should ensure that prospective teachers have a knowledge of, interest in, and sensitivity to global issues and concerns.*

Understanding the context in which children in today's American schools live means understanding the global events and issues that have affected their lives; for example, the reasons for their immigration to the US and the circumstances of that experience; the political developments in other countries that influence life and work in the US or raise tensions here; and the environmental effects of climate change here and abroad. AACTE has created another Topical Action Group on the Internationalization of Teacher Education for those who want to infuse the curriculum and the clinical component of teacher education with international, intercultural, and global perspective so that culturally and globally conscious teachers can help prepare their students for a diverse, globally connected world. Internationalizing teacher education means preparing global citizens who are aware of global problems and can contribute to solutions.

Possibilities for implementation include short-term prepracticum or full student-teaching practicum experiences abroad; research or development projects in and with communities in other countries of benefit to children, families or communities; experiences in using culturally diverse practices to teach content knowledge (e.g., call-and-response techniques, storytelling, movement and music); partnering with campus international student offices to design presentations, discussions, cultural exchanges and peer-to-peer relationships; and partnerships with populations of immigrants in local community organizations and schools for presentations and discussions with cultural and global themes and neighborhood visits. From 2011–2016 for example, students from the education, nursing and biology programs at Salem State University traveled to a rural community in Liberia during their spring break where, in partnership with a Liberian university, they worked on projects related to educational technology, oral histories, healthcare, and aquaculture. In some cases, project work counted toward coursework in their fields.

4. *Programs should emphasize teaching for knowledge we do not yet know, applied to situations and contexts we cannot anticipate, using technology we do not yet have.*

The educational progressive John Dewey urged educators at all levels to teach for critical and creative thinking, rather than emphasize content that might not be relevant, or true, in the future; teach in ways that ask students to apply theories, hypothesizes and strategies to real situations so as to understand the relationship between theory and practice and help move knowledge forward, and use materials and methods that are themselves opportunities for learning and thinking in new ways (Dewey, 1897). His anecdote about his frustration in finding student desks suitable for learning – rather than for "listening" – , described in Chapter 3, is relevant. Linda Darling-Hammond of Stanford and Jeannie Oakes of UCLA and their colleagues from seven teacher preparation programs – in traditional colleges and universities, residency and intern programs – carry the idea forward in *Preparing Teachers for Deeper Learning*. The book describes programs whose curriculum and field experiences prepare teachers who know how to teach for learning that is developmentally grounded, personalized, contextualized, applied and transferred, equitable and oriented to social justice, and that is part of productive communities of practice (Darling-Hammond & Oakes, 2019). Briefly, the cadre of teachers prepared in this way design classrooms where academic content is applied to innovative, experiential activities that collaboratively engage students in analytical and creative thinking in response to new situations. In one example a college instructor presents groups of prospective math and science teachers with a pendulum and asks them to work together to devise an explanation for how it works. The assignment includes norms of behavior, assigned roles, and some procedural guidelines. The instructor asks facilitating questions and encourages interdisciplinary knowledge-sharing, including reflection on the similarities and differences and contributions of each discipline.

5. *Programs should include ways of integrating social-emotional learning, including helping students deal with outside events, and should prepare teachers and students for "digital citizenship."*

In this media-driven age, the world inside a school can no longer be separated from the world outside its walls, if it ever could. The students inside do not leave behind their concerns, their questions, their fears, stressors, nor their talents, their interests, or passions. Their learning is enhanced or distracted by events outside the school. It also rests in good part on their physical and emotional comfort within the classroom. The most creatively designed lesson in the world won't reach a child who is hungry, worried, or unable to interact positively and productively with other children. For this reason, we urge teacher preparation programs to include in their curricula research and practice in social-emotional learning (SEL). The Collaborative for Academic, Social, and Emotional Learning (CASEL), a nonprofit research and development organization specializing in SEL, defines it as a process of developing knowledge, skills, and attitudes that result in the development of healthy identity, emotional self-management, empathy, positive relationships, personal goal-setting, and responsible and caring decisions. Ideally, SEL includes school-family-community partnerships, trusting relationships among all three, and, ideally, it leads to greater equity, stronger and more inclusive voices, and empowerment and safe, healthy, and just school communities. CASEL breaks down SEL to skills of self-awareness, relationship building, self-management, responsible decision-making, and social awareness (CASEL, 2021). The PEAR (Partnerships in Education and Resilience) Institute posits a somewhat broader and more social-psychological definition of "social-emotional development," as an ongoing process of growth in emotional, interpersonal, and resiliency skills and competencies essential to success and thriving throughout life." Their "Clover Model" describes four essential elements that children (and adults) need in order to "thrive, learn, and develop": *active engagement* (a physical connection to the world), as "the body is the foundation of all experience and can become a great concern in psychosomatic, eating, and stress disorders"; *assertiveness/voice* (self-efficacy, the ability to negotiate one's self in relation to others, and make decisions); *belonging* (the ability to build strong relationships with peers and adults, as belonging to a group, a culture, a society is essential for well-being and survival; and *reflection* (the human need to create and make meaning, make sense of one's experiences, emotions, and thoughts to create a sense of personal identity. The clover image conveys elements of growth, luck, nurturance, and balance (Noam & Biggs, 2021).

In this time of multiple, competing, and questionable sources of information and misinformation, and in a nation that purports to give people a voice in government, it is critical that we educate students who use their powers of engagement, assertiveness, sense of belonging and reflection as digital citizens. Buchholz, DeHart, and Moorman (2020) define "digital citizenship" as critical digital literacy combined with responsible participation. He cites John Dewey in describing democracy as not just a form of government but a "mode of associated living, of conjoint communicated experience" (quoted in Buchholz et al., 2020, p. 12) requiring that participants engage responsibly in social and political activities. But democracy cannot be directly taught. It requires practice; that is, participation in democratic communities. Digital literacy means finding ways to engage online as well as face to face. Classrooms and schools, "as well as other educational contexts" (whether face-to-face or online), "must be(come) democratic communities." The political turmoil and pandemic crisis of the last few years have presented opportunities to raise questions about how to prepare youth for democratic citizenship; questions like, How can I stay informed by evaluating the accuracy, perspective, and validity of online sources? How can I locate and/or develop spaces online where I can engage respectfully with people who have different beliefs and experiences than mine? How can I use technology to engage, participate, and be a force for good in my community? How can we prepare students to face future crises; for example, climate change, and "the need for sacrifice and collective action for the good of communities beyond one's own?" (Buchholz et al., 2020, pp. 13, 16).

Recommendations Related to Program Form and Structure

1. *Programs should recruit, prepare, and support a racially/culturally diverse workforce to infuse the curriculum, classroom, and climate with cultural relevance and help students feel that they belong. This initiative must include a significant rise in the number and percentage of BIPOC (Black, Indigenous, and People of Color) teachers.*

The experience of having teachers of color gives Black and brown students a sense of belonging, a common language and common experiences on which to scaffold learning (Boser, Wilhelm, & Hanna, 2014; Gershenson, Holt, & Papageorge, 2016). Teachers' backgrounds can affect the way curriculum is presented. Crowley and Smith (2015) found that white social studies teachers tended to avoid discussions of the ways that structural racism has affected US history and society, including the lives of their students. Irizarry and Raible (2011) found that Latinx teachers with experiences in common with their Latinx students brought that knowledge into the classroom, using those experiences to make meaningful analogies, broaden the subject matter to include culturally relevant examples and models, and convey that they understood students' emotions. The presence in a school of teachers who share Black and brown students' cultural experiences has a mitigating effect on the typically wide disparity between white students and students of color relative to the number and seriousness of disciplinary actions, including suspensions and expulsions

(Holt & Gershenson, 2015; U.S. Department of Education, 2016; Wright, 2015). These students are less likely to be viewed as disruptive or inattentive and are less likely to be chronically absent or drop out before graduation (Bates & Glick, 2013). They are more likely to have opportunities for advanced classes, gifted programs, and extracurricular activities (Grissom, Rodriguez, & Kern, 2017). Teachers of color tend to have higher expectations (Boser et al. 2014; Gershenson et al., 2016), are often driven to teach by a "calling" to give back to their community, and tend to stay longer in high-need schools than their white counterparts (Irvine & Fenwick, 2011). BIPOC students who at some point in their schooling are taught by well-prepared teachers from their own cultures and who attend a school where there is a critical mass of teachers who look like them are more likely to want to come to school, stay in school, and learn (Gershenson et al., 2016; Villegas & Irvine, 2010; Villegas, Strom, & Lucas, 2012).

The need to reduce the great demographic disparity between teachers and students in American schools has led AACTE to create a Diversified Teaching Workforce Topical Action Group. AACTE has also partnered with the Council of Chief State School Officers of nine states as well as national education organizations (e.g., CAEP, the National Association of State Directors of Teacher Education and Certification, the Learning Policy Institute, NEA, AFT, and school boards) that have been sharing research and promising practices in an effort to increase the number of teachers of color in their states (Meola, 2018; Thurman, 2018). The group has produced a video series on strategies that worked, and those that didn't, for the participant university programs.

To counter the decline in the number and percentage of BIPOC students entering teacher preparation programs, we offer three strategies to broaden the pipeline into teaching. Three of them relate to the promising practice of "Grow Your Own" teacher recruitment programs (see Bartow et al., 2014).

- Programs should partner with schools or school districts, reaching down into middle and high schools to offer classroom experiences – e.g., observations, "classroom helper" opportunities, and special programs – to expose young people to the work of teaching and explain the options and routes to a career. School districts should consider recruiting paraprofessionals, tutors, and other non-teacher-licensed personnel who would be interested in becoming teachers.
- Programs should actively recruit candidates from local BIPOC communities, including adults working in childcare, after-school programs, or in other education or human service organizations, and should work with governmental, educational, and philanthropic organizations to secure funding to support their further education and the ancillary costs (childcare, transportation, etc.) of returning to school.
- Programs should partner with area community colleges, Historically Black Colleges and Universities (HBCUs), and other higher education institutions with community-oriented missions (Dilworth, 2012; Irvine & Fenwick, 2011) to create articulation agreements that smooth transitions for prospective

BIPOC teachers from 2–4-year programs or from baccalaureate-to-postbaccalaureate or master's-level teacher preparation programs, sharing advising, academic support, financial and other resources where appropriate.
- Because retaining good teachers is as important as recruiting them, we urge teacher preparation programs to provide organized and consistent support for teachers of color from recruitment through preparation into practice, including working with districts to ensure that hiring schools and districts providing both professional support for new teachers and, importantly, a welcoming and culturally consciousness climate for BIPOC teachers.

2. *Programs should provide multiple pathways to preparation and licensure but adhere to a set of common standards and components.*

Given declining enrollments in teacher preparation programs, the need for more teachers of color, and impending shortages in some subject areas, there need to be pathways available to attract prospective teachers with a variety of educational and experiential backgrounds. We support baccalaureate preparation programs that appeal to and are appropriate for high school graduates or community college students, as well as postbaccalaureate and graduate-level programs for career-changers or others who already have bachelor's degrees or higher. We also support teacher residency programs that place candidates in classrooms as paid interns before full licensure, so long as they have received adequate preparation ahead of time, including graduated classroom experience, work alongside an experienced teacher-mentor and program supervisor, and are not teachers of record. In all cases and forms, however, program content and expectations should adhere to a clear set of standards, including ensuring candidates' knowledge of subject matter content; learning and learning differences; the social, cultural, historical, and economic conditions and systems that impact students, their communities and their schools; and pedagogical strategies effective with diverse students and learning contexts. Programs should offer graduated, supervised, field experiences that include collaborative and community settings. Programs should build in regular analysis and reflection on their growth as prospective teachers. We advocate the use of performance-based assessments alongside grades, test scores, and self-assessments; flexibility in schedules, settings and supports; multiple pathways, given differences in candidates' backgrounds, interests, and needs. Finally, we urge that programs partner with local districts, institutions of higher education, and community organizations to broaden and strengthen pipelines into teaching and to offer and model new kinds of teacher preparation for twenty-first century change (Darling-Hammond & Oakes, 2019).

Flexibility in form and structure should not obviate standard expectations for professional knowledge and skills that should govern every preparation program. We believe that national professional education organizations should have a role in determining standards for the knowledge and skills expected of a licensed teacher. We highlight here two standards we believe essential to the work of teaching:

- All teacher preparation programs, no matter their structure or form, should ensure that teacher candidates have a strong foundation in the subject matter knowledge they will teach. Good teachers must have mastery of the subject matter content they teach. Furthermore, they must be interested in that subject matter. Good teachers are learners; they should love children, and they should also love learning. Teaching is a complex, complicated process, requiring constant alertness, the ability to organize a roomful of students for a variety of activities designed to present the content in ways that each of them can understand, the ability to change approaches at a moment's notice, the ability to respond to unanticipated questions, concerns, and interruptions, all the while monitoring student learning and watching the clock. Teachers must be free of anxiety or questions with regard to their subject matter while they are determining how best to present it in a variety of ways that their students will understand. Programs can ensure candidates' content knowledge in many ways; for example, by requiring major coursework within the preparation program or before admission, by establishing grade-point requirements in content areas, by setting a level of performance on standardized tests. We suggest also that, at several points in their progress, programs ask students to assess and report on their own strengths and weaknesses with respect to the content they will be expected to teach, and what, and how, they hope to learn more in their fields during their professional life.
- All teacher preparation programs should be "clinically rich" and should provide teacher candidates with experience in professional collaboration. Would-be teachers should experience real students, real classrooms, and real schools from the onset of their programs, beginning with guided observations accompanied by discussion and reflection, proceeding to direct work with individual students and small groups, and culminating in to guided pre-practicum and then independent practicum experiences. That graduated field experience should be connected to program courses and include different kinds of school and community settings and opportunities to work with students of different backgrounds, talents and learning needs, including students with disabilities. Candidates should have field-based mentors and supervisors and participate regularly in demonstrations and reflective sessions. They need opportunities to learn about and practice collaboration with teaching and nonteaching professionals (counselors, social workers, specialists) in and out of school. As described above under Recommendation 1, clinical experiences should take prospective students beyond the school into the community that surrounds it so that teacher candidates can learn more about what the community offers its children, what problems this community faces, and how knowledge of the community might deepen or enhance or modify what and how they teach. There is evidence that a formal partnership involving program faculty and school staff, with ample time for exchanges, demonstration, discussion, and reflection, will benefit not only the prospective teacher but the school culture by focusing attention on strengthening teaching and learning (DeMoss & Brennan, 2020, p. 34).

3. *Programs should support new graduates.*

Teachers leave the profession for several reasons, among them, lack of professional coaching in the first few years, weak administrative support, resentment that their voices aren't consulted or heard in school decision-making, and a feeling that the work is overwhelming. According to the Learning Policy Institute, teachers who do not receive mentoring and other supports leave at more than two times the rate of those who do (Darling-Hammond, 2017). It is unfortunate that most teacher preparation programs congratulate their graduates on securing a teaching job and then say goodbye, leaving their further learning in the hands of the school principal, the teacher in the next room, or their own devices. Contemporary pedagogical theory and practice features the idea that students need "scaffolds" to help them negotiate new rungs on the ladder of knowledge and skill; the same is true for their new teachers. New teachers would gain greatly from a continued connection with the program that prepared them. That connection might entail invitations to campus professional presentations and workshops. It might also occasion a visit to the new teacher's classroom at his or her request from a former supervisor who focuses as a friendly observer on something the new teacher needs help with. It might mean providing a place and opportunity to share, reflect, and connect with others new to the work. Regular forums for connection and discussion would also provide an avenue by which working graduates might provide feedback and ideas for program changes/development.

Recommendations for National/Federal Policies and Support

1. *The work of teaching should be understood and treated as a formal continuum of professional development entailing graduated levels of teaching responsibility with support from educator preparation programs as well as professional organizations.*

Just as new doctors undertake internships, residencies, and national certification as they grow in their specific fields, earning state licenses and national board certifications along the way, or as carpenters and electricians move from apprenticeships to journeymen to master levels, so should the careers of teachers proceed along a continuum of support and scaffolding and successive levels of responsibility, including the responsibility to help prepare new para-teachers and teachers for the field. Progress to each level should include extended fieldwork, coaching and supervision, an easing into more responsibility, deeper content-specific pedagogy, and new roles as mentors and peer professional presenters. The scope and range of university-based and other preparation programs should expand to offer professional development support for teachers at various levels in this continuum. That is, in fact, the case in some programs in states that have established hierarchies of "preliminary" or "provisional" or "initial" or "clear" or "professional" licenses, but requirements for preparation or mastery, and the nature of increased responsibility, are not uniform across all states in the US, are not addressed by the federal government, and do not universally involve input from national educational organizations. Many school districts designate "teacher-leaders" and/or "mentors," and some have created combined roles of teacher-principal or teacher-professional development coordinator. BetsAnn Smith (2019) investigated England's system of formal, ranked, differently paid school-based positions that blend teaching with management, comprising a "continuous leadership model." She found that formal advanced teacher roles are accepted and valued by classroom teachers as long as these roles remain rooted in teaching, when leaders' tasks assisted teachers logistically and instructionally, enhancing focus, purpose, quality assurance, support and development, consulting and coordination.

While in the US, similar roles have helped experienced teachers interested in expanding the scope of their work to do so without having to leave the classroom for management roles, these options are not universally available or supported or named. The National Board of Professional Teaching Standards (NBPTS) presents a continuum of professional teaching levels, from "pre-service" to "novice" to "professional" teacher, and a pathway to achieving the highest level, NBPTS Board Certification. Theirs, however, is a voluntary model, and one that is not universally pursued or rewarded by school districts, especially where there are teacher shortages or budget limitations, as teachers with more education and more experience are typically paid more than new teachers with bachelors' degrees. NBPTS touts their certification as an indication of teaching excellence, as a way to improve one's practice, and as an award designed and conveyed by teachers themselves. According to NBPTS (and the authors agree), Board-certified teachers are looked at as leaders in many schools and districts. They are chosen to serve as team leaders, coaches, department chairs, school leaders, and, at times, members of state education panels (Teacher Career Continuum, n.d.) NBPTS has long experience assessing teaching excellence and recognizing that teaching develops along a continuum with successive levels of responsibility within that work. Their model should contribute to a building of consensus among the several national educator preparation organizations and national teachers associations on a continuum applicable across the nation, one that will encourage teacher preparation programs to participate in longer-term career development of the teaching workforce with opportunities for deeper and broader learning, mentoring and coaching preparation, and extended professional experiences, including at preparation programs and policy levels.

2. *The federal government should establish funding streams within the US Department of Education and other federal departments focused on schools, their students, and their content that provide consistent financial support to states, districts, and individuals for recruiting and preparing new teachers, especially BIPOC teachers.*

The funding streams should increase scholarship and ancillary aid to prospective teachers of color, provide loan forgiveness to all preparation program completers who have taught for five years, and fund programs designed to interest and recruit students by strengthening pipelines within communities, especially communities of color. We are encouraged by plans by the Biden administration to expand the federal program to forgive loans incurred by college students heading toward public service careers (including teaching). We are also encouraged by his including in his "Build Back Better" proposal billions of dollars for the creation of teacher-leader and mentorship programs for new teachers and teachers of color, for teacher residency programs and "Grow Your Own" teacher programs, for teacher preparation programs at minority-serving institutions, and for assistance in preparing much-needed special education teachers and teachers of English to speakers of other languages (Fact Sheet, 2021). The fight in Congress over the level of funding needed means there will undoubtedly be less available than the administration hopes; however, what we hope will not disappear is the new and welcome attention to the many problems in public education that can be solved with financial, social, and professional support for more and better teachers whose abilities and values can meet the critical and complex needs of children. In the past several years, there has been too little or inconsistent support for building a new cadre of teachers of color, for teachers committed to teaching in high-need areas, for teacher career ladders, and for scholarships and loan forgiveness and other supports that would help prospective teachers who want to engage in this work complete the programs that will prepare their heads, hearts, and hands.

3. *Through its agencies concerned with international education and development, as well as the Department of Education, the federal government should provide grants and scholarships to educator preparation programs to encourage the design and implementation of international experiences for teacher preparation students, and to support need-based scholarships for teacher education students who participate.*

America has evolved from a nation that assumed education was for some an experiment in democracy that required education for all, with steps along the way that successively included more people in that "all." As the nation evolved, so did knowledge of how people learn and develop, the conditions in which they thrive, and the seriousness with which we took the preparation of teachers. Our reality, however, needs to catch up to our rhetoric, and our practice to our theory. We are a nation of contradictions, which make that correction a slower and more difficult process than many would like. Federal government competes with states' rights. A commitment to individual rights competes with that of democratic social responsibility. The principles of freedom, equal rights, and equal opportunity are haunted by a history that embedded slavery in its original Constitution and inequality in its laws. Those tensions have played out in public education and the education of teachers for the public schools. We agree with those who believe that facing history is essential to moving forward toward American goals, hopes, and dreams. An important place to do that work is the public school, and the important guides are its teachers and teacher-leaders.

The United States has roles to play in the world, as a leader and a participant. We write as the nations of the world meet to set goals and action to stem the deleterious results of climate change, using new technologies and creating new jobs, requiring new education. In this twenty-first century globally interconnected world, we hope that the US government and its separate states also recognize the role that teachers, and teacher educators, play in preparing their students for twenty-first century needs, with wider perspectives, deeper understanding, more creative thinking, more appreciation of the conditions and cultures of other peoples of the world, and a commitment to the responsibility we bear for one another.

References

Bartow, J., Gillette, M., Hallett, A., Johnson, K., Madda, C. L., Salazar, I., & Valle, V. M. (2014). Growing your own teachers in Illinois: Promising practice for urban and rural high-needs schools. In C. E. Sleeter, L. I. Neal, & K. K. Kumashiro (Eds.), *Diversifying the teacher workforce* (pp. 99–110). New York, NY: Routledge.

Bates, L. A., & Glick, J. E. (2013). Does it matter if teachers and schools match the student? Racial and ethnic disparities in problem behaviors. *Social Science Research*, *42*(5), 1180–1190. doi:10.1016/j.ssresearch.2013.04.005

Blumenreich, M., & Rogers, B. L. (2021). Schooling teachers: Teach for America and the future *of teacher education*. New York, NY: Teachers College Press.

Boser, U., Wilhelm, M., & Hanna, R. (2014). *The power of the Pygmalion effect: Teachers' expectations strongly predict college completion*. Washington, DC: Center for American Progress. Retrieved from https://www.americanprogress.org/issues/education/reports/2014/10/06/96806/the-power-of-the-pygmalion-effect/

Brewer, J. T., & deMarrais, K. (Eds.). (2015). *Teach for America counter-narratives: Alumni speak up and speak out*. New York, NY: Peter Lang.

Buchholz, B. A., DeHart, J., & Moorman, G. (2020, July 17). Digital citizenship during a global pandemic: Moving beyond digital literacy. *Journal of Adolescent & Adult Literacy*, *4*(1), 11–17. doi:10.1002/jaal.1076

Carter Andrews, D., Brown, T., Castillo, B. M., Jackson, D., & Vellanki, V. (2019). Beyond damage-centered teacher education: Humanizing pedagogy for teacher educators and preservice teachers. *Teachers College Record*, *121*(6), 1–28. Retrieved from https://www.tcrecord.org

Carver-Thomas, D., Leung, M., & Burns, D. D. (2021, March). *California teachers and COVID-19: How the pandemic is impacting the teacher workforce*. Palo Alto, CA: Learning Policy Institute. Retrieved from https://learningpolicyinstitute.org/sites/default/files/product-files/California_COVID_Teacher_Workforce_REPORT.pdf

CASEL (Collaborative for Academic, Social, and Emotional Learning). (2021, November 10). *Ten years of social and emotional learning in US school districts: Elements for long-term sustainability of SEL*. Chicago, IL: CASEL, Inc. Retrieved from https://casel.org/cdi-ten-year-report/

Christakis, E. (2017, October). Americans have given up on public schools. That's a mistake. *The Atlantic*, pp. 15–18. Retrieved from https://www.theatlantic.com/magazine/archive/2017/10/the-war-on-publicschools/537903/

Cochran-Smith, M., Keefe, E. S., Carney, M. C., Sanchez, J. G., Olivo, M., & Smith, R. J. (2020, Spring). Teacher preparation at new graduate schools of education: Studying a controversial innovation. *Teacher Education Quarterly*, *47*(2), 8–37. Retrieved from https://files.eric.ed.gov/fulltext/EJ1249353.pdf

Cochran-Smith, M., Villegas, A. M., Abrams, L., Chavez-Moreno, L., Mills, T., & Stern, R. (2015). Critiquing teacher preparation research: An overview of the field, part II. *Journal of Teacher Education*, *66*(2), 109–121.

Crowley, R. M., & Smith, W. (2015). Whiteness and social studies teacher education: Tensions in the pedagogical task. *Teaching Education*, *26*(2), 1–19.

Darling-Hammond, L. (2000, May/June). How teacher education matters. *Journal of Teacher Education*, *51*(3), 166–173.

Darling-Hammond, L. (2017, September 20). *Where have all the teachers gone? LPI blog*. Learning Policy Institute. Retrieved from https://learningpolicyinstitute.org/blog/where-have-all-teachers-gone

Darling-Hammond, L., & Oakes, J. (2019). *Preparing teachers for deeper learning*. Cambridge, MA: Harvard University Press.

DeMoss, K., & Brennan, B. (2020, March). *Making teacher preparation policy work: Lessons from and for New York. Prepared to teach*. New York, NY: Bank Street College.

Dewey, J. (1897, January). My pedagogic creed. *School Journal*, *54*(3), 77–80. Retrieved from http://dewey.pragmatism.org/creed.htm

Dewey, J. (1935). The teacher and his world. *The Social Frontier*, *1*(4), 7. Retrieved from https://www.tcrecord.org/Content.asp?ContentId=13000=

Dilworth, M. E. (2012, Spring). Historically Black colleges and universities in teacher education reform. *The Journal of Negro Education*, *81*(2), 121–135. Retrieved from https://www.jstor.org/stable/10.7709/jnegroeducation.81.2.0121

Education Deans for Justice and Equity. (2019). *Seven trends in U.S. teacher education, and the need to address systemic injustices*. Boulder, CO: National Education Policy Center. Retrieved from http://nepc.colorado.edu/publication/seven-trends

Fact Sheet: How the Biden Administration Is Advancing Educational Equity. (2021, July 23). Washington, DC: The White House. Retrieved from https://www.whitehouse.gov/briefing-room/statements-releases/2021/07/23/fact-sheet-how-the-biden-harris-administration-is-advancing-educational-equity/

Fast Facts: Back to School Statistics. (2021). *U.S. Department of Education*. Washington, DC: National Center for Educational Statistics. Retrieved from https://nces.ed.gov/fastfacts/display.asp?id=372#K12-enrollment

Gershenson, S., Hart, C. M. D., Lindsay, C. A., & Papageorge, N. W. (2017, March). *The long-run impacts of same-race teachers*. Bonn: Institute of Labor Economics. Retrieved from https://ftp.iza.org/dp10630.pdf

Gershenson, S., Holt, S. B., & Papageorge, N. (2016). Who believes in me? The effect of student-teacher demographic match on teacher expectations. *Economics of Education Review*, *52*(C), 209–224. Retrieved from https://research.upjohn.org/cgi/viewcontent.cgi?article=1248&context=up_workingpapers

Grissom, J. A., Rodriguez, L. A., & Kern, E. C. (2017). Teacher and principal diversity and the representation of students of color in gifted programs: Evidence from national data. *The Elementary School Journal*, *117*(3), 396–422. Retrieved from https://www.journals.uchicago.edu/doi/abs/10.1086/690274

Hannah-Jones, N., Elliot, M., Hughes, J., & Silverstein, J. (Eds.). (2019, August 14). The 1619 project. In *New York Times Magazine Special Issue*. New York, NY: New York Times.

Hannah-Jones, H., Roper, C., Silverman, I., & Silverstein, J. (Eds.). (2021). *The 1619 project: A new origin story*. New York, NY: One World.

Henderson, M. B., Houston, D., Peterson, P. E., & West, M. R. (2021). Hunger for stability quells appetite for change: Results of the 2021 education next survey of public opinion. Retrieved from https://www.educationnext.org/2021-ednext-poll-interactive/

Hollins, E. (2015, March 31). *Understanding urban communities as context and text for teaching and learning. Ed Prep Matters*. Washington, DC: American Association of Colleges for Teacher Preparation. Retrieved from https://edprepmatters.net/2015/03/understanding-urban-communities-as-context-and-text-for-teaching-and-learning/

Holt, S. B., & Gershenson, S. (2015). *The Impact of teacher demographic representation on student attendance and suspensions*. Discussion Paper 9554. Bonn: Institute for the Study of Labor. Retrieved from https://ftp.iza.org/dp9554.pdf

Irizarry, J. G., & Raible, J. (2011). Beginning with el barrio: Learning from exemplary teachers of Latino students. *Journal of Latinos and Education*, *10*(3), 186–203. Retrieved from https://digitalcommons.unl.edu/cgi/viewcontent.cgi?article=1185&context=teachlearnfacpub

Irvine, J. J., & Fenwick, L. T. (2011). Teachers and teaching for the new millennium: The role of HBCUs. *Journal of Negro Education*, *80*(3), 197–208. Retrieved from https://www.jstor.org/stable/41341128?seq=1#metadata_info_tab_contents

Irwin, V., Zhang, J., Wang, X., Hein, S., Wang, K., Roberts, A., … Parker, S. (2021). *Report on the condition of education 2021 (NCES 2021-144)*. National Center for Education Statistics. Washington, DC: U.S. Department of Education. Retrieved from https://nces.ed.gov/pubs2021/2021144.pdf

Levinson, M., & Fay, J. (Eds.). (2019). *Democratic discord in schools: Cases and commentaries in educational ethics*. Cambridge, MA: Harvard University.

Love, B. L. (2014, May). Urban storytelling: How storyboarding, moviemaking, and hip-hop-based education can promote students' critical voice. *English Journal*, *103*(5), 53–58.

Maslow, A. H. (1954). *Motivation and personality*. New York, NY: Harpers.

Meola, O. (2018, March 21). *CCSSO Launches effort to foster a diverse and culturally responsive teaching workforce*. Council for Chief State School Officers. Retrieved from https://ccsso.org/blog/ccsso-launches-effort-foster-diverse-and-culturally-responsive-teaching-workforce

Milner, H. R., Pearman, F. A., & McGee, E. O. (2013). Critical race theory, interest convergence, and teacher education. In M. Lynn & A. D. Dixson (Eds.), *Handbook of critical race theory in education* (pp. 339–354). New York, NY: Routledge.

Morgan, A., & Amerikaner, A. (2018). *Funding gaps: An analysis of school funding equity across the U.S. and within each state*. Washington, DC: The Education Trust. Retrieved from https://edtrust.org/resource/funding-gaps-2018/

National Board for Professional Teaching Standards. (n.d.). Teacher career continuum. Retrieved from https://www.nbpts.org/teacher-career-continuum/

Noam, G. G. (2020a). *Ten big bets: Transforming education during the pandemic and beyond*. Cambridge, MA: PEAR Institute and Clover Press.

Noam, G. G. (Host). (2020b, April 30). Trends in education: Crisis to opportunity in the new normal. No limit generation. YouTube. Retrieved from https://www.youtu.com/watch?v=WGc1t5NRWVo

Noam, G. G., & Triggs, B. (2021). *The Clover model: A developmental process theory of social-emotional development*. Cambridge, MA: Pear Institute. Retrieved from https://www.pearinc.org/clover-model

Partelow, L. (2019, December 3). *What to make of declining enrolment in teacher preparation programs*. Center for American Progress. Retrieved from https://www.americanprogress.org/issues/education-k-12/reports/2019/12/03/477311/make-declining-enrollment-teacher-preparation-programs/#fn-477311-10

Ray, R., & Gibbons, A. (2021, August). *Why are states banning critical race theory?* Washington, DC: Brookings Institution. Retrieved from https://www.brookings.edu/blog/fixgov/2021/07/02/why-are-states-banning-%20%20%20%20critical-race-theory/

Silverstein, J. (2021, November 14). A nation of argument. *New York Times Magazine*, pp. 44–52. Retrieved from https://www.nytimes.com/2021/11/09/magazine/1619-project-us-history.html

Sleeter, C. E. (2017). Critical race theory and the whiteness of teacher education. *Urban Education*, *52*(2), 155–169.

Smith, B. A. (2019). Leadership for "the all of it": Formalizing teacher-leader networks. *Teachers College Record*, *121*(3), 1–44. Retrieved from https://www.tcrecord.org/search.asp?kw=BetsAnn&x=0&y=0

Sutcher, L., Darling-Hammond, L., & Carver-Thomas, D. (2016, September 15). *A coming crisis in teaching? Teacher supply, demand, and shortages in the US*. Palo Alto, CA: Learning Policy Institute. Retrieved from https://learningpolicyinstitute.org/sites/default/files/product-files/A_Coming_Crisis_in_Teaching_REPORT.pdf

Teacher Shortage Areas by State. (2021). Teach.com. 2UInc. Retrieved from https://teach.com/careers/become-a-teacher/where-can-i-teach/shortage-areas/

Thurman, J. (2018). AACTE and CCSSO partners on new initiative to diversify teaching profession. American Association of Colleges of Teacher Education. Retrieved from https://edprepmatters.net/2018/09/aacte-and-ccsso-partners-on-new-initiative-to-diversify-teaching-profession/

U.S. Department of Education. (2016). *The state of racial diversity in the educator workforce*. Washington, DC: U.S. Department of Education, Office of Planning, Evaluation and Policy Development, Policy and Program Studies Service.

Villegas, A. M., & Irvine, J. J. (2010). Diversifying the teaching force: An examination of major arguments. *Urban Review*, *2*, 175–192. Retrieved from https://www.montclair.edu/profilepages/media/439/user/Villegas_%26_Irvine–2010.pdf

Villegas, A. M., Strom, K., & Lucas, T. (2012). Closing the racial/ethnic gap between students and their teachers: An elusive goal. *Equity and Excellence in Education*, *45*(2), 283–301. Retrieved from https://www.montclair.edu/profilepages/media/439/user/Villegas-Strom-Lucas–2012–EEE.pdf

Wright, A. C. (2015, November). *Teachers' perceptions of students' disruptive behavior: The effect of racial congruence and consequences for school suspension*. Unpublished paper, University of California Department of Economics, Santa Barbara, CA. Retrieved from https://www.researchgate.net/publication/342339365_Teachers'_Perceptions_of_Students'_Disruptive_Behavior_The_Effect_of_Racial_Congruence_and_Consequences_for_School_Suspension/link/5eee8946a6fdcc73be908348/download

Zygmunt, E., & Clark, P. (2015). *Transforming teacher education for social justice*. New York, NY: Teachers College Press.

References

An Act donating public lands to the several states and territories which may provide colleges for the benefit of agriculture and mechanic arts [Morrill Act]. (1862). Washington, DC: National Archives and Records Administration. Chap. CXXX. Retrieved from http://www.ourdocuments.gov/doc.php?doc=33&page=transcript

Altwerger, B., Arya, P., Jin, L., Jordan, N., Laster, B., Martens, P., … Wiltz, N. (2004). When research and mandates collide: The challenges and dilemmas of teacher education in the era of NCLB. *English Education*, *36*(2), 119–133.

American Association of Colleges for Teacher Education. (2018). *Colleges of education: A national portrait*. Washington, DC: American Association of Colleges for Teacher Education.

Anderson, K. (2015). *The Los Angeles state normal school: UCLA's forgotten past: 188-1919*. Anderson, Keith W.

Anderson, L. & Welsh, M. (2000). Making progress: An update on state implementation of federal education laws enacted in 1994. Washington, DC: Policy Studies Associates prepared for U.S. Department of Education.

Appleton and Co, & Harris, W. T. (1894, June). The Curriculum for secondary schools. *Education*, *14*, 586–587.

Banks, J. (1979). *Teaching strategies for ethnic studies*. New York, NY: Pearson.

Banks, J. (1981). *Cultural diversity and education: Foundations, curriculum, and teaching*. New York, NY: Routledge.

Banks, J. (1993). Multicultural education: Development. *Phi Delta Kappan*, *75*(1), 22–28.

Banks, J. (2001). Diversity within unity: Essential principles for teaching and learning in a multicultural society. *Phil Delta Kappan*, *83*(3), 196–198.

Banks, J. (2008). *An introduction to multicultural education*. New York, NY: Pearson.

Barnard, H. (1850). *Extract from the fifth annual report of the superintendent (Henry Barnard) of the common schools of Connecticut to the general assembly*. May session, 1850. Retrieved from https://www.jstor.org/stable/24884994?seq=1#metadata_info_tab_contents

Barnard, H. (Ed.). (1856). *American Journal of Education* (Vol. 1). Hartford, CT, London: Trubner & Company.

Barnard, H. (1858). Samuel read hall. *American Journal of Education*, *5*(14), 372–385. Retrieved from https://ia803103.us.archive.org/21/items/americanjournalo05barn/americanjournalo05barn.pdf

Barros, S. (2020). Paulo Freire in a hall of mirrors. *Educational Theory*, *70*(2), 151–169.

Bartow, J., Gillette, M., Hallett, A., Johnson, K., Madda, C. L., Salazar, I., & Valle, V. M. (2014). Growing your own teachers in Illinois: Promising practice for urban and rural high-needs schools. In C. E. Sleeter, L. I. Neal, & K. K. Kumashiro (Eds.), *Diversifying the teacher workforce* (pp. 99–110). New York, NY: Routledge.

Battaglino, L. (2014). Bridgewater normal school (1840). In M. Breitborde & K. Kolodny (Eds.), *Remembering Massachusetts state normal schools: Pioneers in teacher education* (pp. 48–57). Westfield, MA: Institute for Massachusetts Studies.

Baym, N. (1991, March). Women and the republic: Emma Willard's rhetoric of history. *American Quarterly*, *43*(1), 1–23. Retrieved from https://www.jstor.org/stable/2712964

Beaton, A. E., Rogers, A. M., Gonzalez, E., Hanly, M. B., Kolstad, A., Rust, K. F., ... Jia, Y. (2011). *The NAEP primer*. U.S. Department of Education, National Center for Educational Statistics, Washington, DC.

Beecher, C. E. (1845). *The duty of American women to their country*. New York, NY: Harper & Brothers. Retrieved from https://www.gutenberg.org/files/53739/53739-0.txt

Benjamin, L., & Crouse, E. (2002). The American Psychological Association's response to Brown v. Board of Education: The case of Kenneth B. Clark. *American Psychologist*, *57*(1), 38–50.

Berry, B. (2020). Teaching, learning, and caring in the post-COVID era. *Phi Delta Kappan*, *102*(1), 14–17.

Blackwell, P. (2002, April). Putting the pieces of teacher education together lessons learned by the Eisenhower initial teacher professional development programs. Paper Presented at the Annual Meeting of the American Educational Research Association. New Orleans, LA. Retrieved from https://www.govinfo.gov/content/pkg/ERIC-ED465745/pdf/ERIC-ED465745.pdf

Blumenreich, M., & Rogers, B. L. (2021). *Schooling teachers: Teach for America and the future of teacher education*. New York, NY: Teachers College Press.

Bohan, C. H., & Null, J. W. (2007, Summer-Fall). Gender and the evolution of normal school education: A historical analysis of teacher education institutions. *Educational Foundations*, *21*(3–4), 3–26. Retrieved from https://files.eric.ed.gov/fulltext/EJ831197.pdf

Boser, U., Wilhelm, M., & Hanna, R. (2014). *The Power of the Pygmalion Effect: Teachers' expectations strongly predict college completion*. Center for American Progress, Washington. Retrieved from https://www.americanprogress.org/issues/education/reports/2014/10/06/96806/the-power-of-the-pygmalion-effect/

Boston School Committee. (1848, May 8). *Additional report of committee on high school for girls. City document no. 25 city of Boston archives*. Retrieved from https://cityofboston.access.preservica.com/uncategorized/IO_19d2ab60-c2cd-45da-b1e6-4badc7a701ad/

Boston in the (18)30s: The girls high school experiment. (2018, January 17). City of Boston archives and records management. Retrieved from https://www.boston.gov/news/boston-30s-girls-high-school-experiment

Boyden, A. (1876). *History and alumni record of the state normal school, Bridgewater, Mass, to July 1876*. Boston, MA: Noyes and Snow.

Breitborde, M. (2014). Salem normal school (1854). In M. Breitborde & K. Kolodny (Eds.), *Remembering Massachusetts state normal schools: Pioneers in teacher education* (pp. 58–77). Westfield, MA: Institute for Massachusetts Studies.

Breitborde, M.-L. (2019). "Fitted for their community": Race, power and the transition to vocational education at Penn School. In G. Lauzon (Ed.), *Educating a working society* (pp. 33–58). Charlotte, NC: Information Age Publishing.

Breitborde, M., & Kolodny, K. (2014). *Remembering Massachusetts state normal schools: Pioneers in teacher education*. Westfield, MA: Institute for Massachusetts Studies.

Brewer, J. T., & deMarrais, K. (Eds.). (2015). *Teach for America counter-narratives: Alumni speak up and speak out*. New York, NY: Peter Lang.

Buchholz, B. A., DeHart, J., & Moorman, G. (2020, July 17). Digital citizenship during a global pandemic: Moving beyond digital literacy. *Journal of Adolescent & Adult Literacy*, *64*(1), 11–17. doi:10.1002/jaal.1076

Burch, P. (2020). Federal policy and the push to privatize education. *Phi Delta Kappan*, *102*(2), 14–20.

Burkhalter, B., McLean, J., & Jones, M. (2004). Recipients' views of the role of Christa McAuliffe fellowships in science education. *Science Educator*, *13*(1), 49–57.

Burris, C., & Welner, K. (2011). Conversations with Arne Duncan: Offering advice on educator evaluations. *Phi Delta Kappan*, *93*(2), 38–41.

Butchart, R. E. (2013). *Schooling the freed people: Teaching, earning, and the struggle for Black freedom, 1861–1876*. Chapel Hill, NC: University of North Carolina.

Butchart, R. E., & Rolleri, A. F. (2004). Secondary education and emancipation: Secondary schools for freed slaves in the American South, 1862–1875. *Paedagogica Historica*, *40*(1–2), 157–181. doi:10.1080/00309230310001649243

Butler, A. J. (2013). *A Union of church and State: The Freedmen's Bureau and the education of African Americans in Virginia from 1865—1871*. Ed.D. Dissertation. College of William and Mary in Virginia. 1539618383. doi:10.25774/w4-0k2t-pw52

Caliver, A. (1933). *Education of Negro teachers. Bulletin, No. 10. 4. Office of education, U.S. Dept. of the interior*. ERIC No. ED543652. U.S. Government Printing Office, Washington, DC. Retrieved from https://files.eric.ed.gov/fulltext/ED543652.pdf

Canada, G. (2000). Raising better boys. *Educational Leadership*, *57*(4), 14–17.

Canada, G. (2001). The best way we know how. *Reclaiming Children and Youth*, *10*(1), 54–56.

Capen, E. P., & Laberee, L. W. (1947). Zilpah Grant and the art of teaching: 1829. *The New England Quarterly*, *20*(3), 351–353. Retrieved from https://www.jstor.org/stable/361444

Carter Andrews, D., Brown, T., Castillo, B. M., Jackson, D., & Vellanki, V. (2019). Beyond damage-centered teacher education: Humanizing pedagogy for teacher educators and preservice teachers. *Teachers College Record*, *121*(6), 1–28. Retrieved from https://www.tcrecord.org

Carver-Thomas, D., Leung, M., & Burns, D. D. (2021, March). *California teachers and COVID-19: How the pandemic is impacting the teacher workforce*. Learning Policy Institute, Palo Alto, CA. Retrieved from https://learningpolicyinstitute.org/sites/default/files/product-files/California_COVID_Teacher_Workforce_REPORT.pdf

CASEL [Collaborative for Academic, Social, and Emotional Learning]. (2021, November 10). *Ten years of social and emotional learning in U.S. school districts: Elements for long-term sustainability of SEL*. CASEL, Inc., Chicago, IL. Retrieved from https://casel.org/cdi-ten-year-report/

Catalogue of Cherokee Indian Normal School. (1938). Retrieved from https://lib.digitalnc.org/record/109581#?c=0&m=0&s=0&cv=2&r=0&xywh=2305%2C2570%2C3358%2C2040.

Center on Reinventing Public Education. (2020). *Our families need us. This is what we do: Lessons from LEARN charter school network's COVID-19 response*. Seattle, Washington, DC: Center on Reinventing Public Education.

Chadwick, F. E. (1914). The Woman peril in American education. *Educational Review*, *47*(9), 109–119.

Children's Defense Fund. (2021). *The state of America's children 2021*. Washington, DC: Children's Defense Fund.

Christakis, E. (2017, October). Americans have given up on public schools. That's a mistake. *The Atlantic*, 15–18. Retrieved from https://www.theatlantic.com/magazine/archive/2017/10/the-war-on-publicschools/537903/

Clark, W. (1889). *History of education in Alabama: 1702–1889*. Washington, DC: Government Printing Office.

Clifford, G. J. (1989). Introduction. In G. J. Clifford (Ed.), *Lone voyagers: Academic women in coeducational institutions* (pp. 18–20). New York, NY: Feminist Press.

Clifford, G. J., & Guthrie, J. W. (1983). *Ed school: A brief for professional education*. Chicago, IL: University of Chicago Press.

Cochran-Smith, M., Keefe, E. S., Carney, M. C., Sanchez, J. G., Olivo, M., & Smith, R. J. (2020, Spring). Teacher preparation at new graduate schools of education: Studying a controversial innovation. *Teacher Education Quarterly*, *47*(2), 8–37. Retrieved from https://files.eric.ed.gov/fulltext/EJ1249353.pdf

Cochran-Smith, M., Villegas, A. M., Abrams, L., Chavez-Moreno, L., Mills, T., & Stern, R. (2015). Critiquing teacher preparation research: An overview of the field, Part II. *Journal of Teacher Education*, *66*(2), 109–121.

Cogan, M. (1955). "Master of arts in teaching" at Harvard University. *Journal of Teacher Education*, *6*(2), 135–142.

Cole, N. M. (1957, Winter). The Licensing of schoolmasters in colonial Massachusetts. *History of Education Journal*, *8*(2), 68–74.

Coley, R. E., & Desmond, C. T. (1999, April 23). Parallel lives: The relationship between the sexes at Millersville State normal school, 1855–1927. ERIC ED433274. Paper presented at the national conference of the American Educational Research Association, Montreal. Retrieved from https://files.eric.ed.gov/fulltext/ED433274.pdf

Collins, B., & Schuster, J. (2001). Some thoughts on the history of rural special education: A first hand account. *Rural Special Education Quarterly*, *2*(1/2), 22–29.

Commission on the Reorganization of Secondary Education. (1918). *Cardinal principles of secondary education: A report of the commission on the reorganization of secondary education*. Bulletin 35. Bureau of Education, U.S. Department of the Interior. U.S. Government Printing Office, Washington, DC. ERIC Number: ED541063. Retrieved from https://files.eric.ed.gov/fulltext/ED541063.pdf

Cook, K. (2021). *The burning blue: The untold story of Christa McAuliffe and NASA's Challenger disaster*. New York, NY: Henry Holt and Company.

Coppin, F. J. (1913). *Reminiscences of school life, and hints on teaching*. Philadelphia, PA: A.M.E. Book Concern. Retrieved from https://docsouth.unc.edu/neh/jacksonc/jackson.html

Cordier, M. H. (1997). *Schoolwomen of the prairies and plains: Personal narratives from Iowa, Kansas, and Nebraska, 1860s–1920s*. Albuquerque, NM: University of New Mexico Press.

Corrigan, G. (1993). *A journal for Christa: Christa McAuliffe, teacher in space*. Lincoln, NE: University of Nebraska Press.

Council for Exceptional Children. (2021, November). Students with learning disabilities (LD) have difficulty acquiring basic skills or academic content due to difficulty using or understanding spoken or written language. Retrieved from https://exceptionalchildren.org/topics/learning-disabilities

Craig, S. (2016). The trauma-sensitive teacher. *Educational Leadership*, *74*(1), 28–32.

Cremin, L. A. (1953). The heritage of American teacher education. *Journal of Teacher Education*, *4*, 163–170.

Crowley, R. M., & Smith, W. (2015). Whiteness and social studies teacher education: Tensions in the pedagogical task. *Teaching Education*, *26*(2), 1–19.

Cubberley, E. P. (1920). *The History of education*. Cambridge, MA: Riverside Press.

Cubberley, E. P. (1929). *Public school administration*. Cambridge, MA: Riverside Press.

Darling-Hammond, L. (2000, May/June). How teacher education matters. *Journal of Teacher Education*, *51*(3), 166–173.

Darling-Hammond. (2017, September 20). Where have all the teachers gone? LPI Blog. Learning Policy Institute. Retrieved from https://learningpolicyinstitute.org/blog/where-have-all-teachers-gone

Darling-Hammond, L., & Oakes, J. (2019). *Preparing teachers for deeper learning*. Cambridge, MA: Harvard University Press.

Davidson, O. (1881, September 12). [Letter to Mary Jewett]. Framingham State University Archives and Special Collections.

DeMoss, K., & Brennan, B. (2020, March). *Making teacher preparation policy work: Lessons from and for New York. Prepared to Teach*. Bank Street College, New York, NY.

Department of the Interior. (1910). *For the fiscal year ended June 30 1909: Volume II Indian affairs territories*. Government Printing Office, Washington, DC.

Department of Justice. (September 27, 2011). Massachusetts takes steps to require sheltered English immersion training in response to Justice Department's letter. Retrieved from https://www.justice.gov/opa/pr/massachusetts-takes-steps-require-sheltered-english-immersion-training-response-justice

Dewey, J. (1897, January). My pedagogical creed. *School Journal*, *54*, 77–80. Retrieved from http://dewey.pragmatism.org/creed.htm

Dewey, J. (1902). *The Child and the curriculum*. Chicago, IL: University of Chicago Press.

Dewey, J. (1907). *The School and society*. Chicago, IL: University of Chicago Press.

Dewey, J. (1916). *Democracy and education*. New York, NY: Macmillan.

Dewey, J. (1935a). *Liberalism and social action*. New York, NY: G. P. Putnam's Sons. Retrieved from https://archive.org/stream/dewey_liberalism/dewey_liberalism_djvu.txt

Dewey, J. (1935b). The Teacher and his world. *The Social Frontier*, *1*(4), 7.

Dewey, J. M. (1939). Biography of John Dewey. In P. A. Schilpp (Ed.), *The Philosophy of John Dewey* (pp. 3–45). New York, NY: Tudor Publishing Company. Retrieved from https://brocku.ca/MeadProject/Dewey/Dewey_1939.html

Dilworth, M. E. (2012, Spring). Historically Black colleges and universities in teacher education reform. *The Journal of Negro Education*, *81*(2), 121–135. Retrieved from https://www.jstor.org/stable/10.7709/jnegroeducation.81.2.0121

Dobbs, P., & Hetland, L. (2014). Massachusetts normal art school (1873). In M. Breitborde & K. Kolodny (Eds.), *Remembering Massachusetts state normal schools: Pioneers in teacher education* (pp. 78–97). Westfield, MA: Institute for Massachusetts Studies.

Dodge, M. (2014). Westfield normal school (1839). In M. Breitborde & K. Kolodny (Eds.), *Remembering Massachusetts state normal schools: Pioneers in teacher education* (pp. 34–47). Westfield, MA: Institute for Massachusetts Studies.

Dorsey, C. (1985). Despite poor health: Olivia Davidson Washington's story. *SAGE*, *2*(2), 69–72.

Dr. Booker Taliaferro Washington, founder and first president of Tuskegee Normal and Industrial Institution. (2021). Tuskegee, AL: Tuskegee University. Retrieved from https://www.tuskegee.edu/discover-tu/tu-presidents/booker-t-washington

Du Bois, W. E. B. (1903). The Talented tenth. In *The Negro problem: A series of articles by representative Negroes of to-day*. New York, NY: Teachers College Press. Retrieved from http://moses.law.umn.edu/darrow/documents/Talented_Tenth.pdf

Ducharme, E. R., & Ducharme, M. K. (1998). *The American association of colleges for teacher education: A history*. Washington, DC: AACTE Publications.

Duckworth, E. (1987). *The having of wonderful ideas & other essays on teaching & learning*. New York, NY: Teachers College Press.

Duckworth, E. (2006). *The having of wonderful ideas and other essays on teaching and learning* (3rd ed.). New York, NY: Teachers College Press.

Dykman, A. (1997). Interview with Deborah Meier. *Techniques: Making Education and Career Connections*, *72*(2), 30–35.

Edelman, M. (1999). *Lanterns: A memoir of mentors*. Boston, MA: Beacon Press.

Education Deans for Justice and Equity. (2019). Seven trends in U.S. teacher education, and the need to address systemic injustices. Boulder, CO: National Education Policy Center. Retrieved from http://nepc.colorado.edu/publication/seven-trends

Emerson, J. (1822, January 15). Female education, a discourse, delivered at the dedication of the seminary hall in Saugus, to which is added the little reckoner, consisting principally of arithmetical questions for infant minds. *Maine Bicentennial*, *88*. Retrieved from https://digitalcommons.library.umaine.edu/mainebicentennial/88

English, B. (2020). *Civil wars, civil beings, & civil rights in Alabama's black belt*. Tuscaloosa, AL: The University of Alabama Press.

ETS Praxis. (2021). Praxis. Retrieved from https://www.ets.org/praxis

Fact Sheet: How the Biden Administration is advancing educational equity. (2021, July 23). Washington, DC: The White House. Retrieved from https://www.whitehouse.gov/briefing-room/statements-releases/2021/07/23/fact-sheet-how-the-biden-harris-administration-is-advancing-educational-equity/

Fairchild, J. H. (1860). Joint education of the sexes: An address before a meeting of college presidents at Springfield, Ill. Retrieved from https://www2.oberlin.edu/external/EOG/LucyStonewalk-a-thonTour/FairchildCoEducation.html

Fast Facts: Back to school statistics. (2021). U.S. Department of Education. Washington, DC: National Center for Educational Statistics. Retrieved from https://nces.ed.gov/fastfacts/display.asp?id=372#K12-enrollment

Fast Facts: Historically Black colleges and universities. (2021). Institute for Education Sciences, National Center for Educational Statistics, U.S. Department of Education. Retrieved from https://nces.ed.gov/fastfacts/display.asp?id=667

Feden, P., & Clabaugh, G. (1986). The 'new breed' educator: A rationale and program for combining elementary and special education teacher preparation. *Teacher Education and Special Education*, *9*(4), 180–189.

Firestone, D. (2013, December 17). Q. & A. with Arthur Levine. *The New York Times*. Retrieved from https://www.nytimes.com/2013/12/18/opinion/q-a-with-arthur-levine.html

Flanagan, J. (1941). An analysis of the results from the first annual edition of the national teacher examinations. *The Journal of Experimental Education*, *93*(3), 237–250.

Foner, P. S., & Pacheco, J. F. (1984). *Three who dared: Prudence Crandall, Margaret Douglass, Myrtilla Miner–Champions of antebellum Black education*. New York, NY: Praeger.

Fraser, J. W. (2007). *Preparing America's teachers: A history*. New York, NY: Teachers College Press.

Freedberg, L. (February 12, 2019). *Gov. Newsom names new head of State Board of Education in California*. Retrieved from https://edsource.org/2019/newsom-names-new-head-of-state-board-of-education-in-california/608484

Freire, P. (1967/1976). *Education as the practice of freedom*. Danbury, CT: Writers and Readers Publishing Cooperative.

Freire, P. (1968/2000). *Pedagogy of the oppressed*. New York, NY: Bloomsbury.

Fuller, E. (2014). Shaky methods, shaky motives: A critique of the National council of teacher quality's review of teacher preparation programs. *Journal of Teacher Education*, *65*(1), 63–77.

Fultz, M. (1995). Teacher training and African American education in the South, 1900–1940. *The Journal of Negro Education*, *64*(2), 196–210. doi:10.2307/2967242

Gadotti, M. (1994). *Reading Paulo Freire: His life and work* (Trans. John Milton). Albany, NY: State University of New York Press.

Gardner, H. (1997). Multiple intelligences as a partner in school improvement. *Educational Leadership*, *55*(1), 20–21.

Gershenson, S., Hart, C. M. D., Lindsay, C. A., & Papageorge, N. W. (2017, March). *The Long-run impacts of same-race teachers*. Bonn: Institute of Labor Economics. Retrieved from https://ftp.iza.org/dp10630.pdf

Gershenson, S., Holt, S. B., & Papageorge, N. (2015). "Who believes in me?" the Effect of student-teacher demographic match on teacher expectations. Working Paper 15-231. W.E. Upjohn Institute for Employment Research, Kalamazoo, MI. doi:10.17848/wp15-231

Gillette, F. (1850). First annual circular of the trustees of the state normal school of Connecticut. Retrieved from https://www.jstor.org/stable/44749450?seq=1#metadata_info_tab_contents

Givens, J. R. (2016). *Culture, curriculum, and consciousness: Resurrecting the educational praxis of Dr. Carter G. Woodson, 1875–1950*. Ph.D. Dissertation. University of California, Berkeley. Retrieved from https://escholarship.org/uc/item/38h233rw

Givens, J. R. (2021). *Fugitive pedagogy: Carter G. Woodson and the art of Black teaching*. Cambridge, MA: Harvard University Press.

Gomez, M. (January 14, 2021). Will California students have to take standardized tests at home? Educators are wary. *Los Angeles Times*. Retrieved from https://www.latimes.com/california/story/2021-01-14/will-california-students-take-standardized-tests-at-home

Grant, C., & Zwier, E. (2011). Intersectionality and student outcomes: Sharpening the struggle against racism, sexism, classism, ableism, heterosexism, nationalism, and linguistic, religious, and geographical discrimination in teaching and learning. *Multicultural Perspectives*, *13*(4), 181–188.

Greene, M. (1977). Toward wide-awakeness: An argument for the arts and humanities in education. *Teachers College Record*, *79*(1), 119–125.

Greene, M. (2021). About Maxine Greene. Retrieved from https://maxinegreene.org/about/maxine-greene

Gregorc, A. (1975). Matching in service activities with teacher personalities. *NASSP Bulletin*, *59*(395), 24–28.

Hall, S. R. The old stone House Museum. Retrieved from https://web.archive.org/web/20100405231650/http://www.oldstonehousemuseum.org/srhallbio.html

Hall, S. R. (1830). *Lectures on school-keeping*. Boston, MA: Richardson, Lord and Holbrook. Retrieved from https://play.google.com/books/reader?id=SAETAAAAIAAJ&hl=en&pg=GBS.PP5

Hannah-Jones, N., Elliot, M., Hughes, J., & Silverstein, J. (Eds.). (2019, August 14). The 1619 project. *New York Times Magazine Special Issue*. New York, NY: New York Times.

Hannah-Jones, H., Roper, C., Silverman, I., & Silverstein, J. (Eds.). (2021). *The 1619 project: A new origin story*. New York, NY: One World.

Harden, T. (1981). *The national defense education act: A turning point in federal aid*. Accession number ED212084.

Harlem Children's Zone. (2021). Our history and zone map. Retrieved from https://hcz.org/our-purpose/our-history-zone-map/

Harrell, R., Graves, W., & Foster, J. (1968). *Master of arts in teaching program*. Texas A&M University.

Harris, W. T. (1898). *Psychological foundations of education*. New York, NY: D. Appleton & Company.

Harris, I. (1988). *Peace education*. Jefferson, NC: McFarland & Co.

Hehir, T. (2007). Confronting ableism. *Educational Leadership*, *64*(5), 8–14.

Henderson, M. B., Houston, D., Peterson, P. E., & West, M. R. (2021). Hunger for stability Quells appetite for change: Results of the 2021 Education Next survey of public opinion. Retrieved from https://www.educationnext.org/2021-ednext-poll-interactive/

Herbst, J. (1989). *And sadly teach: Teacher education and professionalization in American culture*. Madison, WI: University of Wisconsin Press.

Higginson, T. W. (1859, February). Ought women to earn the alphabet. *Atlantic Monthly*, p. 3–23. Retrieved from https://www.theatlantic.com/magazine/archive/1859/02/ought-women-to-learn-the-alphabet/306366/

Hildebrand, D. (2018, Winter). John Dewey. In E. N. Zalta (Ed.), *The Stanford encyclopedia of philosophy*. Retrieved from https://plato.stanford.edu/archives/fall2021/entries/dewey/

History of the institute for colored youth. Falvey Library, Villanova University, PA. Retrieved From https://exhibits.library.villanova.edu/institute-colored-youth/institute-history

Hofstadter, R. (1963). *Anti-intellectualism in American life*. New York, NY: Knopf.

Holden, W. (1959). The master of arts in teaching at Yale, 1951–1958. *Journal of Teacher Education*, *10*(4), 393–400.

Hornick, N. S. (1975, October). Anthony Benezet and the Africans' school: Toward a theory of full equality. *Pennsylvania Magazine of History and Biography*, *99*(4), 399–421. Retrieved from https://www.jstor.org/stable/20091000

Howard, J. (1931). *In distant climes and other years*. Buenos Aires: The American Press.

Huddle, M. A. (1997, April). To educate a race: The making of the first state colored normal school, Fayetteville, North Carolina, 1865–1877. *North Carolina Historical Review*, *74*, 147–150.

Institute of Education Sciences. (2020). *The transition to ESSA: State and district approaches to implementing Title I and Title II-A in 2017–2018*. Report on indicators of school crime and safety: 2020. Washington, D.C.: U.S. Department of Education. U.S. Department of Education.Institute of Education Sciences, Washington, DC.

Irizarry, J. G., & Raible, J. (2011). Beginning with el barrio: Learning from exemplary teachers of Latino students. *Journal of Latinos and Education*, *10*(3), 186–203. Retrieved from https://digitalcommons.unl.edu/cgi/viewcontent.cgi?article=1185&context=teachlearnfacpub

Irons, P. (2004, Summer). Jim Crow's schools. American Educator. American Federation of Teachers. https://www.aft.org/periodical/american-educator/summer-2004/jim-crows-schools

Irvine, J. J., & Fenwick, L. T. (2011). Teachers and teaching for the new millennium: The role of HBCUs. *The Journal of Negro Education*, *80*(3), 197–208. Retrieved from https://www.jstor.org/stable/41341128?seq=1#metadata_info_tab_contents

Irwin, V., Zhang, J., Wang, X., Hein, S., Wang, K., Roberts, A., … Parker, S. (2021). *Report on the condition of education 2021 (NCES 2021-144)*. U.S. Department of Education, National Center for Education Statistics, Washington, DC. Retrieved from https://nces.ed.gov/pubs2021/2021144.pdf

Jefferson, T. (1950/1779). A Bill for the more general diffusion of knowledge. In J. P. Boyd (Ed.). *The papers of Thomas Jefferson* (Vol. 2, pp. 526–535). Princeton, NJ: Princeton University Press.

Jennings, J. (2015). ESEA at 50. *Phi Delta Kappan*, *96*(7), 41–46.

Jennings, J., & Rentner, D. (2006). Ten big effects of the No Child Left behind Act on public schools. *Phi Delta Kappan*, *72*(4), 4–9.

Johns Hopkins School of Education. (2021). Joyce L. Epstein. Retrieved from https://education.jhu.edu/directory/joyce-l-epstein-phd/

Johnson, E. A. (1890). *A School history of the Negro race in America, from 1619 to 1890, with a short introduction as to the origin of the race; Also a short sketch of Liberia*. Raleigh, NC: Edwards & Broughton, Printers and Binders. Retrieved from https://docsouth.unc.edu/church/johnson/johnson.html

Johnson, M. (2020). Self-care: The antidote to compassion fatigue. *Educational Leadership*, *78*(2), 46–51.

Johnson, C. J., & Harter, C. (n.d.). Biographical Note. American missionary association archives, 1828–1969, Amistad Research Center at Tulane University, New Orleans, LA. Retrieved from http://amistadresearchcenter.tulane.edu/archon/?p=collections/findingaid&id=19&rootcontentid=12505

Jones, J. (2020). Voice of the fugitive: Newspaper used to communicate with underground railroad supporters. Retrieved from https://blackthen.com/voice-fugitive-newspaper-used-communicate-underground-railroad-supporters/

Kaestle, C. F. (1988, March). Public education in the old Northwest: 'Necessary to good government and the happiness of mankind.'. *Indiana Magazine of History*, *84*(1), 60–74. Retrieved from https://www.jstor.org/stable/27791140\\

Kansas State University. (1975). Kansas State University bulletin. Kansas State University. Retrieved from https://archive.org/details/generalcatalo197576kans/mode/2up

Kaufman, P. W. (1984). *Women teaching on the frontier*. New Haven: Yale University Press.

Keller, H. (1902). *The story of my life*. New York, NY: Grosset & Dunlap Publishers.

Keller, F. R. (1999, Autumn). An Educational controversy: Anna Julia Cooper's vision of resolution. *NWSA Journal*, *11*(3), 49–67. Retrieved from https://www.jstor.org/stable/4316681

Kerber, L. (1976, Summer). The republican mother: Women and the Enlightenment–An American perspective. *American Quarterly*, *28*(2), 187–205.

Kerr, C. (2001). *The Uses of the university* (5th ed.). Cambridge, MA: Harvard University Press.

Kilpatrick, W. H. (1918, September). The project method: Child-centeredness in progressive education. *Teachers College Record*, *19*, 319–334. Retrieved from https://archive.org/details/projectmethodus00kilpgoog

Klein, A. (2015). No child left behind: An overview. *Education Week*, April 10.

Kliebard, H. (1995). The Feminization of teaching on the American frontier: Keeping school in Otsego, Wisconsin, 1867–1880. *Journal of Curriculum Studies*, *27*(5), 545–561.

Kliebard, H. (1999). *Schooled to work: Vocationalism and the American curriculum 1876–1946*. New York, NY: Teachers College Press.

Kohlberg, L. (1975). Moral education for a society in moral transition. *Educational Leadership*, *33*(1), 46–54.

Kolodny, K. (2014). *Normalites: The first professionally prepared teachers in the United States*. Charlotte, NC: Information Age Publishing.

Kolodny, K. (2018). The endorsed and spontaneous reading and writing exercises of students in early state normal schools in Massachusetts (1839–1850). In M. Nash (Ed.), *Women's higher education in the United States: New historical perspectives* (pp. 69–91). Palgrave Macmillan.

Labaree, D. F. (2005, February). Progressivism, schools and schools of education: An American romance. *Paedagogica Historica*, *41*(1–2), 275–288.

Labaree, D. F. (2008). An Uneasy relationship: The History of teacher education in the university. In M. Cochran-Smith, S. M. Nemser, & J. McIntyre (Eds.), *Handbook of research on teacher education: Enduring issues in changing contexts* (3rd ed., pp. 290–306). Washington, DC: Association of Teacher Educators.

Ladson-Billings, G. (1994). *The dreamkeepers: Successful teachers of African American children*. Hoboken, NJ: Jossey-Bass.

Ladson-Billings, G. (2001). *Crossing over to Canaan: The journey of new teachers in diverse classrooms*. Hoboken, NJ: Jossey-Bass.

Lagemann, E. C. (1996, May). Experimenting with education: John Dewey and Ella Flagg Young at the University of Chicago. *American Journal of Education*, *10*(3), 171–185.

Lamson, M. S. (1879). *Life and education of Laura Dewey Bridgman, the deaf, dumb, and blind girl*. Boston, MA: New England Publishing Company.

Latham, A., Gitomer, D., & Ziomek, R. (1999). What the tests tell us about new teachers. *Educational Leadership*, *56*(8), 23–26.

Lengyel, L. S., & Vanbergeijk, E. (2021). A brief history of special education: Milestones in the first fifty years (part I of II). Retrieved from https://www.epmagazine.com/blog/a-brief-history-of-special-education-milestones-in-the-first-50-years-part-i-of-ii

Levinson, M., & Fay, J. (Eds.). (2019). *Democratic discord in schools: Cases and commentaries in educational ethics*. Cambridge, MA: Harvard University.

Levy, T. (1991, Fall). First in his class: The many contributions of Samuel Read Hall. *Organization of American Historians Magazine of History*, *6*(2), 38–41. Retrieved from https://www.jstor.org/stable/25162822

Lewis, L., & Claffey, R. L. (2014). Worcester normal school. In M.-L. Breitborde & K. Kolodny (Eds.), *Remembering Massachusetts state normal schools: Pioneers in teacher education* (pp. 98–107). Westfield: Institute for Massachusetts Studies.

Lightfoot, S. L. (1978). *Worlds apart: Relationships between families and schools*. New York, NY: Basic Books.

Lightfoot, S. L. (2004). *The essential conversation: What parents and teachers can learn from each other*. New York, NY: Ballantine Books.

Liptak, A. (2015, June 26). Supreme Court ruling makes same-sex marriage a right nationwide. *The New York Times*. Retrieved from https://www.nytimes.com/2015/06/27/us/supreme-court-same-sex-marriage.html

Love, B. L. (2014, May). Urban storytelling: How storyboarding, moviemaking, and hip-hop- based education can promote students' critical voice. *English Journal*, *103*(5), 53–58.

Lowe, R. (2004). The strange history of school desegregation. *Rethinking Schools*, *18*(3). Retrieved from https://rethinkingschools.org/articles/the-strange-history-of-school-desegregation/

Lucero, A. (1915). The New Mexico blue book or state official registrar. Santa Fe, New Mexico.

Lutz, A. (1964). *Emma Willard: Pioneer educator of American women*. Boston, MA: Beacon Press.

Maestas, S. (2011). *Children of the normal school: 60 years in El Rito, 1909–1969*. Santa Fe, NM: Sunstone Press.

Mann, H. (1839). *The common school journal for the year 1839* (Vol. 1). Boston, MA: Marsh, Capen, Lyon, and Webb.

Mann, H. (1845). *Lecture on education*. Boston, MA: Marsh, Capen, Lyon and Webb.

Mann, M. (1865). *Life of Horace Mann*. Boston, MA: Walker, Fuller, and Company.

Mapp, K., Carver, I., & Lander, J. (2017). *Powerful partnerships: A teacher's guide to engaging families for student success*. New York, NY: Scholastic Professional.

Marshall, M. (2013). *Margaret Fuller: A new American life*. Boston, MA: Houghton Mifflin Harcourt.

Martin, R. J. (1994). Multicultural social reconstructionist education: Design for diversity in Teacher education. *Teacher Education Quarterly*, *21*(3), 77–89.

Martin, J. R. (2011). *Education reconfigured: Culture, encounter, and change*. New York, NY: Routledge.

Maslow, A. H. (1954). *Motivation and personality*. Harpers.

Matthews, J. (1989). *Escalante: The best teacher in America*. New York, NY: Henry Holt.

McIntosh, A. C. (1920). *Consolidated statues of North Carolina*. Raleigh, NC: Edwards & Broughton Printing Company. State Printers.
McNeil, M. (2012). Duncan sketches out 'long haul' agenda. *Education Week*, *32*(12), 1–31.
Mehta, J. (2015). Escaping the shadow: 'A nation at risk' and its far-reaching influence. *American Educator*, *39*(2), 20–26.
Meier, D. (1996). The big benefits of smallness. *Educational Leadership*, *54*(1), 12–15.
Meier, D. (2002a). Just let us be: The genesis of a small public school. *Educational Leadership*, *59*(5), 76–79.
Meier, D. (2002b). *The power of their ideas: Lessons for America from a small school in Harlem*. Boston, MA: Beacon Press.
Meier, D. (2014). *In schools we trust: Creating communities of learning in an era of testing and standardization*. Boston, MA: Beacon Press.
Meier, D. (2021). Deborah Meier on education. Retrieved from https://deborahmeier.com/about/.
Milner, H. R., Pearman, F. A., & McGee, E. O. (2013). Critical race theory, interest convergence, and teacher education. In M. Lynn & A. D. Dixson (Eds.), *Handbook of critical race theory in education* (pp. 339–354). New York, NY: Routledge.
Minihan, J. (2020). Maintaining relationships, reducing anxiety during remote learning. *Educational Leadership*, *78*(2), 20–27.
Morgan, A., & Amerikaner, A. (2018). *Funding gaps: An Analysis of school funding equity across the U.S. and within each state*. The Education Trust, Washington, DC. Retrieved from https://edtrust.org/resource/funding-gaps-2018/
Muirhead, G. (1999). *Images of America: Central Connecticut State University*. Charleston, SC: Arcadia Publishing.
Mulligan, C. (n.d.). Letter of reference for Christa McAuliffe. Retrieved from https://digitalcommons.framingham.edu/uncategorized/IO_a94c7f1b-3486-428d-a04f-ef01521d6e6e/
NASA. The Teacher in Space Project. (n.d.). Retrieved from https://digitalcommons.framingham.edu/uncategorized/SO_496d86d0-e150-4319-9c93-08893d32df7b/
Nash, M. A. (1997, Summer). Rethinking republican motherhood: Benjamin rush and the Young ladies' academy of Philadelphia. *Journal of the Early Republic*, *17*(2), 171–191. Retrieved from https://www.jstor.org/stable/3124445.
Nash, M. A. (2005). *Women's education in the United States, 1780–1840*. New York, NY: Palgrave-Macmillan.
National Academy of Education. (2021). Deborah Meier https://naeducation.org/our-members/deborah-meier/
National Board for Professional Teaching Standards. (n.d.). Teacher career continuum. Retrieved from https://www.nbpts.org/teacher-career-continuum/
National Center for Education Statistics. (2014). Digest of education statistics: Public and private elementary and secondary teachers, enrollment, pupil/teacher ratios, and new teacher hires: Selected years. fall 1955 through fall 2024. Retrieved from https://nces.ed.gov/programs/digest/d14/tables/dt14_208.20.asp
National Center for Education Statistics. (2019). Digest of education statistics: Number and percentage distribution of teachers in public and private elementary and secondary schools, by selected teacher characteristics: Selected years, 1987–88 through 2017–18. Retrieved from https://nces.ed.gov/programs/digest/d19/tables/dt19_209.10.asp

National Center for Education Statistics. (2020). *The condition of education 2020*. Washington, DC: U. S. Department of Education.

Navarre, J. P. (1977). *The female teacher: The beginnings of teaching as a "woman's profession"*. Ph.D. Dissertation. Bowling Green State University, Ohio. Retrieved from https://etd.ohiolink.edu/apexprod/rws_etd/send_file/send?accession=bgsu1566463048515457&disposition=inline

Nettles, M. T., Scatton, L. H., Steinberg, J. H., & Tyler, L. L. (2011). *Performance and passing rate differences of African American and white prospective teachers on Praxis examinations*. Princeton, NJ: Educational Testing Service. Retrieved from https://www.ets.org/Media/Research/pdf/RR-11-08.pdf

Nieto, S. (2004). Black, white, and us: The meaning of Brown v Board of Education for Latinos. *Multicultural Perspectives*, *6*(4), 22–25.

Nieuwejaar, K. (2015). *Learning through living together: The educational philosophy of Jane Addams,"*. Ph.D. dissertation. Columbia University. Retrieved from https://academiccommons.columbia.edu/doi/10.7916/D84J0CXF

Noam, G. G. (2020a). *Ten big bets: Transforming education during the pandemic and beyond*. Cambridge, MA: PEAR Institute and Clover Press.

Noam, G. G. (Host). (2020b, April 30). Trends in education: Crisis to opportunity in the new normal. No Limit Generation. YouTube. Retrieved from https://www.youtu.com/watch?v=WGc1t5NRWVo

Noam, G. G., & Triggs, B. (2021). *The Clover model: A developmental process theory of social-emotional development*. Cambridge, MA: Pear Institute. Retrieved from https://www.pearinc.org/clover-model

Noddings, N. (1984). *Caring: A relational approach to ethics and moral education*. Berkeley, CA: University of California Press.

Noddings, N. (1992). *The challenge to care in schools: An alternative approach to education*. New York, NY: Teachers College Press.

Noddings, N. (2003). *Happiness and education*. New York, NY: Cambridge University Press.

Noddings, N. (2008). Caring and peace education. In M. Bajaj (Ed.), *Encyclopedia of peace education* (pp. 87–92). Charlotte, NC: Information Age Publishing, Inc.

Noddings, N. (2012). *Peace education: How we come to love and hate war*. New York, NY: Cambridge University Press.

Norton, A. (1926). *The first state normal school in America: The journals of Cyrus Peirce and Mary Swift*. Cambridge, MA: Harvard University Press.

Ogren, C. A. (1995, Spring). Where coeds were coeducated: Normal schools in Wisconsin, 1879–1920. *History of Education Quarterly*, *35*(1), 1–26.

Ogren, C. A. (2000). "A Large measure of self-control and personal power": Women students at state normal schools during the late-nineteenth and early-twentieth centuries. *Women's Studies Quarterly*, *28*(3/4), 211–232. Retrieved from http://www.jstor.org/stable/40005486

Ogren, C. (2005). *The American state normal school: An instrument of great good*. New York, NY: Palgrave Macmillan.

O'Hara, E. (n.d.). Letter of reference for Christa McAuliffe. Retrieved from https://digitalcommons.framingham.edu/uncategorized/IO_ceb61c38-ce2e-4179-a89e-ada8d1fc99c1/

Old Deluder Satan Act. (1647). *The Laws and liberties of Massachusetts*. Reprinted from the Copy of the 1648 Edition in the Henry E. Huntington Library, with an introduction by Max Farrand. Cambridge, MA: Harvard University Press. Retrieved from https://www.mass.gov/files/documents/2016/08/ob/deludersatan.pdf

Omeola (2018, March 21). CCSSO Launches effort to foster a diverse and culturally responsive teaching workforce. Council for Chief State School Officers. Retrieved from https://ccsso.org/blog/ccsso-launches-effort-foster-diverse-and-culturally-responsive-teaching-workforce

O'Neil, J. (1997). Building schools as community: A conversation with James Comer. *Educational Leadership*, *54*(8), 6–10.

An Ordinance for the government of the Territory of the United States northwest of the River Ohio (1787). Washington, DC: The National Archives and Records Administration. Retrieved from https://www.ourdocuments.gov/document_data/document_transcripts/document_008_transcript.html

Palmer, G. H. (1909). *Ethical and moral instruction in schools*. Boston, MA: Houghton Mifflin. Retrieved from https://www.google.com/books/edition/Ethical_and_Moral_Instruction_in_Schools/42pIsDmeHZEC?hl=en&gbpv=1&dq=Palmer,+Ethical+and+Moral+Instruction&printsec=frontcover

Partelow, L. (2019, December 3). *What to make of declining enrollment in teacher preparation programs*. Center for American Progress. Retrieved from https://www.americanprogress.org/issues/education-k-12/reports/2019/12/03/477311/make-declining-enrollment-teacher-preparation-programs/#fn-477311-10

Pawlo, E., Lorenzo, A., Eichert, B., & Elias, M. (2019). All SEL should be trauma-informed. *Phi Delta Kappan*, *101*(3), 37–41.

Perkins, L. M. (1982). "Heed life's demands": The educational philosophy of Fanny Jackson Coppin. *The Journal of Negro Education*, *51*(3), 181–190. Retrieved from https://www.jstor.org/stable/2294688

Pierce, P. S. (1904). *The Freedmen's Bureau: A chapter in the history of reconstruction*. Iowa City, IA: University of Iowa Press.

Pincham, L. B. (2005, Spring). A League of willing workers: The Impact of northern philanthropy, Virginia Estelle Randolph and the Jeanes teachers in early twentieth-century Virginia. *The Journal of Negro Education*, *74*(2), 112–123. Retrieved from https://www.jstor.org/stable/40034537

Pruitt, S. (2019). How 'duck-and-cover drills channeled America's cold war anxiety. History. Retrieved from https://www.history.com/news/duck-cover-drills-cold-war-arms-race

Quinn, K., Mollet, N., & Dawson, F. (2021). The compassionate schools framework: Exploring a values-driven, hope-filled, relational approach with school leaders. *Educational and Child Psychology*, *38*(1), 24–36.

Racial discrimination by colleges restricted. (1890, August 30). U.S. Code, Title 7, agriculture, Ch. 13, agricultural and mechanical colleges, subchapter II. College aid annual appropriation, section 323. Retrieved from https://www.law.cornell.edu/uscode/text/7/323

RAND Education. (2007). *State and local implementation of the No Child Left Behind Act: Volume III – Accountability under NCLB: Interim report*. RAND, Santa Monica, CA.

RAND Education. (2009). *No Child Left Behind educational options: Availability expands, but participation remains low*. RAND, Santa Monica, CA.

Ravtich, D. (1991). A culture in common. *Educational Leadership*, *49*(4), 8–11.

Ray, R., & Gibbons, A. (2021, August). *Why are states banning critical race theory?* Washington, DC: Brookings Institution. Retrieved from https://www.brookings.edu/blog/fixgov/2021/07/02/why-are-states-banning-%20%20%20%20critical-race-theory/

Rayman, R. (1981, Winter). Joseph Lancaster's monitorial system of instruction and American Indian education, 1815–1838. *History of Education Quarterly*, *21*(4), 395–409. Retrieved from https://www.jstor.org/stable/367922

Reid, D. (2015). People's colleges for other citizens: Black land-grant institutions and the politics of educational expansion in the post-Civil-War South. In A. Marcus (Ed.), *Science as service: Establishing and reformulating American land-grant universities, 1865–1930* (pp. 141–174). Tuscaloosa, AL: University of Alabama Press.

Reigart, J. F. (1916). *The Lancasterian system of instruction in the schools of New York City*. Ph.D. Dissertation. Columbia University. Retrieved from http://www.columbia.edu/cu/lweb/digital/collections/cul/texts/ldpd_6316626_000/ldpd_6316626_000.pdf

Romo, V. (2018, February 19). Teens 'lie in' at White House to push for stronger gun control. NPR. Retrieved from https://www.npr.org/sections/thetwo-way/2018/02/19/587089773/teens-lie-in-at-white-house-to-protest-for-stronger-gun-control

Rush, B. (1787). Thoughts upon female education. The Albert M. Greenfield Digital Center for the History of Women's Education. Retrieved from http://greenfield.brynmawr.edu/items/show/2828

Santee Normal Training and Missionary Association, American. (1885). Santee normal training school. Santee Agency, Nebraska, for the year ending 1885. Santee Normal Training School 4. Retrieved from https://digitalcommons.unomaha.edu/santee_school/4

Scherer, M. (2012). A conversation with Linda Darling-Hammond. *Educational Leadership*, *69*(8), 18–23.

Sciaraffia, M., Zeanah, P., & Zeanah, C. (2018). Understanding and promoting resilience in the context of adverse childhood experiences. *Early Childhood Education Journal*, *46*(3), 343–353.

Shugurensky, D. (2011). *Paulo Freire*. London: Bloomsbury Academic.

Shuman, B. (1981). An MAT program to meet future needs. *Improving College and University Teaching*, *29*(1), 9–11.

Silverstein, J. (2021, November 14). A Nation of argument. *New York Times Magazine*, 44–52. Retrieved from https://www.nytimes.com/2021/11/09/magazine/1619-project-us-history.html

Simmons, D. (2021). Why SEL alone isn't enough. *Educational Leadership*, *78*(6), 30–34.

Sizer, T. (2009). Ted Sizer's opening remarks. *Horace Feature*, *25*(2–3), 1–3.

Sklar, K. K. (1973). *Catharine Beecher: A study in American domesticity*. New Haven, CT: Yale University Press.

Slaughter, E. (1960). The use of examinations for state certification of teachers. *Journal of Teacher Education*, *11*(2), 231–238.

Sleeter, C. E. (2017). Critical race theory and the whiteness of teacher education. *Urban Education*, *52*(2), 155–169.

Sleeter, C. E., Neal, L. I., & Kumashiro, K. K. (Eds.). (2014). *Diversifying the teacher workforce*. New York, NY: Routledge.

Smith, B. A. (2019). Leadership for "The All of It": Formalizing teacher-leader networks. *Teachers College Record*, *121*(3), 1–44. Retrieved from https://www.tcrecord.org/search.asp?kw=BetsAnn&x=0&y=0

Snedden, S. (1922). *Educational sociology*. New York, NY: Century Press.

Speicher, A. (2016–2017, Winter). Catharine Beecher educates the West. In *Connecticut explored: The magazine of connecticut history*. Retrieved from https://www.ctexplored.org/catharine-beecher-educates-the-west/

Stallings, D. T. (2002). A brief history of the U.S. Department of Education, 1979–2002. *Phi Delta Kappan*, *83*(9), 677–683.

Standerfer, L. (2006). Before NCLB: The history of ESEA. *Principal Leadership*, *6*(8), 26–27.

Steiner, B. C. (1919). *The life of Henry Barnard: The first United States Commissioner of education, 1867–1870*. Bulletin No 8 (pp. 89–93). U.S. Department of the Interior, Bureau of Education, Washington, DC. Retrieved from https://files.eric.ed.gov/fulltext/ED541144.pdf

Stevenson, B. (1988). In B. Stevenson (Ed.), *The journals of Charlotte Forten Grimke*. New York, NY: Oxford University Press.

Stewner-Manzanares, G. (1988). *The bilingual education act: Twenty years later. The national clearinghouse for bilingual education: Occasional papers in bilingual education. Number 6* (pp. 1–8).

Stinnett, T. M. (1960). Certification requirements and procedures among the states in 1960. *Journal of Teacher Education*, *11*(2), 173–184.

Strober, M. H., & Lanford, A. G. (1986, Winter). The feminization of public school teaching: Cross-sectional analysis, 1850–1880. *Signs*, *11*(2), 212–235. Retrieved from https://www.jstor.org/stable/3174046

Sutcher, L., Darling-Hammond, L., & Carver-Thomas, D. (2016, September 15). *A coming crisis in teaching? Teacher supply, demand, and shortages in the US*. Learning Policy Institute, Palo Alto, CA. Retrieved from https://learningpolicyinstitute.org/sites/default/files/product-files/A_Coming_Crisis_in_Teaching_REPORT.pdf

Swarthmore College. (1965). *Swarthmore College bulletin: 1965–1966* (*Volume LXIII*, Number 1). Swarthmore, PA: Swarthmore College. Retrieved from https://digitalcollections.tricolib.brynmawr.edu/object/sc11979

Sweet, L. I. (1985, March). The female seminary movement and woman's mission in antebellum America. *Church History*, *54*(1), 41–55. Retrieved from https://www.jstor.org/stable/3165749/

Taggart, R. (1979, October). Philanthropy and Black public education in Delaware, 1918–1930. *Pennsylvania Magazine of History and Biography*, *103*(4), 467–483. Retrieved from https://www.jstor.org/stable/20091405

Taggart, R. J. (1988). *Private philanthropy and public education: Pierre S. Du Pont and the Delaware schools, 1890–1940*. Newark, DE: University of Delaware Press.

Talladega College. (n.d.). Talladega College: Our history. Retrieved from http://www.talladega.edu/our-history/

Tamir, E., & Wilson, S. (2005). Who should guard the gates? Evidentiary and professional warrants for claiming jurisdiction. *Journal of Teacher Education*, *56*(4), 332–342.

Teach for America. (2021). History. Retrieved from https://www.teachforamerica.org/what-we-do/history

Teacher Shortage Areas by State. (2021). Teach.com. 2UInc. Retrieved from https://teach.com/careers/become-a-teacher/where-can-i-teach/shortage-areas/

The American Institutes for Research. (1999). *Designing effective professional development: Lessons from the Eisenhower program*. Washington, DC: U. S. Department of Education.

The Independent Review Panel on the Evaluation of Federal Education Legislation. (1999). Measured progress: An evaluation of the impact of federal education legislation enacted in 1994. Washington, DC.

The National Commission on Excellence in Education. (1983). *A nation at risk: The imperative for educational reform*. Washington, DC: U. S. Department of Education.

The National Council for the Social Studies. (2021). Christa McAuliffe reach for the stars award. Retrieved from https://www.socialstudies.org/membership/christa-mcauliffe-reach-stars-award

The White House Office of the Press Secretary. (1999). Educational accountability and excellence. Retrieved from https://clintonwhitehouse6.archives.gov/1999/05/1999-05-19-fact-sheet-on-educational-accountability-and-excellence.html

Thickstun, E. (1907, October). Education department. *The Indian School Journal*, *7*(32), 33–41. Retrieved from https://catalog.archives.gov/OpaAPI/media/2745460/content/nrf/chilocco/the_indian_school_journal_october_1907.pdf

Thorndike, E. L. (1905). *The elements of psychology*. New York, NY: A. G. Seiler.

Thorndike, E. L. (1913, July–December). Eugenics: With special reference to intellect and character. *Popular Science Monthly*, *83*, 125–138. Retrieved from https://archive.org/details/popularsciencemo8313newy

Thurman, J. (2018). AACTE and CCSSO partners on new initiative to diversify teaching profession. American Association of Colleges of Teacher Education. Retrieved from https://edprepmatters.net/2018/09/aacte-and-ccsso-partners-on-new-initiative-to-diversify-teaching-profession/

Tolley, K. (2015). *Heading south to teach: The world of Susan Nye Hutchison, 1815–1845*. Chapel Hill, NC: University of North Carolina Press.

Transcript of Morrill Act. (1862). Washington, DC: The National Archives and Records Administration. Retrieved from https://www.ourdocuments.gov/doc.php?flash=false&doc=33&page=transcript

Tushnet, M. (1995). *Brown v. Board of Education: The battle for integration*. New York, NY: Franklin Watts.

United States Department of Education. (2010). An overview of the U.S. Department of Education. Retrieved from https://www2.ed.gov/about/overview/focus/what.html

United States Department of Education. (2021). About ED. Retrieved from https://www2.ed.gov/about/landing.jhtml

United States Senate. (2021). Sputnik spurs passage of the National Defense Education Act. Retrieved from https://www.senate.gov/artandhistory/history/minute/Sputnik_Spurs_Passage_of_National_Defense_Education_Act.htm

University of California at Irvine. (1965). University of California at Irvine initial bulletin: 1965–1966 catalogue. Retrieved from https://www.reg.uci.edu/catalogue/1965-1966Catalogue.pdf

University of Illinois at Urbana-Champaign. (1980). Courses catalog 1980–82 at the University of Illinois at Urbana-Champaign. Retrieved from https://archive.org/details/coursescatalog198082univ/page/n5/mode/2up?view=theater

University of Washington. (2021). James A. Banks home. Emeritus professor. Retrieved from https://education.uw.edu/people/faculty/jbanks/

U.S. Department of Education. (2016). *The State of racial diversity in the educator workforce*. Washington, DC: U.S. Department of Education, Office of Planning, Evaluation and Policy Development, Policy and Program Studies Service.

Valant, J. (2020). Good schools for a troubled democracy. *Phi Delta Kappan, 102*(3), 28–31.

Velez, D. O. (2013, December 8). Myrtilla Miner: Teaching 'colored girls' to teach. *Daily Kos*. Retrieved from https://www.dailykos.com/stories/2013/12/8/1260525/-Myrtilla-Miner-Teaching-colored-girls-to-teach

Wakeman, S., Browder, D., Meier, I., & McColl, A. (2007). The implications of No Child Left behind for students with developmental disabilities. *Mental Retardation and Developmental Studies, 13*(2), 143–150.

Walker, D. (1995/1829). *David Walker's appeal, in four Articles: Together with a preamble to the coloured citizens of the world, but in particular, and very expressly, to those of the United States of America*. Revised edition with an Introduction by Sean Wilentz. New York, NY: Hill and Wang.

Wang, C., & Chen, X. (2009). The characteristics and enlightening of NCATE. *International Education Studies*, *2*(2), 72–76.

Washington, B. T. (1901). *Up from slavery: An autobiography*. New York, NY: Doubleday & Company.

Washington, B. (1995/1901). *Up from slavery*. Mineola, NY: Dover Publications.

Westhauser, K., Smith, E., & Fremlin, J. (2005). *Life and learning at Montgomery's black university*. Tuscaloosa, AL: The University of Alabama Press.

White, A. (1913). *Biennial report of the superintendent of public instruction to the governor of New Mexico: For the years 1910–1911 and 1911–1912*. New Mexican Printing Co, Santa Fe, NM.

Willard, E. (1819). *An address to the public particularly to the members of the Legislature of New York proposing a plan for improving female education*. Middlebury, VT: J.W. Copeland. Retrieved from https://ia802702.us.archive.org/13/items/aplanforimprovi01willgoog/aplanforimprovi01willgoog.pdf

Woodson, C. (1922). *The Negro in our history*. Washington, DC: Associated Publishers. Retrieved from https://archive.org/details/negroinourhisto01woodgoog/page/n12/mode/2up

Woody, T. (1966/1929). *A History of women's education in the United States*. New York, NY: Farrar, Strauss & Giroux.

Wraga, W. (2006). The heightened significance of Brown v. Board of Education in our time. *Phi Delta Kappan*, *87*(6), 425–428.

Wright, F. W. (1930, January). The evolution of the normal schools. *The Elementary School Journal*, *30*(5), 363–371. Retrieved from https://www.jstor.org/stable/994569

Wright, A. C. (2015, November). Teachers' perceptions of students' disruptive behavior: The Effect of racial congruence and consequences for school suspension. Unpublished paper. University of California Department of Economics, Santa Barbara, CA. Retrieved from https://citeseerx.ist.psu.edu/viewdoc/download?doi=10.1.1.713.8228&rep=rep1&type=pdf

Yale University Child Study Center. (2021). Comer school development program. Retrieved from https://medicine.yale.edu/childstudy/communitypartnerships/comer/

Yale University School of Medicine. (2021). James Comer, MD, MPH. Retrieved from https://medicine.yale.edu/profile/james_comer/

Zimmerman, J. (2009). *Small wonder: The Little red schoolhouse in history and memory*. New Haven, CT: Yale University Press.

Zoracki, S. M. (2006). Vermont's tradition of education and the Vermont Constitution. *Albany Law Review*, *69*, 581. Retrieved from http://www.albanylawreview.org/Articles/Vol69_2/69.2.0581-Vermonts_Tradition_of_Education_and_the_Vermont_Constitution.pdf

Zygmunt, E., & Clark, P. (2015). *Transforming teacher education for social justice*. New York, NY: Teachers College Press.

"Nothing Servile": Native resistance at the Santee Normal Training School. (n.d.). Beloit, WI: Beloit College Logan Museum of Anthropology Online Exhibition, Beloit College. Retrieved from https://www.loganmuseumexhibits.com/preserving-the-dakota-language

Index